RURITANIA

RURITANIA

A CULTURAL HISTORY, FROM *THE PRISONER OF ZENDA* TO *THE PRINCESS DIARIES*

NICHOLAS DALY

OXFORD

UNIVERSITY PRESS

OXFORD
UNIVERSITY PRESS

Great Clarendon Street, Oxford, OX2 6DP,
United Kingdom

Oxford University Press is a department of the University of Oxford.
It furthers the University's objective of excellence in research, scholarship,
and education by publishing worldwide. Oxford is a registered trade mark of
Oxford University Press in the UK and in certain other countries

First Edition published in 2020

Impression: 1

Published in the United States of America by Oxford University Press
198 Madison Avenue, New York, NY 10016, United States of America

British Library Cataloguing in Publication Data
Data available

Library of Congress Control Number: 2019946146

ISBN 978–0–19–883660–5

Printed and bound by
CPI Group (UK) Ltd, Croydon, CRO 4YY

Acknowledgements

Small countries can run up big debts, and even in writing about pocket kingdoms I seem to have done the same. Warm thanks to Jacqueline Norton and Aimee Wright and their colleagues at Oxford University Press for their help with this book, to Luciana O'Flaherty at Oxford World's Classics in supporting its sister publication, a new edition of *The Prisoner of Zenda*, and to Priyanka Swansi and Wade Guyitt for production support. An earlier version of chapter 4 appeared in *Popular Modernism and Its Legacies* (Bloomsbury, 2018), and I am grateful to the editor of that collection, Scott Ortolano, for a number of suggestions, and to Bloomsbury for permission to reproduce it here. For their help in locating Ruritanian texts and artefacts, I would like to make special mention of the staff of the libraries of University College Dublin and Trinity College Dublin, the British Library, and the V&A Theatre and Performance Archives at Blythe House. For financial help with different parts of the project, I am grateful to UCD College of Arts and Humanities and to the NUI.

This book has benefited immeasurably from the generous comments and queries of audiences at conferences and invited talks. There are many, many Ruritanian novels, plays, and films, and people have taken the trouble to point me towards variants I had not come across, from Hindi films to ballet-school novels to made-for-television Christmas movies. I would particularly like to thank my hosts and audiences at the University of Glasgow, Padua University, Exeter University, Trinity College Dublin, the University of Erlangen, the British Association for Victorian Studies conference at Leeds Trinity in 2015, and of course my own university, UCD. Richard Pearson invited me to talk about Ruritania at NUI Galway, and I was deeply saddened to hear of his untimely death.

In the UCD School of English, Drama and Film, I would to give a special mention to Danielle Clarke, Lucy Cogan, Fionnuala Dillane, Porscha Fermanis, Karen Jackman, Margaret Kelleher, Emilie Pine, James Ryan, Pauline Slattery, and Leanne Waters. At UCD and elsewhere, thanks to Nancy Armstrong,

Maurice Bric, Susan Cahill, Clare Clarke, Sarah Comyn, Aileen Douglas, Declan Downey, Dino Felluga, Christine Ferguson, Peter Ferry, Carolin Hahnemann, Jason Hall, Scott Hamilton, Jo Hofer-Robinson, Darryl Jones, Roger Luckhurst, Jo McDonagh, Matt McGuire, Rohan McWilliam, Pablo Mukherjee, Katy Mullin and Hannah Roche, Francis O'Gorman and Kate Williams, Marilena Parlati, Paige Reynolds, Fariha Shaikh, Harry White, and colleagues at the *Journal of Victorian Culture*. Special thanks to Tom Roueché of *Tank* magazine and to Conor Reid of the *Words To That Effect* podcast, for interviewing me about this project and helping me to clarify my thoughts.

For their hospitality and tolerance of my Ruritanian interests, thanks to my friends and family in Dublin, Cork, and London, especially the Dalys, Brian Murphy and Miriam O'Brien, Clare Hayes-Brady and Maz Al-Alawi, Claire Connolly and Paul O'Donovan, Catherine Kirwan, David Glover, and Peter and Nicola Byrne.

This book started as a planned collaborative project with Stephanie Rains, before it somehow turned into a single-author monograph; readers may still discern the vestiges of an absent chapter on John Buchan and Dornford Yates. But Stephanie has continued to be an unofficial collaborator on things Ruritanian, and she should really have her name on the cover too. The other member of our household, Pola, has right from the start preserved a sensible disdain for the whole business and will not be pleased even to be mentioned.

None of the above, of course, is to be held responsible for the content.

Contents

List of Illustrations

List of Plates

Introduction

Locating Ruritania

Each player takes seven pieces of the same color, one arranging his pieces on any of the black spots on or near the Palace at Strelsau, the other placing his pieces on any of the black spots on or near the Castle of Zenda.

(Rules For Two Players, *The Prisoner of Zenda*, a board game by Parker Brothers, 1896)

Alaine, Alasia, Axphain, Balaria, Bomania, Bovinia, Cadonia, Dawsbergen, Freedonia, Genovia, Glottenberg, Grand Fenwick, Graustark, Hohenwald, Karaslavia, Karlsburg, Krasnia, Livonia, Marsovia, Monteblanco, Murania, Novia, Panoplia, Pontevedro, Sylvania, Thermosa, Vulgaria, Wallaria. These are the names of small, semi-feudal, imaginary countries, and they have provided the settings for late-Victorian adventure stories, musicals and operettas, romantic Hollywood costume dramas, Cold War fantasies, and children's novels. There are scores of similar such pocket kingdoms, which are usually termed 'Ruritanian'. But where did this term come from? It is scarcely the case now, but many readers would once have readily recognized Ruritania as the fictional setting of Anthony Hope's 1894 novel of adventure *The Prisoner of Zenda* and its 1898 sequel *Rupert of Hentzau*. In Hope's tale an idle English gentleman, Rudolf Rassendyll, encounters royal intrigue, sword-play, and romance when he takes a holiday in the picturesque German statelet of Ruritania, not far from Dresden, where King Rudolf has just acceded to the throne. Because of his remarkable resemblance to the King, Rassendyll is recruited to impersonate him at the coronation in Strelsau in order to foil a coup by the King's half-brother, Michael. But his role has to be extended when the real King is kidnapped, and to complicate matters he finds himself falling for the real King's fiancée, Princess Flavia. Torn between love and honour, he strives to rescue the King from the Castle of Zenda, clashing with the ruthless Rupert of Hentzau, Michael's most able hench-man. But all the time he knows the price that he and Flavia must pay if he succeeds.

A bestseller when it first appeared, Hope's romantic swashbuckler cast its spell on readers long after and inspired countless imitations on both sides of the Atlantic; a series of successful stage and screen versions consolidated its position in international popular culture. But tastes change. *Zenda* itself remains as a late-Victorian classic, but the stream of adaptations has dried up, and most of the imitations have been swallowed up by the swirling mists of literary history. There is magic in Ruritania still, but it is, perhaps, finally waning.

Here I have attempted to recover the glory days of Ruritania and to fol-low the long career of copycat pocket kingdoms in popular culture. This is a book, then, about Hope's late Victorian bestseller *The Prisoner of Zenda*, but it is for the most part about the long cultural shadow cast by that novel. In its day Hope's novel was famous enough to inspire everything from North American place names (there are or were Zendas in Idaho, Kansas, Missouri, Virginia and Wisconsin in the United States, as well as in Ontario, Canada) to a stage illusion to a Parker Brothers board game.

Its more direct narrative and dramatic offspring include lucrative stage productions in the 1890s; a Sigmund Romberg operetta, *Princess Flavia* (1925); films in the 1910s, 1920s, 1930s, 1950s, and 1970s; and a television adaptation in the 1980s. Ronald Colman, Stewart Granger, and Peter Sellers, among others, have swashbuckled their way through the double lead, and such stars as Madeleine Carroll and Deborah Kerr have played the alluring Flavia. Irreverent retellings have included George MacDonald Fraser's *Royal Flash* (1970), and K. J. Charles's homoerotic romance *The Henchmen of Zenda* (2018). The novel's greatest cultural impact, though, has been the new subgenre of 'Ruritanian romance', romance in this case meaning light fiction that deals with the extraordinary rather than the ordinary.[1] This term was already in use by the early 1900s to describe a legion of stories in which the protagonists find themselves happily ensnared in political and romantic intrigues in such pocket European territories as Laurania, Gerisau, Ehrenfelberstein, Hohenphalia, Montara, Grimland, Montalba, and Scarvania.[2] By 1900 one reviewer already felt that 'the minor states of Germany are by this time somewhat outworn as fields for romantic adven-ture'.[3] But they continued to come, with fictional Balkan countries some-times replacing fictional German ones. Writing in 1906, another weary reviewer calculated that by then there had appeared 'probably a hundred' of these formulaic novels.[4] New Ruritanian tales continued to appear for decades on both sides of the Atlantic, from the pens of a diverse army of writers, including P. G. Wodehouse (Mervo, in *The Prince and Betty*, 1912); Edgar Rice Burroughs (Lutha, in *The Mad King*, serialized 1914, 1915); E. Phillips Oppenheim (England itself, in *The Great Impersonation*, 1920, and Jakovia, in *Jeremiah and the Princess*, 1933); Dornford Yates (Riechtenburg in *Blood Royal*, 1929, and *Fire Below*, 1930); John Buchan (Evallonia, in *The House of the Four Winds*, 1935); Leslie Charteris (Roldavia in *Le Saint Refuse une Couronne*, 1954), and Leonard Wibberley (Grand Fenwick, *The Mouse that Roared* series, 1954–81). Among its American cousins, George Barr McCutcheon's *Graustark* series (1901–27) was easily the most successful, the basis of a plethora of stage and screen adaptations. Though now largely forgotten, McCutcheon's Graustark was once as well known to American readers as Hope's imaginary land, and the term 'Graustarkian' was interchangeable with 'Ruritanian'.

Aspects of Hope's fantasy leached into other cultural forms too. In children's fiction there are, for instance, Frances Hodgson Burnett's Samavia, in *The Lost Prince*, 1915, and Hergé's Syldavia, in *King Ottokar's Sceptre*, *Destination Moon*, and other Tintin adventures, from 1938 on. Science fiction and alternative history variants include Balkania in William Holt-White's *The Man Who Stole the Earth*, 1909, and Mars in Robert Heinlein's *Double Star*, 1956. Detective novels have occasionally found Ruritania a useful sort of place: Agatha Christie deploys Herzoslovakia, in *The Secret of Chimneys*, 1925, and Margery Allingham invents Averna for *Sweet Danger*, 1933.[5] Versions of *Zenda* even found their way into the work of more 'literary' writers, including Thomas Mann's *Royal Highness* (1909); Ford Madox Ford's *The New Humpty Dumpty* (1912) and *Vive Le Roy* (1937); Antal Szerb's *Oliver VII* (1942); and Vladimir Nabokov's *Pale Fire* (1962).[6]

Nor has Hope's influence been confined to fiction. The musical stage had long had a few of its own chocolate-box kingdoms, but it readily took to the new model, with its scope for ice-cream uniforms, splendid gowns, and sweeping waltzes. In the early 1900s *Zenda* inspired such popular musical comedies as *The King of Cadonia* (1908), *The Balkan Princess* (1910), and *Princess Caprice* (1912). This Ruritanian strain was later revived in the spectacular West End musical theatre of Ivor Novello in *Glamorous Night* (1935) and *King's Rhapsody* (1949), and, with the coming of the sound era, film musicals naturally followed.

After the Second World War, just when we might expect the old formula to have become hopelessly outdated, it was retailored for the new geopolitical order, and we see a clutch of Cold War narratives set in such territories as Barovia, Lichtenburg, Concordia, Gaillardia, and Grand Fenwick. With the fall of the Iron Curtain, pocket kingdoms finally went into something of a decline, but the runaway success of Meg Cabot's young-adult comic novel *The Princess Diaries* (2000) and its Disney film adaptations have put the fantasy country back on the map, so to speak: in the form of Genovia, it now resides somewhere on the Riviera.

What is the appeal of such pocket kingdoms? Imaginary territories are a commonplace of fantasy: their importance in the imaginative world of children is such that psychologists have argued that the tendency to create 'paracosms' is in fact innate rather than cultural.[7] Fictitious lands have also, of course, long been used by writers of all stripes. They have offered among other things a resource for those who wish to make political points—Thomas More's Utopia, for instance, and Jonathan Swift's Lilliput—and those who want to create a space in which magic exists, like H. Rider Haggard's Kôr, J. R. R. Tolkien's Middle Earth, and James Hilton's Shangri-La. However, Ruritania is something else again, neither a site for thought experiments nor a faery land forlorn. In terms of its relation to the everyday, it is only very mildly exotic: while it cannot be found on any map, and has some fairy-tale and daydream qualities, Rudolf Rassendyll's adventure playground is not in the distant reaches of Empire, nor in a magical realm, but a short train journey from Dresden. The people speak German; and its national air is almost certainly the waltz. And yet it is a country apart, in time as well as space: in a period in which technology was making the world a smaller place, Ruritania, as the name hints, offers an escape hatch from modernity into an old-fashioned, rural, and feudal kingdom in which true heroes and heroines can still flourish. (To use Mikhail Bakhtin's term, it is a distinct 'chronotope', a particular arrangement of time and space.)[8] Part of its original charm was that it provided all the swashbuckling adventure of the historical novel in the more-or-less present. Sequestered from the tide of progress, pastoral Ruritania cherishes not just court pageantry but the old-fashioned virtues of duty and honour; a man of spirit can find himself crowned king in such a place and win the love of a princess. In this light the kingdom's diminutive size is important: it works to make the heroic individual loom all the larger, and it also imbues the adventure story with a certain snug intimacy. In his 1973 history of science fiction *Billion Year Spree*,

Brian Aldiss describes certain post-apocalyptic stories as offering 'cosy catastrophes'; Anthony Hope launches a tradition of cosy adventure. Part of this cosiness is that whatever happens in Ruritania stays in Ruritania: however bloody the fighting, however serpentine the skulduggery, it will never spill over into international politics. This self-containment gives Ruritania a certain metafictional quality—books too are their own small worlds, after all, safely bounded by covers.

How, though, do we explain the extraordinary longevity and adaptability of the pocket-kingdom trope? Considering its pervasiveness, it has attracted very little in the way of critical attention, though a few critics have pointed the way. Raymond P. Wallace some thirty years ago described such novels as 'Cardboard Kingdom' fictions.[9] For Wallace the strongly plotted formula offered the 'romance and adventure that were missing from the daily life of the industrial age' (28); they and their successors were 'designed to move the heart and to instill the sense of romance' (34). As helpful as this is, it does not entirely explain how the Ruritanian formula in particular works to those ends, since many of the ingredients that Wallace isolates as Ruritanian/ Graustarkian—e.g., the presence of a hero and villain, coincidence, a chase, a confrontation—appear in other sorts of adventure fiction too. More recently, following the approach developed by Edward Said in *Orientalism* (1978), Vesna Goldsworthy has argued that Ruritanian fiction was part of the 'narrative colonisation' of the Balkans, a process by which writers imagined and projected images and fantasies of southeastern Europe that have had a lingering influence outside the literary realm.[10] This is a persuasive argument, and it certainly helps to illuminate a particular variety of the Ruritanian. There is a clear line, for instance, from such works as Anthony Hope's Balkan novel *Sophy of Kravonia* (1906) to interwar thrillers along the lines of John Buchan's *The House of the Four Winds* (1935) and subsequent political fantasies from the Balkan imaginary. However, such a hypothesis does not get us very far in explaining the German setting of the original *Zenda*, to say nothing of the varied locations of its many successors, from the Mediterranean island Mervo in *The Prince and Betty* to the Alpine Grand Fenwick in *The Mouse that Roared* to the Monaco-like Genovia in *The Princess Diaries*. Ruritania can be relied on to be a small, politically unstable monarchy, but its location has been a movable feast.

The later success of Ruritanian romance had both generic and historical underpinnings. Generically, *Zenda*'s plot of disguise, royal love intrigues, and swashbuckling was easily copied, though few writers matched Hope in creating a satisfactorily bijou setting for these elements. It also proved extremely adaptable to other media: the story's scope for royal pageantry and spectacle, as well as swordplay and romantic intrigue, made it a valuable theatrical property and attracted the early film industry. But popular culture does not exist in a vacuum, and I will suggest that Ruritania's resilience has also owed much to its capacity to model a whole series of political imaginaries. To this extent the fictional territory did indeed sometimes operate as a screen onto which Britain and the United States projected their images of Eastern Europe, as Goldsworthy argues, but more importantly it was a glass in which they saw their own distorted and miniaturized reflection. Ruritania is not a utopia, in which everything is better, or a dystopia, in which things are worse, but a heterotopia in which everything is different and yet the same.[11]

In the 1890s Ruritania provided a refracted version of Britain in which industrialization and the middle classes have yet to make any significant impact and in which modern policing is unheard of, allowing for feats of derring-do that would not be out of place in the seventeenth-century world of *The Three Musketeers*. At the same time, Ruritania caught the imagination because it was not in fact so very different from the Britain of the 1890s: the latter too, after all, was an unevenly developed Germanic monarchy, much given to ceremony, pageantry, and the importance of rank and still deploying cavalry armed with swords and lances. (Germany itself was by the 1890s a formidable, unified, military and industrial power, no longer a set of Ruritanian statelets, though it too was still run by the landed and titled.) The modern, industrial British state that took shape across the nineteenth century was always shadowed by this second self, the semi-feudal kingdom of tradition and spectacle that Tom Nairn describes in *The Enchanted Glass* (1988) as 'Ukania'. Likewise, the American version of Ruritania is a refracted version of American realities in the early 1900s. In McCutcheon's *Graustark* series, for instance, we initially encounter a space that seems to be the opposite of modern America, offering a semi-exotic testing ground for American character, but as the series continues Graustark converges with the America from which it is supposed to represent an escape, troubled by trade unions and Bolshevik subversives. Subsequent variations on the Ruritanian formula tend to replay this refractive logic. Ivor Novello's Krasnia is at once a musical fantasy land that recycles the recent history of the Romanian throne and an anamorphic image of Britain and its own royal troubles in the 1930s. Leonard Wibberley's Grand Fenwick in *The*

Mouse that Roared (1955) is a comic pocket kingdom in the French Alps but also a version of post-war Britain, a shrunken former Great Power, left behind in the atomic arms race between the US and Russia.

In what follows I have not attempted to give an encyclopedic account of all of the adventures of Ruritania. Such a book would, I feel, weary most readers, who may already regret that the effervescence of the original novels, plays and films has been transmuted into the still water of cultural history. Instead I have tried to spotlight the more significant episodes in the history of this curious country. Chapters 1 and 2 explore the origins of Anthony Hope's novel and its busy afterlife on the stage and screen. A surprise hit in 1894, *Zenda* was not without antecedents, from the swashbuckling *romans de cape et d'épée* of Alexandre Dumas to the Victorian stories of doubles and impostors of Mark Twain, R. L. Stevenson, and even Oscar Wilde. It appeared as part of a more general seismic shift in the market for fiction that saw stirring adventure romances vie with the older and more expansive domestic novel. Some contemporary critics hailed this 'revival of romance' as a wholesome alternative to such contemporary trends as 'New Woman' fiction, Zolaesque Naturalism, and aesthetic refinement, and *Zenda* became identified with a sort of counter-decadence. From the beginning, though, the novel's success was also bound up with its versatility, and hit stage versions followed in New York and London, offering royal pomp, spectacle, and athletic swash-buckling and creating a new breed of matinee idol. Again some saw these plays as an antidote to the more intellectual currents in the theatre of the day. As we shall see, these popular adaptations in turn led directly to the first screen *Zenda* in 1913, when Adolph Zukor persuaded the veteran stage lion James K. Hackett to reprise his stage performance for one of the very first American feature films. Many more screen *Zenda*s followed, including David O. Selznick's gorgeous 1937 version, which trades on the American fascination with royalty in these years and comments obliquely on the recent abdication of King Edward VIII. Subsequent adaptations fail to cap-ture the vitality of the 1937 film, and by the 1970s the trend was resolutely towards parody, with the 1979 Peter Sellers film effectively signalling that *Zenda* was exhausted as a big-screen property.

Chapter 3 considers the meteoric rise and slow descent of the once enor-mously successful *Graustark* series (1901–27) by George Barr McCutcheon, which Americanized Hope's plot. At a time when American heiresses were being presented at Buckingham Palace and marrying European aristocrats in significant numbers, McCutcheon's works explore the fantasy of a love match between American vigour and lingering European prestige. He also significantly changes the gender dynamics of the Ruritanian formula in the second novel in the series, *Beverly of Graustark*, in which a young American woman wins the love of a good prince and founds a royal American line. As with *Zenda*, the early success of the novels was bolstered by multiple stage productions, and in later years the series' popularity attracted Hollywood. The sumptuous 1920s screen versions feature such stars of the day as John Gilbert, Marion Davies, and Norma Talmadge, though what might have been the greatest adaptation, maverick director Erich von Stroheim's take on *East of the Setting Sun* (1927), never made it into production. After its zenith in the 1920s Graustark began to sink, at first gradually and then suddenly, so much so that, while *Zenda* lingers on in popular culture, *Graustark* is now largely forgotten, even among literary scholars.

Although the opera had long had its own chocolate-box principalities, Hope's bestseller gave musical pocket kingdoms a new lease of life, and in chapter 4 we explore this rich parallel tradition. Among the more famous examples are Marsovia (originally Pontevedro) in Franz Lehár's *The Merry Widow* (*Die lustige Witwe*, 1905), Karlsburg in Sigmund Romberg's *The Student Prince* (1924), and Krasnia in Ivor Novello's *Glamorous Night* (1935). But there were many minor variants, and the *Stage* could claim with some justice in 1949 that 'every Englishman who can write a musical comedy or light opera turns sooner or later...to the territory of those Balkan nations that were once rather uneasy kingdoms', lands of manly choruses, splendid hussars uniforms, and chiming bells.[12] Musical Ruritania has its own characteristics: romance rather than swashbuckling predominates, for example. And where Hope's Germanic kingdom is both a land of adventure and a site of self-denial, on the stage these qualities are sometimes divided between the petty kingdom and some other territory to which the principals escape: the fleshpots of belle époque Paris are in contrast to offstage Marsovia, while Heidelberg offers sweet romance and beery comradeship to the young Prince of Karlsburg. On screen too there have been innumerable musical principalities, including such classics as Ernst Lubitsch's Sylvania in *The Love Parade* (1929) and the Marx Brothers' delightfully daft Freedonia in *Duck Soup* (1933). The last major instance I discuss here is *Chitty Chitty Bang Bang* (1968), whose surprisingly sinister Vulgaria evokes some of the darker memories of the 1930s and 1940s. But that we may not be done with musical Ruritania yet, though, is suggested by the runaway success of the stage version of *Chitty Chitty Bang Bang* (2002, with many revivals) and indeed *Princess Diaries 2* (2004).

After the Second World War the chivalric world of Ruritania appeared very remote indeed. However, as we shall in chapter 5, it soon found itself dusted off for a string of Cold War narratives, in which fictional tiny countries provide a way of reflecting on life in the shadow of the Bomb. This strand includes the Bob Hope comedy *Where There's Life* (1947); the Ethel Merman musical *Call Me Madam* (1950; filmed 1953); Peter Ustinov's play *Romanoff and Juliet* (1956; filmed in 1961) and the Boulting Brothers' *Carlton Browne of the F. O.* (1959), set in, respectively, Barovia, Lichtenburg, Concordia, and Gaillardia. Perhaps the most impressive contribution to Cold War Ruritania, though, was made by Leonard Wibberley in his Grand Fenwick series, which began under the Eisenhower administration with *The Mouse that Roared* (1954–5) and lasted into the Reagan years with *The Mouse that Saved the West* (1981). Grand Fenwick, a tiny Anglophone duchy nestled somewhere between France and Switzerland, invades the United States, beats the USA and Russia to the moon, and comes generally to punch above its geopolitical weight. These bestselling novels and the films they inspired rejuvenated the old formula for the atomic age, bringing levity to a deeply anxious time.

With the end of the Cold War, Ruritania could no longer function as an imaginary space outside the 'spheres of influence' of the superpowers. However, variants on the bijou kingdom linger on in young adult fiction, as we see in chapter 6. Ruritania has been useful to children's writers since at least as early as Frances Hodgson Burnett's *The Lost Prince*, and many later children's writers also dipped into the Ruritanian well. For instance, Biggles helps out the state of Maltovia in Captain W. E. Johns' *Biggles Goes to War* (1938), and in Lorna Hill's ballet-school novel, *Rosanna Joins the Wells* (1956), the young dancer is helped by Leopold, the former King of Slavonia. But a whole new dynasty of Ruritanian fiction sprang up in 2000, when the American writer Meg Cabot published a bestselling young adult novel, *The Princess Diaries*, the first in what has become at the time of writing a series of eighteen. The books follow the comic tribulations of Mia Thermopolis, an American teenager who discovers one day that she is really the Princess of Genovia. *The Princess Diaries* was given a further boost by the Disney film that appeared in 2001, featuring Anne Hathaway as Mia and Julia Andrews as her formidable royal grand-mère. While Ruritania has outlived Graustark, here the American version of the formula has its revenge, so to speak, since

our central character has more in common with George Barr McCutcheon's
Beverly of Graustark than with Rudolf Rassendyll. But underwritten by
shifts in geopolitics as well as in popular culture, the *Diaries* introduces a
significant transformation of the old formula, as the fantasy moves away
from one of marrying royalty to discovering that one simply *is* a princess. In
fact in the novels, as opposed to the films, Genovia itself is scarcely needed
except as underwriting Mia's status as an American princess.

Across these variations in the Ruritanian formula, one of the most striking features is the lingering fascination with royalty, and with royal romance
in particular, and perhaps it will be as well to say something about this
before we move on. When *Zenda* was published in 1894, royal families were
still significant players on the European political stage. But after the First
World War, the Habsburg, Hohenzollern, and Ottoman dynasties were finished, the Romanovs of Russia had been killed or exiled, and the smaller fry
had largely gone too. The old empires, in Roy Fuller's phrase, broke like
biscuits. One reviewer observed in 1918 that the 'Ruritanian romance' was
'based upon the antiquated manners and customs of the minor courts of
Europe, which have been swept away by the world war'.[13] Indeed, as Adam
Tooze has recently outlined, Europe more generally had been crippled by
the war, leaving the United States as a sole superpower.[14] And yet, for decades to come, eligible European princes and princesses continued to walk
gracefully through the pages of Ruritanian novels and to don lovely gowns
and braided uniforms for the stage and screen. We might understand this
fixation with royalty in terms of the romance form's literary heritage:
as Northrop Frye argues, the literary romance can be read as a more sophisticated reworking of the folk or fairy tale, and life-altering encounters with
lovely princesses and valiant princes are very much the stuff of such popular
tales.[15] This narrative legacy may carry a modern political charge, of course.
Jeffrey Richards argues that in the twentieth-century screen swashbuckler
the monarchy continues to operate as a 'metaphor for the Establishment',
and the same might be said here: Ruritanian romance may be read as conservative in its politics, presenting the state as something to be preserved at
all costs to the self.[16]

I would suggest, though, that there might also be other ways of reading
this interest in blue bloods and royal romance. For one thing, later Ruritanian
tales in part reflect the changing position of royals, as they become less
political actors and more participants in modern celebrity culture. Popular
enchantment with the surviving royal families was fuelled by media coverage

of what they were doing and wearing, and whom they were marrying, coverage that increased, if anything, in the 1920s and 1930s, after the great thinning of dynasties. The British royal family became the most prominent of all, and if the Windsors were never wholly assimilated into an expanding culture of celebrity—never 'just celebrities', as Tom Nairn points out—they were not immune to its gravitational pull either.[17] Frank Prochaska has shown that America had been fascinated with Britain's royalty throughout the nineteenth century, and in the Edwardian years the country's elite sent their daughters to be presented at the British court.[18] But we see an investment in royalty as celebrity spectacle in the media coverage of the abdication crisis in 1936; the coronations of George VI in 1937 and Elizabeth II in 1953; the marriage of Prince Charles and Lady Diana Spencer in 1981; and the installation of their very own princess, when Grace Kelly became Princess Grace of Monaco in 1956.[19] The marriage of the American actress Meghan Markle to Prince Harry, Duke of Sussex, in 2018 created a similar excitement.

We can, then, interpret the lingering appeal of Ruritanian royalty and tales of cross-caste marriage as a reflex of a more pervasive celebrity culture. No doubt it is. I would suggest, though, that we might also see a utopian dimension to this fascination and a longing for forms of value beyond those of the market economy. Just as Ruritania itself is imagined as a pocket kingdom that escapes the rising tide of modernity, so too do its princes and princesses stand outside the quotidian world of pence or cents. To be such an individual—or to fall in love with one—is, perhaps, to be removed not simply from the everyday but from capitalism itself. At any rate, what exactly these royal reveries mean is something that we can consider further as we go along. Rather than speculate any further, let us turn now to *The Prisoner of Zenda*, the origin story for all of these fantasies of pocket kingdoms and instant coronation, and to its author, struggling young barrister and aspiring Liberal politician Anthony Hawkins. Under the name Anthony Hope, he first charmed the magic casement opening upon Ruritania and became one of the most successful authors of his time.

I

Anthony Hope Hawkins, George Alexander, and *The Prisoner of Zenda*

On an overcast day in November 1893, Ruritania came into being somewhere between St Martin's Lane in Covent Garden and Brick Court in Middle Temple. Anthony Hawkins, an ambitious young barrister who wrote light fiction under the name Anthony Hope, was sauntering back from court when the outline came to him of a story of lookalikes set in a fictional Mitteleuropean kingdom. Out of this kernel grew *The Prisoner of Zenda*, a suspenseful tale about an aristocratic English holidaymaker who happens to bear a strong resemblance to the King of Ruritania and who is persuaded to impersonate him in order to foil a coup by his half-brother, Michael, Duke of Strelsau. The novel spellbound its original readership and became the publishing sensation of 1894; a steady seller long after, it inspired scores of copycat tales of royal intrigue in pocket principalities. Here I want to follow the story of this late Victorian bestseller and to suggest some of the reasons for its original impact, as well for its power to enchant long afterwards. What its blend of suspense, swashbuckling, and romance seemed to offer for some of its first readers was a bracing alternative to the intellectual and introspective fare of the fin de siècle, including the literature of Aestheticism, Decadence, and the New Woman. But, almost from the beginning, the novel's runaway success was inseparable from its adaptability, since from 1895 onward stage versions of *Zenda* drew eager audiences on both sides of the Atlantic. In the United States, first E. A. Sothern and then James K. Hackett made the play into an athletic stage swashbuckler that toured around the country for years. In Britain, at the upmarket St James's Theatre, the actor-manager George Alexander transformed Edward Rose's adaptation of *Zenda* into a sumptuous romantic spectacle and reinvented himself as a matinee idol. These plays in turn ensured the continuing popularity of the novel. By the early 1900s Anthony Hawkins' street reverie had become the 'Ruritanian romance', an established subgenre on page and stage and one well placed to conquer the new medium of film.

Anthony Hawkins

Anthony Hawkins was a somewhat unlikely candidate to be the author of one of the great adventure stories of modern times. To his Oxford contemporaries, and indeed to himself, success at the Bar and a political career would have seemed a far more natural course. Born Anthony Hope Hawkins in Clapton, Hackney, in London on 9 February 1863, Hawkins was the son of Jane Isabella Grahame and a prominent clergyman, the Reverend Edwards Comerford Hawkins, headmaster of St John's Foundation School for the Sons of Poor Clergy and later vicar of a fashionable church, St Bride's on Fleet Street. His mother's family hailed from Scotland, and through her he was related to the Scottish writer and banker Kenneth Grahame, author of *The Wind in the Willows* (1908). The Hawkins family, long settled in Hitchin, Hertfordshire, had long produced respectable professional men: doctors, lawyers, and clergymen, though the author's grandfather had married into an affluent Irish family, the Comerford-Caseys, who had prospered through the manufacture of soap.[1] After a period at his father's school, Anthony went on to shine academically at Marlborough, then a relatively new public school, and from there he won an exhibition scholarship to Balliol College, Oxford. The renowned Oxford reformer Benjamin Jowett was master of Balliol at this time, and the college trained many of Britain's leaders in various fields. Hawkins's contemporaries, for instance, included Lord Curzon, future viceroy of India, and Edward Grey, later a leading Liberal politician. Among his more immediate circle at Balliol were L. T. Hobhouse (who became an academic and theorist of Liberalism), J. A. Spender (future editor of the *Westminster Gazette*), Cosmo Lang (later Archbishop of York, and of Canterbury), and Charles Mallet, later Sir Charles Mallet, liberal politician and Hawkins's biographer. From Corpus Christi there was Henry Newbolt, whose line 'Play up! Play up! and play the game!' from the poem 'Vitaï Lampada' stirred imperial hearts, before becoming an object of scorn for a later generation. Keenly interested in sport as well as politics, a staunch

Liberal, and a gifted debater, young Hawkins played rugby, worked on the *Oxford Magazine*, and was president at different times of the Liberal Russell Club and the Oxford Union. Among the visiting speakers he met in this period were the Irish Land League campaigner Michael Davitt, whom Hawkins took to dinner and later recalled quite warmly, and William Morris (another old Marlburian), writer, socialist, and proponent of the Arts and Crafts movement.

Oxford was a more-than-congenial environment for Hawkins, and he would have prolonged his stay if he could, but despite achieving a first-class honours degree in Greats (i.e., Classics), he failed to obtain a fellowship. A career as a barrister was the obvious choice for someone with his debating talents and political interests, and he returned to London to read for the Bar, to which he was called in 1887. Like those of many young barristers, his first years in chambers were dispiriting; finding it hard to get briefs, he depended on the income from a small inheritance and lived with his widowed father in the vicarage of St Bride's on Fleet Street, which was conveniently close to London's legal quarter, if a rather quiet setting for a sociable young man. In this lean period young Hawkins was grateful to obtain some work as marshal, or assistant, to his cousin, the prominent judge, Sir Henry 'Hanging' Hawkins, later Lord Brampton. (It is worth noting in passing that Sir Henry had acted as a Queen's Counsel in Victorian Britain's most famous case of impersonation, that of the Tichborne claimant, in which Thomas Castro, a butcher living in Wagga Wagga, claimed to be the long-lost Sir Roger Tichborne, heir to the sizeable Tichborne baronetcy.)[2] H. H. Asquith, head of Hawkins's legal chambers and later Liberal prime minister, also helped Hawkins's career in this period, and briefs eventually began to trickle in, partly through his Balliol connections. A wider prospect opened before him when he was asked to run as a Liberal candidate for Wycombe in Buckinghamshire, but, despite a walking tour in Ireland to brush up on Home Rule, the great topic of the day, he failed to oust the sitting Conservative, Viscount Curzon (not Hope Hawkins's Oxford contemporary). He was convincing enough in his campaign to be offered opportunities to stand for election again in 1895 and 1900, but ill health prevented him from pursuing his political ambitions, something that he regretted all his life.

Throughout his time at the Bar, Hawkins was also trying his hand at fiction. In 1890, under the name Anthony Hope, he published at his own expense his first novel, *A Man of Mark*, a semicomic tale of political intrigue and corruption in Aureataland, an imaginary South American republic, a very different place to Ruritania. Despite its engagingly rackety first-person narrator, it failed to attract many readers. Another novel in this line, *Half A Hero* (1893), is set in New Lindsey, a fictional British colony, in which a determined politician with a past fails to achieve his ambitions. Not all of Anthony Hope's work turned on politics, and other early efforts included *Father Stafford* (1891), a story of religious crisis, presumably inspired by Mrs Humphry Ward's bestselling novel of religious doubt of three years before, *Robert Elsmere*. The *Athenaeum* complained that, despite its serious subject, Hope's novel was largely comprised of 'clever, cynical, generally disjointed, and sometimes epigrammatic conversation, or, often more accurately, slang.'[3] He enjoyed more success with a society story, *Mr Witt's Widow* (1892), a humorous tale of a prosperous widow whose petty-criminal past returns to haunt her. One of its admirers was the prolific late-Victorian man of letters Andrew Lang, another Balliol graduate, who puffed the novel in his influential column in *Longman's Magazine*, 'At the Sign of the Ship'. (We will encounter Lang again as an important advocate for *The Prisoner of Zenda*.) Hope's most successful work at this time was also in the comic line, the *Dolly Dialogues*, which he published in the *Westminster Gazette*, where his old college friend J. A. Spender worked. Breezily sketching the running flirtation between our narrator, Mr Carter, and the lively Dorothea 'Dolly' Foster, later Lady Mickleham, the *Dialogues* were popular with readers of the *Gazette* and were published in volume form after the success of *Zenda*. Their society setting and vaguely amoral tone led one magazine to dub Hope the 'chief etcher' of a counter-Victorian 'New Hedonism'.[4]

There is one piece from this period that directly anticipates *The Prisoner of Zenda*. 'Sport Royal', the title story of a collection Hope published in 1893, is the light-hearted, first-person narrative of a British traveller, Julius Jason, who is mistaken for a Colonel Despard in Heidelberg and drawn into the affairs of the Prince and Princess of the fictional Glottenberg. He fights a duel, unknowingly acts as a go-between for the Princess in a clandestine affair, and is stabbed by her when he tries to force her to return to her husband. Recovering from his injuries, he keeps the knife as a memento of his chivalrous career: 'I have it still, a little tortoise-shell-handled thing, with a sharp—a very sharp—point. On the blade is engraved, in German letters, "Sophia". It is a pretty toy, and in its delicacy, its tininess, its elegance, its seeming harmlessness, and its very sharp point, it reminds me much of Princess Ferdinand of Glottenberg.'[5] Julius Jason shares Rudolf Rassendyll's wry humour and appetite for adventure, but the story does not have the narrative drive of the later novel. As Sir Charles Mallet notes, Hawkins was 'on his way to Ruritania, but had not yet arrived' (68). Glottenberg reappears in a post-*Zenda* collection of Ruritanian tales, *The Heart of Princess Osra* (1896), in which Ludwig, Prince of Glottenberg, comes to Strelsau to court the Princess, so perhaps Hawkins thought of them as contiguous territories.[6]

According to his own account, on Tuesday, 28 November, of that year, Hope was strolling back to his chambers in Middle Temple from a sitting of the Westminster County Court in St Martin's Lane when he thought up another story of adventure in a fictional kingdom, one that would turn not just on mistaken identity but on the idea of doubles.[7] The name Ruritania and the plot came to him quickly, and within a month he had a full draft of the novel. Our hero and first-person narrator, Rudolf Rassendyll, is a 6-foot 2-inch, 29-year-old English gentleman of leisure, the younger brother of Lord Burlesdon, enjoying a very comfortable income of 2,000 pounds a year. Educated in Germany, the confident young Englishman speaks 'German as readily and perfectly as English', and, as a former army officer, he is also a skilled rider, 'a strong, though hardly a fine swordsman, and a good shot' (11). He is also, as it happens, distantly related to the royal family of Ruritania, the Elphbergs, through an eighteenth-century dalliance between King Rudolf the Third and Rassendyll's ancestress, the Countess Amelia.[8] Rassendyll himself has the distinctive red hair, long nose, and blue eyes of the Elphbergs, and his father has named him Rudolf because of his 'sneaking fondness for the Elphbergs'.[9] At a loose end, he decides to visit Ruritania, a small German-speaking principality, where the coronation of his distant cousin Rudolf is about to take place at the capital, Strelsau. He stops off in Paris, where he meets his old friends George Featherly and the poet and journalist Bertram Bertrand; Bertrand is in love with one Antoinette de Mauban, who for her part is more interested in the Duke of Strelsau, half-brother to the King of Ruritania. Our hero and this lady travel on the same train to Ruritania via Dresden (then capital of the Kingdom of Saxony) but rather than competing for accommodation with the coronation crowds, Rassendyll leaves the train at Zenda, 'a small town fifty miles short of the capital, and about ten from the frontier' (23). There his adventures really begin, after a chance meeting with the King, whom he discovers to be his double. Because of this striking resemblance our hero is almost immediately drawn into national affairs: when Duke Michael drugs the bibulous King Rudolf's wine on the eve of his coronation, two of his followers—the grizzled veteran Colonel Sapt and young Fritz von Tarlenheim—persuade the Englishman to impersonate him and be crowned in his place. Otherwise the crown is likely to fall to the scheming Duke of Strelsau, alias Black Michael, who covets not just the throne but also the King's fiancée, Princess Flavia. It is all rather far-fetched, but then the novel is quite self-conscious about its daydream qualities: before he meets with Sapt and von Tarlenheim, our hero falls asleep in the forest of Zenda and dreams that he is King of Ruritania and husband of the beautiful Flavia. In the waking world, and amid much pomp and ceremony, Rassendyll is duly crowned King and meets the 'pale and lovely' (67) Princess, who also has the distinctive red hair of the Elphbergs. Meanwhile, Michael abducts the real King and imprisons him in the impregnable Castle of Zenda, where he is guarded by the Duke's loyal henchmen, who include three international swordsmen: a Frenchman, De Gautet, a Belgian, Bersonin, and an Englishman, Detchard. As we learn later, if the castle is attacked, their orders are to kill the King and throw his body down 'Jacob's Ladder', a large pipe feeding directly into the castle moat. Rudolf has by this time fallen for the flame-haired Flavia, and when she returns his love he is briefly tempted to continue his impersonation and leave the real King to languish, before his better self prevails. While Rudolf, Sapt, and Tarlenheim plot to storm the Castle of Zenda, the Englishman is stabbed in the shoulder in an encounter with the wicked but debonair Rupert of Hentzau, the most formidable of Michael's allies. But the player-king shrugs off his injury, and the ultimate assault on Zenda is an elaborate and violent set piece that sees him swim a moat and cut down Michael's three foreign henchmen. Detchard is the last to go, defeated in an extended swordfight as the real King watches. The hired blade has the better of our hero until he slips in a pool of blood, giving Rudolf has his chance: 'Like a dart I was upon him. I caught him by the throat and... drove my point through his neck' (253). Michael, though, dies at the hands of his own ally, Rupert, summoned by Madame de Mauban's screams to her room, where the predatory young cavalier has gone 'determined to have his will' (271). Rupert escapes from the Castle of Zenda, and he and our hero clash again in the forest, before his enemy rides off to fight another day, 'singing as he went, for all that there was [a] gash on his cheek' (266). As the real King recovers, Rudolf finally reveals his identity to Flavia, and, heartbroken, they must now part. Rudolf returns to England, where he wonders if he will ever see his lovely princess again. She sends a single red rose each year via Fritz, whom he meets in Dresden. With the rose comes a slip of paper that simply says 'Rudolf—Flavia—always' (309).

It did not take long to place this stirring romantic tale. Impressed by the serialized *Dolly Dialogues*, the Bristol-based publisher J. W. Arrowsmith had already solicited a novel from Hawkins, and, though he would have preferred a novel set in England, he readily accepted the manuscript of *Zenda*. In the first week of April, 1894, *The Prisoner of Zenda; Being the History of Three Months in the Life of an English Gentleman* appeared in the firm's mid-priced 3/6 series, alongside such light reading as Jerome K. Jerome's *Three Men in a Boat* (1889) and the Grossmith brothers' *Diary of a Nobody* (1892).[10] Many of its first readers were reminded of the historical novels of an earlier era and were particularly struck by the curious mixture of the modern and the chivalric. The *Times* compared Hope to Alexandre Dumas père and admired the way he 'interpolates a medieval romance in the civilization of the nineteenth century', creating in the process a 'singular mixture of epochs': 'no tale of adventure in far-off, mysterious countries surpasses the strange excitements [of] this story of the three months spent by an English gentleman in the petty kingdom of Ruritania, in Germany' ('Recent Novels', 21 May 1894). In the *Academy* ('New Novels', 2 June 1894), the reviewer also saw the French connection and enthusiastically greeted this 'roman de cape et d'épee' [sword and cape novel]. *The Pall Mall Magazine*, on the other hand, was reminded of the Knights of the Round Table ('Reviews: Two Novels', 22 May 1894): 'The hero of this brilliant little extravaganza is no medieval knight errant, but a thoroughly modern young man about town... yet the adventures which befall him would put those of "Arthur's Knights" into the shade'. In the United States, similar views prevailed: the *New York Times* heard echoes of Dumas, and Sarah Barnwell Elliott in the *Sewanee Review* stressed the time-travel aspect of the novel: 'beginning in the Park Lane of to-day, in half a dozen little pages we are landed in the Middle Ages, and only now and then are we shocked back to the nineteenth century by the mention of a railway train'. She also praised the 'tender gleam of love that in the end proves to be the "love that loves alway[s]"'.[11] This romantic aspect of the story was a significant departure from the light and ironic treatment of personal relations in Hope's earlier work, especially the *Dolly Dialogues*.

Hope's chocolate-box adventure story soon became a considerable commercial as well as critical success. In its first couple of months it sold almost 7,000 copies in Britain, an impressive number in this period for a novelist who was still a relatively obscure figure. (By way of comparison, the following year, Thomas Hardy, then at the height of his fame as a novelist, recorded sales of 20,000 for *Jude the Obscure* in its first three months.)[12] Now aged 30, only a year older than his red-haired hero, the author decided that this was a fateful moment, and in July he wrote to his clients to say he was leaving the Bar: Anthony Hope the writer had outpaced Anthony Hawkins the barrister. Nor was his belief in the novel misplaced: by the end of the year it was *the* bestselling book in Britain according to the wholesale lists, outselling Sarah Grand's controversial 'New Woman' novel of the previous year, *The Heavenly Twins*. It stayed on the bestseller lists until 1898, though it was replaced at the top by such novels as George du Maurier's sensational tale of Bohemia and mesmerism *Trilby* and Marie Corelli's supernatural melodrama *The Sorrows of Satan*.[13] *Zenda* remained a steady seller for the next thirty years.[14] By 1933 Arrowsmith's alone had sold 300,000 copies in Britain, and other British publishers had sold 200,000, but those figures understate the novel's commercial value, even in Anglophone editions, since it is likely that large numbers were sold throughout the Empire, including school editions in India and Egypt. The American rights had been bought by the firm of Henry Holt, who also published the work of Thomas Hardy and Robert Louis Stevenson; when the novel had sold profitably for a number of years, they released the rights for newspaper syndication.[15] Further income accrued to Hope from his reading tours of the United States, from the highly successful dramatic, musical, and film versions, and of course from the novel's prequel and sequel, *The Heart of Princess Osra* (1896) and *Rupert of Hentzau* (1898), as we shall see. Outside the Anglophone world, the novel's success was more uneven: a German translation, *Der König von Ruritanien: Romantische Erzählung*, appeared as early as 1897, and the Hungarian *A zendai fogoly* in 1900; these were followed by Spanish-language editions, with *El rey de Ruritania* published in Chile in 1901 and *El prisionero de Zenda* published in Argentina in 1909. Both *Zenda* and its sequel were serialized in the *Corriere* of Milan in 1902 (Mallet 168). However, the French *Le Roman d'un roi* did not arrive until 1911, the same year as the Danish *Fangen paa Zenda*. A Hebrew translation, published in Paris, followed in 1925, and there was a Japanese newspaper serial version.[16]

   Zenda's greatest international success was in the United States, where its vogue led to one unusual source of licensing revenues: in 1896 Parker Brothers manufactured a board game based on the novel, in which players compete for advantage on a stylized map of Ruritania (see Figure 1.1).

Figure 1.1. Detail of the Parker Brothers board game, *The Prisoner of Zenda* (1896)

The cover illustration features a stylized cameo image of James K. Hackett, sword in hand, in the American stage version of *Zenda*.[17] It is unlikely, though, that Hope or his publishers ever saw any return from such spin-offs as the 1903 stage illusion called 'The Prisoner of Zenda', in which the magician, bound with steel bands, escapes from a locked room. And while it must have been gratifying to his ego, if he ever knew about them, no money accrued from the various North American towns that were named Zenda in honour of the novel.[18] (As we shall see in the next chapter, one of these towns went on to provide a useful source of ballyhoo for the 1937 screen adaptation.)

In 1896 Arrowsmith published *The Heart of Princess Osra*, a sort of pre-quel, in which the sister of the eighteenth-century King Rudolf the Third (Rudolf Rassendyll's distant ancestor) appears. It is a collection of inter-linked stories, rather than a novel, and focuses on the love and acts of courage inspired by the lovely Osra. Much better known is the sequel to the *Prisoner of Zenda* entitled *Rupert of Hentzau*, which seems to have been written shortly after the first novel but not published until the end of 1897, when it came out in serial form in the *Pall Mall Gazette*; the book was published by Arrowsmith in 1898, with illustrations by the American artist Charles Dana Gibson (see Figure 1.2). Swashbuckling and chivalry are again to the fore, with Rudolf Rassendyll, Fritz, and Sapt rallying

The Decision of Heaven.

Figure 1.2. Charles Dana Gibson, 'The Decision of Heaven', between pp. 378 and 379 of the first edition of Anthony Hope's *Rupert of Hentzau*

around the Queen to defend her honour and the handsome but vicious Hentzau returning as the principal villain. This time Fritz is our first-person narrator, and the action turns on the love token that he brings every year from Princess Flavia to our hero. One year she abandons her usual caution and encloses a love letter with the single rose, only for Rupert and his minions to steal it from Fritz. To prevent the incriminating document being given to the King, Rudolf once again impersonates him, but the scheme goes awry, and when His Majesty is killed by Rupert, Rassendyll is forced to continue in his role. He defeats Rupert in the climactic duel—despite the latter's characteristic attempts to cheat—and our hero is then left on the horns of a dilemma: should he go on pretending to be the real King, as Fritz, Sapt, and Flavia want; or should he renounce his illegitimate power, and once again leave? He must choose the path of love or that of honour. His passionate feelings for Flavia tempt him sorely, and, of course, he has proven himself to be an excellent leader, a better King than the real one; moreover it will be difficult to leave without exposing the Queen. But in the end he is spared this difficult decision, shot dead by one of Rupert's faithful henchmen, Bauer. Canny readers might have anticipated such an ending, given that Fritz rather than Rudolf is our narrator. The real King is secretly interred in the forest, and the player King, Rassendyll, is buried in the royal vault in the Cathedral of Strelsau, over which the Queen orders a Latin inscription to be placed, which Fritz translates as: 'To Rudolf, who reigned lately in this city, and reigns for ever in her heart—QUEEN FLAVIA'.[19]

The novel ends with Fritz taking his 10-year-old son to see the tomb, to 'tell him what I may of brave King Rudolf, how he fought and how he loved, and how he loved the Queen's honour and his own above all things in this world' (384). This might have done very well as an ending, but Hope decides to sound one last plangent chord: the very last words go to the boy: '"God save the Queen, father", said he' (385). Despite, or perhaps because of, this teary ending, *Rupert of Hentzau* was warmly received, with the *Times* rating it as in some respects even better than its original ('Rupert of Hentzau', 25 July 1898). The death of Rudolf seems to have been accepted, perhaps in part because it was widely known beforehand that this would be the last of Ruritania. As the *Pall Mall Gazette* put it, 'Wonderland is not easily re-entered through the Looking-glass' ('Review', 2 August 1898). By February 1899, some 46,000 copies of *Rupert of Hentzau* had been sold in Britain and the colonies, and sales in the United States were probably at least as good, helped by the fact that *The Prisoner of Zenda* was selling briskly there in an edition of 100,000, priced at 50 cents.[20]

Made financially comfortable by his Ruritanian income, in 1903 Hope married Elizabeth Somerville Sheldon, a Titian-haired American whom he had met on one of his lecture tours, and they bought a substantial house on the south side of Bedford Square.[21] There they lived until his ill health led them to move to Surrey in 1925. Although none of his subsequent books did quite as well as *Zenda*, he had been able to make a good living from his pen, not least because he had in 1894 very wisely put his future publishing arrangements in the hands of A. P. Watt, Britain's first real literary agent.

By the time he married he was already a household name, well-known enough to be parodied by Bret Harte in his *Condensed Novels: New Burlesques* (1902), where *Zenda* appears as 'Rupert the Resembler, by A-th-y H-pe', a tale set in Trulyruralania. (Harte scores a few hits: the castle of Bock is described as 'a fine old medieval structure', but one with 'all the appliances of modern times': it was 'lit by electricity, had fire-escapes on each of the turrets, four lifts, and was fitted up by one of the best West End establishments...[T]he sanitary arrangements were excellent.')[22] But others were happy to imitate rather than parody, and soon there was a throng of Ruritanian novels from other pens on both sides of the Atlantic. In Britain these included Sydney C. Grier's *An Uncrowned King*; Samuel Gordon's *The Queen's Quandary* (1903); Percy Brebner's *Princesss Maritza* (1906); and Louis Tracy's *A Son of the Immortals* (1912); and in the United States there were, among many others, Richard Harding Davis's *The Princess Aline* (1895); Harold McGrath's *Arms and the Woman* (1899) and *The Puppet Crown* (1901); and, most successfully, as we shall see, George Barr McCutcheon's *Graustark* series (1901–27).[23] The term 'Ruritanian romance' was already in use by the early 1900s to describe the new subgenre, in which protagonists found themselves happily ensnared in political and romantic intrigues in such territories as Gerisau, Ehrenfelberstein, Hohenphalia, Montara, Grimland, Montalba, and Scarvania.[24] (Romance is used here in the sense of a fiction of the extraordinary rather than the ordinary; it is a term with a long history, often as the foil to the 'proper' novel.)[25] In the *Academy* of October 1906, a reviewer reckoned that there were by then 'probably a hundred' of these Ruritanian adventures, and as a result 'the device has become stale', but stale or not they were eagerly consumed for decades.[26] Long after many of continental Europe's real royal families had been swept away by the First World War, descendants of the House of Elphberg continued to appear in such interwar adventure stories as Dornford Yates's *Blood Royal* and *Fire Below* (1929 and 1930, set in Riechtenburg) and John Buchan's *The House of the Four Winds* (1935, set in Evallonia). More playful reworkings of the formula in these years include Ronald Firbank's *The Flower Beneath the Foot* (1923), which turns Ruritania into an exotic camp space, returning Hope's fantasy to the 1890s decadence that it seemed to so ardently reject.

Anatomy of a Bestseller

What was the appeal of such Ruritanian fare? What were the narrative ingredients of the first 'Ruritanian romance' that made it so irresistible and so imitable? We should note at the outset, of course, that the telling of the tale was a significant factor in the success of Hope's novel and one not easily captured as part of a formula. As many reviewers observed, Hope's prose is lively and crisp, and the plot unfolds at a brisk clip. Our first-person narrator, though scarcely self-deprecating, is a direct and engaging character, and, despite his chivalrous ways, there is something in him of the rackety hero of Hope's first novel, *The Man of Mark*. He is a type that would prove quite portable even outside of the Ruritanian subgenre: John Buchan's resourceful Richard Hannay, hero of *The 39 Steps* and its sequels, owes something to him, for instance.

Modifying Raymond P. Wallace's 'Cardboard Kingdom' list from the Introduction a little, we can see that the narrative features include mistaken identity, a threat to be overcome, a villain, swordplay, and romantic interest in a fictitious kingdom.[27] But far from being unique to the Ruritanian romance, these are in fact the staples of adventure narratives more generally. As John G. Cawelti somewhat archly phrases it: 'the central fantasy of the adventure story is that of the hero... overcoming obstacles and dangers and accomplishing some important and moral mission. Often, though not always, the hero's trials are the machinations of a villain, and... the hero frequently receives... the favors of one or more attractive young ladies'.[28] Such stories are rooted in the tradition of literary romance (e.g., the medieval tales of King Arthur), which in turn, as Northrop Frye notes, takes us back to the folk or fairy tale.[29] One of Hope's boldest moves, in fact, was to return the modern adventure story to these roots. In *Zenda* the fairy tale is unusually close to the surface, since the hero's mission involves him becoming a king who is to marry a beautiful princess, but Hope disguises this

fairy-tale aspect in various ways. For one thing, our hero is no woodcutter
or farmer's youngest son but quite a grand gentleman, the younger brother
of Lord Burlesdon; and, however remotely, he is descended from a King.
The novel's ending likewise mutes the fairy-tale aspect, ultimately making
Rassendyll and Flavia part ways, though for a time we are allowed to imagine
that he might remain as King, with Flavia his Queen. This barely suppressed
fairy-tale/wish-fulfilment element provides a powerful narrative hook.

The novel's central device of the double has also been a narrative trope
since the earliest times, as Hope himself acknowledged, and in this period it
was a commonplace of stage farce and operetta, as well as of such novels as
Mark Twain's *The Prince and the Pauper* (1881). Again, though, *Zenda* gives
the old device a modern finish, not least through its references to heredity,
very much a topic of the times, as we shall see. With his red hair, Rassendyll
is physically a throwback to his Elphberg ancestor, a romantic figure out of
the past, a swashbuckling hero who, as several reviewers remarked, would
not be out of place in *The Three Musketeers*. In this respect the novel is following as well as advancing a contemporary trend, since it is around this
time that the term 'swashbuckling' begins to be used to describe plays and
novels, though there is a whole school of nineteenth-century fiction that
fits the bill: some of the novels of Scott, for example, and the French *roman
de cape et d'epée* or '*bretteur*' (e.g., the work of Dumas père and Paul Féval).[30]
Swashbuckling is not an incidental detail of the novel but provides a sort of
theatre of manliness in which masculinity is performed through feats of
arms. Thus while there is some gunplay in *Zenda*, the real set pieces are the
sword fights, like that with Duke Michael's English henchman, Detchard, in
the final assault on the castle; likewise an extended duel with dashing villain
Rupert of Hentzau provides the climax of the sequel to *Zenda*.

Along with the freedoms of swashbuckling, though, come the restraints
of old-fashioned chivalry.[31] As Jeffrey Richards observes of screen swashbucklers, their 'values are the values of the knightly class'.[32] Our hero abides
by certain rules, and he uses his courage and strength only in defence of the
realm. In *Rupert of Hentzau* this chivalric nature is made even clearer: his
mission is the defence of the Queen's good name, positioning him as
Lancelot to her Guinevere. One can, of course, overstate the knightly aspect
of Ruritania. For example, there is nothing particularly chivalrous about the
way in which Rassendyll in chapter 14 stabs the sleeping minion who is
supposed to guard the moat outside the king's cell: 'Of all the deeds in my
my life I love the least to think of this, and whether it was the act of a man

or a traitor I will not ask. I said to myself: "It is war—and the king's life is the stake"' (197). This is more in the practical spirit of guerrilla warfare than Round Table courtesy. But by and large the swashbuckler must play by the rules, and one's senior adversaries are treated with a certain respect. Foremost among these is Rupert, whose wicked but dashing ways are admired by Rassendyll, even as he escapes at the end of chapter 19: 'Thus he vanished—reckless and wary, graceful and graceless, handsome, debonair, vile, and unconquered' (266). Killing him at all costs is not playing the game; our hero has already passed up a fine chance to shoot Rupert in the back earlier in the same chapter.

Chivalry also governs the treatment of the relations between the sexes in the novel. The female characters do not take part in the swashbuckling, even schemers like Madame de Mauban; instead they are beautiful and soulful, prizes worth fighting for. We are in a world, then, at odds not just with the realities of warfare but also with the developing image of the modern woman as participant in life outside the home; the New Women, that 1890s icon of educated and politically active femininity, has no place here. True womanhood means that where men must fight hand to hand, relations between lovers are pushed onto a higher plane, so while the love between Rudolf and Flavia is passionate, it is more a matter of them being twin souls as magnetically attracted bodies. Theirs is a passion that thrives on self-sacrifice and can survive not just their geographical separation but even Flavia's dutiful marriage to the real King; she is expected to close her eyes and think of Ruritania. This idea of an ennobling passion find its greatest realization in their final scene together. A requiem mass for the fallen is being sung in the background as Rassendyll and Flavia say their tender goodbyes:

> The soft, sweet, pitiful music rose and fell as we stood opposite one another, her hands in mine.
>
> 'My queen and my beauty!' said I.
>
> 'My lover and true knight!' she said. 'Perhaps we shall never see each other again. Kiss me, my dear, and go!' (294)

It is not the resolution of a conventional happy ending that is being offered us but some kind of transcendent love and a vision of self-denial in a higher cause. The fairy-tale fantasy of marrying a princess is over-painted with an arguably more grown-up fantasy of self-sacrifice for a greater good.

But we have skirted around the most important ingredient in Hope's genre-shaping romance: the factor that enables all the others to operate successfully is Ruritania itself. The name hints at its pastoral qualities but more specifically at its status as a time-space world (a chronotope, in Mikhail Bakhtin's terms). Ruritania combines the archaic and the modern in a bijou form. It is the kingdom's size and semi-modernity that makes possible Rassendyll's involvement at the highest levels of national affairs, that licenses the swordplay, and that underpins the chivalric romance. Such adventures, after all, would have been deeply implausible in a larger and more modernized state, with all the inconveniences of modern policing and parliamentary democracy. As Rassendyll dryly reminds us in chapter 15, 'Ruritania is not England, or the quarrel between Duke Michael and myself could not have gone on, with the remarkable incidents which marked it, without more public notice being directed to it' (203). Again Hope was not the first to see the possibilities such settings offered, and he may have been influenced by, for instance, Robert Louis Stevenson's *Prince Otto* (1885), which describes court intrigue around an ineffective German prince in fictional Grünewald.[33] Nor was Stevenson entirely a pioneer: George Meredith's *The Adventures of Harry Richmond* (1871) and, as we shall see in chapter 4, Jacques Offenbach's *La Grande-Duchesse de Gérolstein* (1867) offer earlier instances of such unevenly developed pocket German states. But it was Hope who set the pattern for years to come: some thirty-five years later, the protagonist of Dornford Yates's *Fire Below* could still describes that novel's adventure territory along the same lines: 'Riechtenburg is ancient and modern as is no other country that I have ever seen. Immemorial habits and customs march with the mode.'[34] For the reader there is something cosy in this miniature world that it is so small that order can be restored to it by a single man; there is also, perhaps, a feeling that this is a contained territory whose exciting turmoil and violence cannot spread beyond its boundaries any more than a book can escape its covers. In his 1973 history of science fiction, *Billion Year Spree*, Brian Aldiss describes a strain of post-apocalyptic fiction as offering 'cosy catastrophes'; Anthony Hope, it might be argued, launches a tradition of cosy adventure.[35] At the same time, of course, his chocolate-box kingdom resembles in certain ways the monarchy in which it was written, so we might now turn to Britain at the end of the nineteenth century.

Fiction and Society in 1894

Mistaken identity, swashbuckling, and chivalric love in a pocket kingdom: what made these narrative elements so irresistible in 1894? To answer that question we need to look outside the novel itself, its tropes and motifs, and establish some sense of the literary and cultural context in which the novel appeared. Hope was writing at a time when the novel as a form was undergoing something of a sea change. While there were a few survivors like George Meredith (d.1909) and Mrs Braddon (d.1915), most of the great mid-Victorian novelists were dead and gone by the 1890s. Dickens had been dead since 1870; Bulwer Lytton since 1873; George Eliot since 1880; Anthony Trollope since 1882; Wilkie Collins since 1889. With them went the three-volume novel, that 'loose and baggy monster', as Henry James once described it, which ceased to be the main form in which new fiction appeared. In June 1894, the two major subscription libraries, Mudie's and W. H. Smith, announced that they would only take novels in the old format if they could get massive discounts and other advantageous terms. By 1895, one article cited various publishers on the declining appetite for the 'three-decker' before opining that 'though the long novel will die hard, it will die'.[36] In two years it was indeed no more, with just two books in the old format published in 1897, as the circulating libraries wearied of trying to find storage space for an ever-increasing number of needlessly bulked-up novels.[37] The new wave of novels that began to develop in the 1880s tended to be shorter, and there was a drift towards more sensational content: crime and adventure stories, for instance, began to supplant domestic sagas concerned with issues of courtship, marriage, family affairs, and the disposition of property.[38]

One of the most important transitional figures in what is sometimes termed the 'revival of romance' was Robert Louis Stevenson. Notwithstanding the views of his reviewers, Hope did not in fact have to reach all the way back to Dumas and Scott for a model, as the Scottish writer had already almost single-handedly created a vogue for suspenseful, swashbuckling fiction. Stevenson was quite self-conscious about this project, arguing that English fiction had become too much given over to 'the clink of tea-spoons and the accents of the curate'. What was needed was romance rather than realism, a fiction of adventure in which incident rather than character was to the fore: 'Then we forget the characters; then we push the hero aside;

then we plunge into the tale in our own person and battle in fresh experience'.[39] His *Treasure Island*, a runaway success in 1883, was just such a romance. As Conan Doyle would boil down the mid-Victorian sensation novel to create the Sherlock Holmes stories, Stevenson reduced the more capacious adventure tales of Frederick Marryat and R. M. Ballantyne to their essence. Originally written under an alias ('Captain George North') for the children's magazine *Young Folks*, Stevenson's tale of pirates and buried treasure was found to appeal just as much to adult readers. Soon H. Rider Haggard took Stevenson's basic formula and translated it from the realm of romantic history into the imperial present: the result was *King Solomon's Mines* (1885), another great popular success. The idea that another country could be the past was not lost on young Anthony Hope, whose Ruritania locates a pocket of the more adventurous past within Europe itself.

Dramatic changes in the literary market did not take place in a political vacuum. Tales of exotic adventure and treasure-hunting were very much to the taste of a Britain which was entering an explicitly acquisitive and martial period. Queen Victoria's diamond jubilee in 1897 provided an occasion for unparalleled imperial pageantry, and the country continued to add huge swathes to its overseas territory in this period. These were the years of the 'scramble for Africa', and even pocket kingdoms could be put to use, as colonial administrators like Frederick Lugard saw them as enabling a useful form of indirect rule through native leaders. *Zenda* is hardly an 'empire novel' in the usual sense, in that we never leave Europe, but the insouciant confidence of Rassendyll the ex-soldier is that of the imperial moment. Indeed, with its celebration of swashbuckling masculinity, and of playing the game, the novel fitted very well with the heroic mythos of Empire, which tended to disavow the more squalid realities of exploitation and expropriation.

However, Empire was not the only extra-literary factor at work in shaping responses to the revival of romance. For some commentators, fin-de-siècle Britain, despite its vast empire, was under siege at home. Not only were there fears of Prussian invasion, fuelled by such military fantasies as William Le Queux's *The Great War in England in 1897* (1894), but there were also anxieties about enemies within in the form of decadence, degeneration, and feminism. Murky pseudo-scientific ideas about heredity, the national stock, and the perils of modern culture swirl about in contemporary accounts of Britain's peril. One of the shrillest voices in such jeremiads was Stevenson's friend, and one of Hope's first champions, Andrew Lang, an influential critic and amateur anthropologist. Lang contributed to contemporary debates about the merits of realism versus romance by arguing that one kind of fiction is healthy and the other is not; in this respect he considers adventure fiction an antidote to Naturalism—the grittily realist work of Emile Zola and others—which he portrays as 'morbid'.[40] In a particularly reactionary article in the *North American Review* he is scathing about the 'hysterical' tendency of contemporary New Woman fiction, including Sarah Grand's bestselling *The Heavenly Twins*, which highlighted the social and political position of women. Clearly uncomfortable with such adult material, Lang is happier to see other trends at work, especially 'the good old tendency to love a plain tale of adventure, of honest loves and fair fighting' (160). His exemplars in this case are Stanley Weyman's historical novel *A Gentleman of France*, the work of Haggard and Stevenson, Arthur Conan Doyle's historical fiction, and, of course, *The Prisoner of Zenda*, 'that pleasingly incredible scion of German royalty' (160): 'Here is primitive fiction: here is what men and boys have always read for the sheer delight of the fancy.' These are 'honest, upright romancers who make us forget our problems, and the questions that are so much with us' (160).[41] One of 'our problems', evidently, was that some women were striving to change their prescribed social role as domestic angels, and this struggle against the natural order of things was being abetted by unhealthy and unreadable novels. Far better for us to be reading of the knight-errantry of Rudolf Rassendyll and the self-sacrificing true womanhood of Princess Flavia.[42]

Even those who were less hostile to social change saw Hope's adventure romance as a panacea for some aspects of modern life. The American suffragist Sarah Barnwell Elliott's review of the novel stresses, as Lang does, the novel's escapist qualities, but in her account it is the strain caused by the pace of modern living rather than the gender politics of the time that were banished by the tale's magic. Citing 'these strenuous days when nerves are strained like fiddle-strings and played upon momently by all the modern inventions for annihilating time and space...world fairs, and expositions, and telephones, and electric cars, and all the other crazy machines and life-absorbents', she suggests that the 'unstrung wretch of a worker should take up Anthony Hope's *Prisoner of Zenda*'.[43] As with Lang's attack on the New Woman novel, narrative here is seen as providing a restorative escape from contemporary ills.

Pseudoscientific discussions of hysteria, morbidity, and nervous exhaustion were widespread in the 1890s and have no single source, though the work of Cesare Lombroso and Max Nordau was highly influential. Lombroso's *L'Uomo delinquente* (1876) argued that criminality was often hereditary, the result of atavistic survivals among the population, and elsewhere he suggested that genius and madness were often close companions. Nordau was a disciple of Lombroso, and his *Entartung* (1892), published in English as *Degeneration* (1895), played no small part in circulating the idea that modern life was in and of itself harmful and that hysteria and degeneracy were its consequences.[44] Nordau is usually remembered for his savage attacks on modern art and literature, damning everyone from the Pre-Raphaelites to Ibsen to Wilde, but it is his etiology of the modern malaise of hysteria that is most interesting for our purposes. From around 1840, Nordau argues, there was a dramatic increase in newspaper-reading, rapid travel, and exposure to urban stimuli of various kinds, all of which had exacted a terrible physical and mental toll: 'Every civilized man furnishes, at the present time, from five to twenty-five times as much work as was demanded of him half a century ago.'[45] The result, for Nordau, could only be permanent damage to the nervous system: the first generation of the industrial age suffered from 'acquired hysteria'; their offspring suffer from the hereditary kind. Hysteria, once associated with women only, is presented here as all-pervasive, and most modern art and literature is hysterical and degenerate. The modern world had a bad case of nerves. How could it not be otherwise? Hope's novel was seen by reviewers as a wholesome tonic to such anxieties, not least because it toys with some of these fashionable ideas before dismissing them. With a plot that turns on the idea of familial throwbacks, Hope even allows the reader to momentarily think of the degenerate modern world described by Nordau before dissolving it, as the *Saturday Review* observed: 'That blessed word 'Heredity' is likely to occur to the reader of the first few pages; but the thing itself, the pseudoscientific thing, lifts not its horrid head and multiple issues for a single page to chill the romantic spirit.'[46] The *New York Times* likewise described the novel as a 'bright story' constructed out of 'atavism'.[47]

However, the extent to which Ruritania represented an escape from Britain's perceived ills can be overstated. We might speculate that the ultimate reason for the novel's success was that the fictional territory it described was in fact uncannily familiar. In a novel of doubles, Ruritania's double is none other than Britain itself. The pocket kingdom is, after all, not so very different from 1890s Britain, also a monarchy and a place in which past and present overlapped. Heavily industrialized, and a major commercial power, Britain was still largely ruled, like Germany, by a landed aristo-military caste, even if its elite had long made an accommodation with the world of business. The same landed families dominated the military, where older ways survived too: we should not be surprised to learn that Rassendyll has learned his swordsmanship in the service of his Queen, since as late as the First World War Britain was still putting cavalry in the field armed with swords and lances. The two countries were aligned in other ways too. Germany began to emerge as a rival imperial power after unification in 1871, and in the years of Bismarck it also began to seen as an industrial rival, for instance in Ernest Edwin Williams' polemic of 1896, *Made in Germany*. But for most of the century Britain's main continental enemy was France, and Prussia was an ally. Britain and the German states remained close, politically, commercially, and culturally, and were linked through their monarchies. While it had been quite some time since a German-born King (George II) had occupied the throne of Britain, Queen Victoria herself was from the house of Hanover, and her mother was Princess Victoria of Saxe-Coburg-Saalfeld. Her husband (and cousin) was Prince Albert of Saxe-Coburg-Gotha, and Kaiser Wilhelm II of Germany was her grandson. The political proximity of Germany and Britain came to an abrupt end with the First World War, and famously the British royal family reinvented themselves as the Windsors. But in 1894 German-speaking Ruritania could still provide a perfectly good mirror image for Britain. Ruritania, then, is in many ways less an exotic space than a miniaturized Britain with no industrial middle class and little in the way of law and order; it is a heterotopia of Britain, the same but slightly different. The English Rassendyll and the German King of Ruritania are almost exactly doubles, indistinguishable to all but the most careful observers.[48]

Ruritania on Stage

The novel's early success owed a good deal to its contemporary resonances and to Ruritania's looking-glass quality. But, almost from the beginning, *Zenda*'s popularity was also bound up with its translation to the stage. As early as June 1894, Hope had decided to allow Edward Rose, a well-known playwright and theatre critic, to adapt *Zenda*, rather than doing so himself, though he was to receive 25 per cent of the adapter's profits.[49] Rose's version was relatively faithful to the plot and tone of the original, with some fancy footwork to ensure that Rassendyll and King Rudolf are never seen together. The most significant changes were the introduction of a prologue in which we see the romantic entanglement of Rudolf of Ruritania and Rassendyll's ancestress, the young Countess Amelia; and the enlargement of the minor character of Bertram Bertrand (now an artist rather than a poet), who accompanies Rassendyll to Ruritania.[50] The prologue closes with a candlelit duel between Amelia's much older husband and the young Prince Rudolf, and then the action skips along 150 years to the Forest of Zenda, where Bertram Bertrand is discovered at his easel before Rassendyll himself appears. The rest of the play broadly follows the novel, though all of the action unfolds in just four settings: the Forest of Zenda in Act 1; the Winter Palace at Strelsau in Act 2; the Castle of Tarlenheim in Act 3; and the dungeon of the Castle of Zenda in the final act.

Rose's adaptation was first produced by the American impresario Daniel Frohman (brother of the even more successful Charles) at the Lyceum in New York on 4 September 1895. Frohman had not stinted in preparing the play, sourcing suitable costumes in London and lining up for the lead E. H. Sothern, then a rising Anglo-American actor and son of the famous E. A. Sothern.[51] Young Sothern was a talented comic performer, and the production kept the humour of the novel, adding in a little more in places. Despite the warm and humid weather and the rival outdoor attractions of the season, the play was a critical and commercial success. The *New York Times* pronounced it a 'very great triumph', and there were full houses for the three matinees and six evening performances per week that were soon offered.[52] Sothern's performance was lauded, and Grace Kimball was deemed to play the Princess Flavia in a 'sweet, dainty and sincere' fashion.[53] One newspaper joked that red hair would soon be all the rage, making fortunes for 'the hair regenerator folks'.[54] For Sothern, in his triple role (counting the Prologue), it was a physically demanding part, involving multiple changes of costume and make-up. As he noted at the time, 'the only time I have to rest in this play is when I am acting on the stage'.[55] *Zenda* proved to be the hit of the season: the New York run with Sothern was extended, and the theatre's stock company was sent on the road, a reversal of the traditional practice. It helped to make Sothern not just a star but a 'matinée idol': *Munsey's Magazine* later declared him to be 'the foremost favorite of feminine audiences in America', with 'first call on the impressionable matinée girl's heart', illustrating this claim with a photograph of him from *The Prisoner of Zenda*.[56]

In the end Sothern was not the one who reaped the greatest benefits from the play. *Zenda* went on tour in November of 1895, and the stock company took over at the Lyceum. But in February 1896, Frohman calculated that New York audiences might have an appetite for Ruritania even without Sothern: from 10 February the play was staged by Frohman's stock company. The young James K. Hackett, who had only recently joined the Lyceum company, appeared in the lead role, having studied Sothern's technique for the rapid costume and make-up changes the role required.[57] It was to be a fateful moment in Hackett's career. The son of a well-known Shakespearean actor, Hacket—with his tall good looks and physicality in the part—was soon recognized as a new 'matinée idol'.[58] *The New York Times* opined that if he lacked some of Sothern's subtlety as an actor, he 'was much the handsomer, and [had] the larger share of vocal power'.[59] According to David Carroll's colourful account, Hackett had studied fencing with the expert French swordsman Louis Serai and was an amateur dueling champion, so he soon made the role his own: 'so magnificently did he duel, leaping off seven-foot platforms and laughing as he tossed his sword in the air and caught it again before his assailant was upon him, that he soon overshadowed Sothern in the part'.[60] In September of that year, he and the stock company toured *Zenda* to Chicago, San Francisco, and other cities, where it was as successful as it had been in New York, thanks to Hackett's dynamic performance and the elaborate swordplay. While some critics had carped at Rose's prologue and its duel, now the duel was a draw in its own right: 'the most tragic and sensational effect in it occurs in the first act in the form of a wonderful sword combat', enthused one California paper.[61] In later years Hackett brought *Zenda* to every corner of America, playing the dual role thousands of times and travelling in his private railroad car with his mother on hand as his 'matinée advisor'. He became synonymous with the role of Rassendyll/the King, rather as James O'Neill, father of the famous playwright, became inseparable from Dantès/the Count of Monte Cristo, a role he played more than 5000 times.[62] (To vary his routine, the matinee idol seems to have supplied a happier ending in one Washington performance, killing off the real King.)[63] Hackett's exuberant performance in *Zenda*, *Rupert of Hentzau*, and similar fare played no small part in the rise of the stage swashbuckler as hero: sword in hand, 'he first showed that the up-to-date hero must needs be able to exterminate a dozen enemies alone and single-handed'.[64]

Echoing reviews of the novel, some critics declared the play's success to be a sign that a sea change was under way in theatrical taste from the anxious and pessimistic to the wholesome: 'on the stage, as in the literary world, there is at present a great revulsion from the problem plays and problem stories of the past ten years towards a fresh and healthy romanticism, such as held undisputed sway in the middle of this century'. No more would the theatre-going public be drawn to 'women with pasts and men who delight in discussing unpleasant subjects'.[65] The naturalistic Scandinavian gloom of Henrik Ibsen and his followers would be dispersed by swash-buckling romantic fare. The same note was sounded some three years later when the dramatization of *Rupert of Hentzau* also drew the crowd: 'let realists howl and naturalists scowl and Tolstoi brethren rage', but Rudolf Rassendyll has 'kindled anew the sacred flame of pure romance in the general heart'. This knightly and 'wholesome' hero would be 'deeply refreshing to those whose way is dark and dusty'.[66] Absent the turgid prose, this did indeed appear to be what many people wanted, to judge from the commercial success of Hackett as Rassendyll, O'Neill as Dantès in *The Count of Monte Cristo*, and Kyrle Bellew as Gaston, Sieur de Marsac, in *A Gentleman of France*.[67] This was an athletic theatre of action that appeared to resonate with the strenuous American life that President Theodore Roosevelt recommended in 1898.

However, there is also another facet to the popularity of such costume dramas: part of the *Zenda*'s drawing power was that it presented Hackett not just as an action hero but as a dashing 'matinée idol', a visual feast and object of romantic investment. Such 'idols' were performers whose principal appeal was thought to be to the young women—'matinee girls'—who, unescorted by men, attended cheaper matinee performances rather than evening ones. The 'matinee girl' is first described in American magazine articles in the 1890s and 1900s and has her equivalent in English publications of the same period; on both sides of the Atlantic she comes to stand for an undiscerning feminized consumer culture.[68] (The chocolate-eating matinee girl, with her over-sized hat, was a less threatening version of the New Woman.)[69] An article in *Munsey's Magazine* from 1897, for example, explains that the matinee 'affords the impressionable maiden two to three hours of almost uninterrupted adoration of her hero, the leading man'. At the nearest photographer's shop 'she stands before his latest photographs, and worships them, and longs for them' and ultimately enshrines him as her latest idol in her 'Hero Book', or scrapbook.[70] If some women came to worship the performers rather than the play, this was hardly surprising in light of the way in which the Frohmans and others had been creating a theatrical star system from 1885 onwards, selling photographs and generating press releases.[71] *The Prisoner of Zenda* was ideal grist for this marketing mill, and Hackett, gorgeously attired and sword in hand, provided a suitably photogenic subject. If *Zenda* on stage was offering a model of the 'healthy', manly action hero, it also seemed to be offering something rather different, something more like a sex symbol, to use a later term. As we shall see, this emphasis on spectacle rather than action was even more to the fore in the London production.

Zenda and the English Stage

Daniel Frohman had bid for the English rights to *Zenda* too, but they went to actor-manager George Alexander at the St James's Theatre in King Street, where the play became if anything an even greater hit than it had been in the United States. To understand the extraordinary success of *The Prisoner of Zenda* at the St James's, it is useful to know a little about that house and about its recent role in one of the most infamous episodes in Victorian theatre history. The St James's was a West End theatre—it was in fact the most westerly of the West End theatres—with more of a reputation for drawing-room comedy and serious drama than for action and spectacle. A small theatre with maximum nightly takings of £200, it was also a fashionable theatre drawing a society audience, a status it shared in this period with the Criterion, The Garrick, and the Haymarket.[72] Actor-manager George Alexander—Alec or Aleck to his friends—had forged a reputation as a polished actor in society roles, and under his management the St James's had seen the debut of Oscar Wilde's *Lady Windermere's Fan* (20 February 1892), Arthur Wing Pinero's *The Second Mrs Tanqueray* (27 May 1893), and Henry Arthur Jones's *The Masqueraders* (28 April 1894), all of which had been successes. Alexander was prepared to push his audience in the general direction of the 'new drama' that derived from Ibsen, but he did not like to push them too hard, sticking largely to work by English playwrights. But in later years Alexander would largely be remembered not so much for this relatively challenging fare but for being a matinee idol. As one keen theatre-goer put it, he was 'the immaculate George . . . darling of the matinée girl. . . [with] a slight suggestion of bounderishness to give him flavor [but] inexpressibly "gentlemanly".'[73] *The Prisoner of Zenda* (7 January 1896) would play no small part in this repackaging; it would also have a very positive effect on the theatre's bank balance and contribute to a more general shift in late Victorian culture, which we might think of as a 'counter-decadent' tendency.

At the beginning of 1896, Alexander and the St James's desperately needed a hit: 1895 had been a bleak year for the theatre and for its star. Henry James's turgid costume drama about priestly renunciation, *Guy Domville*, had its disastrous premiere on 5 January 1895. When Alexander as Domville delivered the line 'I'm the last, my lord, of the Domvilles', some wit in the cheaper seats had responded, 'It's a bloody good thing y'are.' Despite other signs of restlessness, the actor misinterpreted the mood of the audience and led James on stage after the curtain, only for him to be loudly booed.[74] While *Guy Domville* limped along for a month to ever-dwindling houses, Alexander managed to acquire *The Importance of Being Earnest* from Charles Wyndham of the Criterion Theatre, where Wilde's sparkling comedy, a 'trivial play for serious people', was meant to have its first performance.[75] After rapid rehearsals, *The Importance of Being Earnest* opened on Valentine's Day, 1895, with Alexander as Jack Worthing; it was an immediate success, but disaster in the pugnacious form of the Marquess of Queensberry was only just kept outside the door, where he ranted at the queuing public.[76] He could not be held at bay forever, and soon Wilde was embroiled in the famous libel case that led to his own prosecution and his eventual conviction for gross indecency on 25 May. When the scandal grew impossible to ignore, Alexander at first ran the play without Wilde's name, but in the end he was forced to end its run on 8 May, when it was swiftly replaced by Henry Arthur Jones's *The Triumph of the Philistines: And How Mr Morgan Preserved the Morals of Market Pewbury Under Very Trying Circumstances*.[77] Alexander, it seems, was making a point, since the play deals with the efforts of provincial puritans to close down the local art studios and replace them with a 'Boot and Shoe and Closed Uppers Orphanage Asylum'; the tolerant man of the world, Sir Valentine (played by Alexander himself) is driven away and plans to live on the Continent.[78] It is hard not to see the choice of the play as a none-too-oblique commentary on the official morality that destroyed Wilde. Unsurprisingly, perhaps, the play lost money, and Jones was jeered on the opening night. A series of short revivals of former favourites eked out the rest of the season and the start of the following season, before

Alexander tried another challenging play.[79] This was H. V. Esmond's *The Divided Way*, which explores the tortured feelings of the heroine, Lois (Evelyn Millard), who marries the half-brother of her dead fiancé, Gaunt (George Alexander), only to find that the latter is not dead at all. For the *Times* it was a 'depressing study...as unreal...as the optimistic and romantic drama against which the new school are understood to be in revolt' and a grim representation of 'the perversion of the sex instinct'.[80] The play closed after twenty performances. Nor was Alexander's off-stage life running smoothly: he was in some danger of following Wilde into legal hot water when he was arrested in the early hours of the morning near his house in Pont Street with one Elizabeth Davis and charged with engaging in 'disorderly conduct', a euphemism for purchasing sex. The judge chose to believe the version of events proposed by his legal counsel—that the woman had been begging, and he had given her half a crown—and he was discharged.[81]

The Pavilion Road incident blew over, but after such a year it is not surprising that Alexander felt that it might be time to forsake the 'new school' for one of those optimistic and romantic dramas mentioned by the *Times*. And so, on 7 January 1896, *The Prisoner of Zenda* opened (see Figure 1.3).

Alexander himself played the challenging triple role of Prince Rudolph/ Rudolf (for some reason the script changes the spelling of the two) Rassendyll and the King; E. Allan Aynesworth was Bertram Bertrand; Evelyn Millard played Princess Flavia; Lily Hanbury appeared as Madame de Mauban; Herbert Waring played Michael; W. H. Vernon had the juicy role of the grizzled Colonel Sapt; Arthur Royston was young Fritz von Tarlenheim; a young George Bancroft debuted as Lord Topham; and Frank Dyall was the servant, Josef. Besides Alexander, the original Jack Worthing/Earnest, a number of the others were veterans of *The Importance of Being Earnest*: Millard was the original Cecily Cardew, Allan Aynesworth was the original Algernon Moncrieff; and Frank Dyall had played Merriman, the butler.[82] Most had also appeared in other St James's society and problem plays: for example, Evelyn Millard had been the innocent daughter Ellean in *The Second Mrs Tanqueray* and later replaced Mrs Patrick Campbell in the title role; and Lily Hanbury was the original Lady Windermere.

Rose had opted to play down action in favour of romance and spectacle, and the much-anticipated London production of *Zenda* was billed as a 'Romantic Play, in a Prologue and Four Acts'. Advance publicity helped to shape audience expectations, and, in an interview with the *Pall Mall Gazette*,

Figure 1.3. George Alexander as Rudolf Rassendyll, promotional postcard for *Zenda*, 1896

Rose explained that the play, 'set in an imaginary German Kingdom', had only two fights, and nobody would be killed on stage: 'If we had wanted that we might have tried to turn the story into a melodrama with a succession of big scenes. We might even have had a tank with real water—a good deal of the action of the story passes, you will remember, in the moat of the castle of Zenda.'[83] At the same time the eye would not be disappointed, and colour and spectacle would not be wanting in the representation of German court ceremony:

> [The coronation] is the big scene from the spectacular point of view...Mr [Walter] Hann, the artist, has got a distinct German note into it by the use of the splendid, almost barbaric, reds and yellows—the Saxe-Meiningen company, you remember, used those hot colours. They give a rich and gorgeous effect, that is still characteristically German. Then of course there is a blaze of colour in the costumes, the uniforms of the soldiers, and diplomats, and court functionaries.[84]

Colour, spectacle, and romance, then, were to be the main attractions of the stage version, and swashbuckling was to take a lesser role, though it was still a good deal more prominent than Rose was willing to suggest. (Writing many years later, W. Macqueen Pope remembered that his nine-year-old self had to be kept in his seat, so exciting was the action, and others in the audience were likewise physically moved [146].) The play itself is in fact fairly explicit about its theme: the making of an old-fashioned hero out of modern materials. When Rassendyll retells to Bertram Bertrand the story of the ancestral romance and subsequent duel, the following dialogue ensues:

> BERTRAND: A duel—but that was 150 years ago. There was some vestige of romance in the world then. People are not so picturesque in this nineteenth century.
>
> RUDOLF: My dear boy, you are mistaken. Believe me, even in these pro-saic days, you may find your heroes and heroines every morning in the newspaper. Heroism, my dear Bertrand, is innate in every bosom, and awaits but the occasion to call it forth.
>
> BERTRAND: Nonsense. Man is a degenerate animal and you are the hor-rible example.[85]

The play, of course, proves Rassendyll right and Bertrand—and such social diagnosticians as Nordau—wrong: even the idlers of the supposedly degenerate 1890s could become heroes under the right circumstances. Ruritania, then, is the quaint Germanic mirror that reveals British man-hood as it could be. *Zenda* makes a dashing hero of Rassendyll, but the production also transformed George Alexander, turning the erstwhile champion of modern British drama into a glamorous matinee idol. The *Pall Mall Gazette* picked up on the play's potential for spectacle even before rehearsals, when word of the new production's lavishness had been spread: 'Mr Alexander himself in a white uniform with a silver helmet should make a fine figure in the photographic shop windows' ('Theatrical Notes', 18 December 1895).

Zenda was almost universally praised, and Alexander and the mise en scène came in for particular plaudits. For the *Era*, the major theatrical news-paper of the time, it was a 'complete success'.[86] The *Times* regretted that some of the lightness of Hope's novel had been lost in the transfer to the stage but was nonetheless impressed by the heroic energy that Alexander brought to the part of Rassendyll and by the play's 'pictorial' quality:

'there is in the interior of the Winter Palace of Ruritania such a display of uniforms and court costumes as, we venture to say, has never been surpassed on the stage' ('St James's Theatre', 8 January). Among the weekly papers, *Lloyd's* proclaimed that the 'Court dresses in the coronation act [were] in themselves a magnificent spectacle' ('Public Amusements', 12 January), while the *Pall Mall Gazette* admired the way in which the theme of love versus duty had come to the fore in the 'lively, thrilling and picturesque' production, and thought that Flavia's coronation dress 'was a glittering dream of delight' ('Zenda Victorious, 8 January).[87] Even Clement Scott in the *Telegraph*, who disapproved of the sparkling production and its 'cardboard and tinsel' characters, admitted that there had been 'three or four calls after every act, cheers for author, double cheers for actors' and that the 'triumph of America ha[s] been repeated in critical London' ('*The Prisoner of Zenda* at the St James's', 8 January).

The spectacular costumes, which had been chosen by Alexander's wife, Florence, made their mark on contemporary fashion journalism. The *Glasgow Herald* expected that 'Tulle and sequin spangled chiffon or net will be used to veil the dresses of debutantes and brides, many of these being modeled on the lovely Empire gown worn by Miss Millard in the second act of *The Prisoner of Zenda*, while the play's court gowns 'may suggest many of the dresses to be worn at the coming season's Drawing Rooms' ('Our London Correspondent', 3 February 1896). In her fashion column in the *Graphic*, Lady Violet Greville argued that Zenda was doing the public good by showing the attractions of colourful clothes for men: the Coronation robes and uniforms worn by Alexander were so much more fetching than the drab modern dress worn by Bertram Bertrand ('Place aux dames', 11 April 1896).

The souvenir programme produced for the 100th performance of the play in London reproduces some of the photographs of the cast that had been produced for sale, and it gives us a good idea of just how eye-catching the costumes and sets were.

George Alexander in his dazzling coronation costume resembles a character from operetta, and Princess Flavia is a shimmering vision in chiffon and costume jewellery; the sets are just as lavish and detailed as contemporary reviews suggested (see Plates 1.1 and 1.2).

What kind of cultural work was *Zenda* performing here? Oscar Wilde's three trials in 1895 are sometimes seen to represent a watershed in social and cultural history, and the beginning of a period of reaction, after a moment in which gender had sometimes been imagined in more fluid terms. There is some danger of overestimating the role of one man's demise and underestimating the conservative currents that had been present throughout the 1890s, even when Wildean 'Decadence' was in vogue. But there is clearly some kind of shift taking place when we see a theatre so closely linked to Wilde switch to masculine heroics complemented by female self-sacrifice against a backdrop of sumptuous feudal display. The Saint James's had often pursued a house policy of variety, but this was a significant change of course. Alexander, the self-indulgent Jack Worthing of February, 1895, who invents a scapegrace younger brother so that he can escape to the fleshpots of London from his duties as guardian, becomes the dashing Rudolf Rassendyll, who saves a country and sacrifices his own happiness. Evelyn Millard had played the delightfully capricious Cecily Cardew, and in *The Divided Way* she had been Lois, the character that the *Times* felt was more suitable for a medical text on 'the perversion of the sex instinct'. But in *Zenda* she becomes the lovely and 'womanly' Princess Flavia, who subordinates her love to her sense of duty. Only E. Allan Aynesworth, the Algernon of 1895, can be seen to have kept something of his old character in the new play as the artist Bertram Bertrand. Role-playing and confused identities link *Earnest* and *Zenda,* but all else is changed utterly, and the playfulness of Wilde's play is replaced by soulful passion and ideas of commitment and self-abnegation in a noble cause.

Wilde's *Earnest* playfully gerrymandered gender and also contained a number of in-jokes for those of Wilde's circle, as Richard Ellmann and Christopher Craft have shown, and even the name Earnest recalls not just the contemporary term Uranist (sc. a man who loves men) but more directly the Uranian poems in John Gambril's Nicholson's *Love in Earnest* (1892).[88] In the general stampede away from Wilde in 1895, George Alexander behaved relatively well, but one cannot help feeling that the embrace of 'romantic drama', swashbuckling heroics, and lavish sets in 1896 was more than happenstance, returning himself and the St James's to safer, more conservative ground.[89] George Alexander was himself being remade here as that safe object for heterosexual desire, the matinee idol. Ironically, this involved a fetishization of male beauty and masculine dress that is very much in keeping with the Wildean 1890s. In fact, Alexander fencing in his tight eighteenth-century breeches or posing in his immaculately tailored coronation uniform seems to be engaged in a sort of over-performance of masculinity that is distinctly camp. It is, perhaps, this aspect of stage Ruritania that drew Ivor Novello to it in the 1930s, when he sought to create his own musical fantasy lands out of these ingredients (see chapter 4).

In commercial terms, the turn to romantic spectacle paid off handsomely for George Alexander and his theatre—and indeed for Anthony Hope, who shared in the profits. Such was the enthusiasm of audiences for Ruritania that the way they greeted each actor as they entered became by April 'almost disconcerting'.[90] *Zenda* ran at the St James's from 7 January until 19 July, when there was a break before the company went on tour from 24 August, returning to the St James's on 20 October. On their return, the *Daily Mail* noted that there was as much public excitement 'as though not for a night (much more 250 such) had they been the talk of the town'.[91] The often acerbic George Bernard Shaw observed that *Zenda* had become 'a permanent institution, like Madame Tussaud's' and thought that the October production, which featured some new cast members, was 'perfectly delectable', with Alexander still 'fresh as paint' in the triple role.[92] When it finally finished at the St James's on 29 November, it had clocked up 303 performances there.[93] (We might note in passing that on 24 August a tall and striking-looking young actor, one C. Aubrey Smith, joined the cast in the part of Duke Michael, also playing Duke Wolfgang in the prologue; we will meet him again when we turn to film versions of the novel.) In addition to the main company, there was a successful touring production run by C. J. Abud, with Yorke Stephens in the lead role. All told, Alexander's net profits from the play and revivals in later years, including touring productions, came to £18,000, most of which was earned in 1896. The £3,000 he had spent on the play—an extravagant amount in 1896—had been a sound investment (see Figure 1.4).[94] Nor did Hope fare badly: his diary entry for 28 December 1896 records that by then he had made '17 or 18 hundred' from the *Zenda* adaptation and from advances on other plays.[95] Presumably he also benefited modestly from the copies of the novel that were on sale at the theatre throughout its long run.

As the theatrical season drew to a close, a number of reviewers tried to make sense of the runaway success of Hope and Rose's costume drama; a bestselling novel did not always a hit play make, after all. As in the United States, some critics chose to interpret *Zenda*'s vogue as a symptom of a sea change in British theatre. The *Pall Mall Gazette*, for instance, saw it as marking the 'revolt of the intellectual playgoer against the intellectual play' ('Theatrical Notes', 5 August 1896), identifying *Trilby* and Wilson Barrett's

Figure 1.4. Poster for *The Prisoner of Zenda* at the St James's, 1896
© Victoria and Albert Museum, Theatre and Performance Collection, Museum Number S.2003-1995

biblical drama *The Sign of the Cross* as part of the same rebellion—all three were melodramas of one kind or another. On its first appearance in January some had hailed the play as a relief 'from the dull and morbid realism of plays of the modern Scandinavian school', and that note is sustained in later press coverage: *Zenda* was an escape from the 'morbid work of the Norwegian' [sc. Ibsen].[96] Sword in hand, Rassendyll was not just saving Ruritania; he appeared to be leading the counter-revolution against the forces of change abroad in Britain itself. But long after the culture wars of the 1890s, the play's mixture of pageantry, romance, and heroics continued to appeal to audiences who were not interested in modern fare, and there were revivals in 1900 and 1909 at the St James's and in 1911 at the Lyceum. Even in 1923, when Rex Ingram's lavish film version of *Zenda* was on release, there was enough interest in the play to sustain a three-month run for Louis Parker's production at the Haymarket (Frank Dyall, once the servant Josef, played Black Michael; and Allan Aynesworth, the former Bertram Bertrand, was Sapt). This is to say nothing of the many provincial productions in the intervening years.

Rupert of Hentzau on Stage

In 1898 playgoers were offered a chance to revisit stage Ruritania through Hope's own adaptation of *Rupert of Hentzau*. Again America went first, and naturally Hackett was the star of Frohman's production of *Rupert of Hentzau*, which premiered in Philadelphia on 21 November 1898 before coming to New York's Lyceum in April of the following year. A 'Gibson Girl', the former artist's model Jobyna Howland, played Flavia.[97] She had been the model for Princess Flavia in Charles Dana Gibson's illustrations for the novel, so now readers could quite literally see the novel realized. The next day's *New York Times* praised Hackett, noting his particular success as the 'virile and picturesque double, the quick-witted and fire-eating Englishman…vigorous, tender and picturesque' as the occasion warranted. It also singled out the vividness of the fight scenes, which called for 'clever sword-play and a couple of very realistic wrestling bouts'. Howland, however, was 'always a model, never a Queen'.[98] In its 'American Amusements' column, the *Era* of 22 April 1899 was more impressed than the *New York Times* had been with her, noting that the final bier scene was a 'reproduction of Charles Dana Gibson's famous picture in the book'.

The first production of *Hentzau* on the other side of the Atlantic was at the Theatre Royal, Glasgow, Thursday, 5 October 1899, with Alexander reprising his role as Rassendyll/King Rudolf and the American actress Fay Davis taking the part of Queen Flavia, which she had already played in touring versions of *Zenda*. H. B. Irving was again the scheming Rupert, and W. H. Vernon and Ernest Lawford (later replaced by H. V. Esmond) took the parts of Sapt and Fritz. Like its American predecessor it stuck close to the novel, with a climactic duel between Rudolf and Rupert and a lavishly realized funeral scene at the coda. Even Boris, the King's loyal boarhound, put in a short and tragic appearance. Hope himself considering it a 'pretty mixture of murder, farce, love-making and funerals' (Mallet 138). The *Times* thought the adaptation was 'magnificently staged' and felt that the novel had been reworked with 'remarkable theatrical effect', even if a few episodes were of a 'strongly melodramatic character' ('Rupert of Hentzau in Glasgow', 6 October 1899). On 1 February 1900, *Hentzau* moved to London, where there was considerable interest not just in Alexander's return but in the reopening of his theatre after six months of reconstruction. The actor-manager had ploughed his Ruritanian profits into the wholesale remodelling of the St James's, and the new building boasted a glass awning for queuing theatre-goers, more seating capacity, a larger stage, new safety exits, electric light throughout, and striking 'transitional period' (sc. early French Renaissance) decor by designer Percy MacQuoid.[99] The first night was accordingly a grand affair, with the opera star Madame Albani secured to sing the national anthem. Patriotism was very much in the air, as the second Boer War had been under way since the previous October: the *Era* for Saturday, 3 February, noted that the action-packed play was 'quite in tune with the present military spirit of the public' and praised the 'superbly alert, virile and vigorous fencing scene' in a performance that featured 'any amount of masculinity and movement'. Complementing such manly vigour was the performance of Davis, who, as Flavia, was seen to be 'fascinatingly gentle and gracious' and whose costumes were widely praised. But overall reviews of *Hentzau* were mixed, with many feeling that the new play did not match up to its predecessor and depended too much on crude effects. The *St James's Gazette*, for instance, felt that the tone of the play came 'not from the fantastical land of Ruritania, but from the Surrey-side of London'—that is, from the cheaper theatres in which old-fashioned melodrama dominated. Perhaps sensing that the wind was changing, Alexander offered matinees of *The Prisoner of Zenda* for a period, so that a keen fan could see the two plays in a day, but *Rupert* closed after just 8 weeks; only the receipts from the matinees of *Zenda* ensured that it broke even (Mason 138–9). Macqueen Pope observes that the real violence of the South African war may have blunted the public's appetite for the romantic stage variety, and certainly the lying-in-state scene *was* removed from the London version of the play after just a few days, as it was felt 'at the present moment a needlessly painful spectacle' and too morbidly realistic.[100] But this scene was almost certainly not the only reason for the play's relative failure in the capital, given *Hentzau*'s already noted resonance with the 'military spirit of the moment'. Hope's was, perhaps, just less successful as a piece of theatre than Rose's *Zenda* had been, at least for jaded London audiences who had plenty of other plays to see. On tour in the provinces, on the other hand, the back-to-back performances of *Zenda* and *Rupert* did very well and turned a profit, rather as Hope himself had anticipated (Mason 159; Mallet 137–8).

The two versions of *Zenda* made George Alexander one of the most successful actor-managers of the day. To mark his identification with the role, he had his portrait painted as King Rudolf, complete with sword: he had moved a long way from Aubrey Tanqueray and Jack Worthing. 'Ruritania' even became the St James's telegraphic address, a further tribute to the play that had paid for the lavish remodeling.[101] As the *Daily Telegraph* noted some years later, '*The Prisoner of Zenda*, with its romantic note and gay coloring[, had] opened up a new vista of possibilities' for Alexander and his theatre. But it had also suggested these possibilities to others, and a whole series of Ruritanian romantic dramas appeared on the London stage, including A. N. Homer's *Count Tezma* (1901); Sydney Grundy's *The Garden of Lies* (1905); James Bernard Fagan's *Hawthorne, U.S.A.* (1905); Walter Howard's *Her Love Against the World* (1907); F.G. Kimberley's *The Power of the King* (1907); and Herbert Skardon's *Send Him Victorious* (1908).[102] Audiences delighted in the troubled royalty of such tinsel territories as Illyria, Ravonia, Ravensburg, Sylvania, and Uldersiburg. As the *Stage Year Book* put it in 1909, 'since the early nineties...dramatists have dealt with imaginary realms, either small German Kingdoms or Principalities or States somewhere in the troubled regions of the Balkans; but, whatever their locale may have been styled, it has always been Ruritania and Strelsau all over again'.[103] Aimed squarely at middlebrow audiences, such plays helped to ensure the survival of lavish spectacle and romantic melodrama, despite the rise of 'little' theatres, from London's Independent Theatre Society to Dublin's Abbey. In Ruritania, their 'morbid' intellectual fare could be kept at the border a little while longer.

Conclusion

When Sir George Alexander—he had been knighted in 1911—died on 15 March 1918, he was warmly remembered by the *Times* as having 'preserved through his long career...the charm and what is known on the stage as "distinction", which made him a "matinée idol" from youth to old age'. Among the long list of his hits the *Times* recalled 'that *succès fou*, Anthony Hope's *The Prisoner of Zenda*'.[104] Evelyn Millard, who lived on until 9 March 1941, was still remembered in her obituary for her 'striking success as Princess Flavia'.[105] After many years of touring James K. Hackett managed to finally escape the part of Rudolf Rassendyll: financially buoyed by a substantial inheritance, he became known for his performances as Macbeth and his work for war charities, for which he received the French Legion of Honour; he died in Paris on 8 November 1926. Before then, though, as we shall see in the next chapter, he immortalized his performance as Rudolf Rassendyll for the cinematograph.

Sir Anthony Hope Hawkins died on Saturday, 8 July 1933. He never enjoyed the political career he had once coveted, though he was knighted in January 1918 for his service to the nation during the war, chiefly his propaganda work for the fledgling Ministry of Information at Wellington House.[106] (John Buchan, in some ways Hope's successor in adventure fiction, also worked at Wellington House, overseeing the new Department.) He never lost his interest in politics, but it was as a novelist that he was remembered. Hawkins's obituary in the *Times* was subtitled 'The Creator of Ruritania' and described him as the inventor of 'Ruritania, a country of his imagination in the Balkans...and thus the father of the many romantic stories that have since entertained lovers of gaily-coloured fiction'.[107] Thanks to Hope's many imitators, it had been forgotten that the original Ruritania was not in the Balkans but somewhere in Germany. Germany, of course, had come to occupy quite a different place in the popular imagination because of the First World War, and it was about to shift again. The same issue of the *Times* carries detailed reports of the World Economic Conference in Lausanne and the plan to suspend the payment of war reparations; among those who had been opposed to the acknowledgement of any war debts was Herr Hitler, who had denounced the government's position to an audience of 15,000 people at Berechtesgaden in Bavaria. Ruritania would have to take up residence elsewhere. By then Ruritania had also moved from the page and stage to the cinema screen, and it is there that we pursue it in our next chapter.

2

Zenda on Screen

The Prisoner of Zenda's longevity has been in no small part due to its rapid transition to the screen, where its scope for splendid pageantry, star-crossed romance, and masculine heroics made it an early favorite. The story's full action potential could be realized on film, and it became a classic swashbuckler, a form which, as Jeffrey Richards lyrically describes, offers 'an exhilarating excursion into pure style, a heady blend of male beauty and agility, the grace and colour of historical costume, the opulence and splendour of period sets, and the spellbinding legerdemain of horseback chases, chandelier-swinging and dazzling swordplay'.[1] Designed to lure the 'carriage trade' to the then somewhat declassé cinema by showcasing the stage idol James K. Hackett, the first screen *Zenda* in 1913 was in fact by later standards a relatively static affair. As film-makers explored the possibilities of the new medium, subsequent versions took the original in different directions: Rex Ingram's stylish 1922 film is a visual feast that also develops the story's comic aspects, while David O. Selznick's landmark 1937 *Zenda* is a romantic homage to monarchy and Englishness, mining a rich seam of American Anglophilia. Later films show that the formula was wearing thin: the 1952 *Zenda* is an almost shot-by-shot Technicolor remake of Selznick's version; and Peter Sellers' 1979 romp is a parody that appears to be intent on killing off the story once and for all. However, even parody helped to keep Hope's pocket kingdom alive, while the paucity of adaptations since the 1980s indicates that *Zenda*'s hold on popular culture has weakened, even if some elements of the Ruritanian formula continue to thrive.

Zenda Before Hollywood

As with the stage productions, the first film of *Zenda* was American rather than British. By the early 1910s the American film industry had moved on from its dingy nickelodeon parlour days to being a more highly capitalized business.[2] Two- and three-reel films were already common, and complex narrative storylines with developed fictional characters had replaced a more novelty-driven 'cinema of attractions', in Tom Gunning's phrase.[3] As actors such as Florence Lawrence ('The Biograph Girl') and Florence Turner ('The Vitagraph Girl') began to appear under their own names, an industry-specific star system began to emerge. Though the close-up was still found somewhat disconcerting by some audiences, film-makers were experimenting with the possibilities of the camera for capturing more naturalistic performance styles.[4] Production companies mushroomed, sometimes despite the best efforts of the Motion Picture Patents Company, also known as 'the Trust'; this group, led by Thomas Edison, held many of the technical patents for cameras and projectors and tried to use them to control film production, distribution, and exhibition. Studios initially flourished in cities such as New York, Chicago, and Philadelphia, but companies also began to film exterior location shots in the more light-saturated settings of California and Florida. Trade magazines such as *Moving Picture World* and *Motography* thrived, giving detailed synopses of new films, as well as industry news and advertisements.

In its endless quest for new content, the nascent industry turned to contemporary popular novels and short fiction, as well as the 'classics' of the past, from Homer to Dickens. Naturally, it also began to cannibalize its older and more prestigious rival, the theatre. Not only did early cinema borrow many of the techniques of stage melodrama, but there were sometimes direct connections at the level of management. Adolph Zukor's Famous Players Film Company, with its slogan 'Famous Players in Famous Plays', is a case in point. (Famous Players would later become Famous Players-Lasky which in turn became Paramount.) Zukor was one of a number of immigrant entrepreneurs who were struggling to create a film industry independent of the 'Trust', but he was also working on another front: Famous Players was trying to lure middle-class audiences to see motion pictures and planned to remove the barrier between the theatre and its upstart rival by making 'photoplays' starring leading stage actors in hit plays. His collaborator in this was none other than Daniel Frohman, whom we encountered as the theatre impresario behind the New York production of *Zenda*. Their ultimate aim was probably that expressed in a 1914 trade ad by their distribution company, Paramount: 'The Dawn of a New Era: Better Pictures, Finer Theatres, Higher Prices'.[5]

Zukor's first serious bid for the carriage trade was the French-made film of Sarah Bernhardt in one of her great stage successes, *Queen Elizabeth*, originally *Les amours de la reine Élisabeth*. He fronted $40,000, and the Swiss film-maker Louis Mercanton handled the production.[6] Released in the US on a states-rights basis in 1912, *Queen Elizabeth* made a profit and, just as gratifying to its producer, enticed to the theatre a new, educated audience, who sat reverently through Bernhardt's one-and-a-half-hour performance. When Zukor turned to stars of the American theatre to anchor a feature, Frohman immediately suggested James K. Hackett in *The Prisoner of Zenda*; the other stage lions rounded up for capture on film were Minnie Maddern Fiske in *Tess of the d'Urbervilles* and James O'Neill in *The Count of Monte Cristo*. (Terry Ramsaye suggests that in fact O'Neill's *Monte Cristo* was to be released first, until it was pre-empted by a version by another company.)[7] The rights to *Zenda* were secured by offering Hope a good lump sum and assuring him that the film version would not interfere unduly with profits from the stage rights (73). Hackett also needed some persuading, but according to Zukor he was won over by the substantial if not princely sum of $5,000, the example of Bernhardt, and the suggestion that he owed it to his public (76). Hackett remained a revered matinée idol, but he was no longer the dashingly athletic swordsman of the 1890s and was reportedly as fond of a drink as Hope's King Rudolf. His career was at this point on a downward spiral. Having tried to escape from *Zenda* into more challenging material in 1906 by leasing his own theatre in New York, he was forced after a couple of poor seasons to resuscitate the old cape-and-sword favourite.[8] Even this was not enough to save him, and, declared bankrupt in July, 1909, the stage lion was forced to sell off his stage properties and scenery, including those for *Zenda*.[9] Hackett's luck would finally turn in 1914, when an inheritance from his half-brother of more than a million dollars freed him forever from melodrama and allowed him to play the meaty Shakespearean roles he had always coveted.[10] But in 1913 there was no inheritance in sight, and, back on the road in yet another Frohman production of *Zenda*, Zukor's $5,000 was impossible to resist, even if it meant yet another swashbuckle through Ruritania.

The Prisoner of Zenda was filmed in New York at a former Armory building at 213 West 26th Street, now the Chelsea Television Studios, directed for Zukor by Edwin S. Porter and Hugh Ford. Zukor claims that the set had to be well guarded from Trust spies, though it seems that Edison's group subsequently licensed this particular 'outlaw' production.[11] With an eye to a middle-class audience, the entrepreneur was willing to spend: costumes were borrowed from Frohman's stock company, but even so the film had a budget of $40,000 to $50,000, at a time when most American films cost a tenth of that. Richard Murphy designed the elaborate sets, and alongside Hackett (see Plate 2.1) there were several other well-known figures from the stage: the English-born Beatrice Beckley (the second Mrs Hackett) as Flavia; the Scottish-born David Torrence as Duke Michael; Fraser Coulter as Colonel Sapt; and Minna Gale as Madame de Mauban.[12] When Hackett's enthusiasm waned, Frohman urged him on by saying, 'Jim, this is a historical moment. You're starting on the first feature picture ever made in America' (82).[13]

The star warmed to the production once he could see that Porter and the others knew their business, and he was even persuaded, after several large whiskies, to swim the castle moat, in reality 'a canvas trough filled with two or three feet of water', in which he splashed around 'like a huge water spaniel' (85, 86). Originally Frohman had planned to shoot a more dramatic version of this scene on the Florida coast, in which Hackett was to 'jump into the sea, and swim for his life, with his sword between his teeth'—it is perhaps just as well that this idea was shelved.[14] Porter's brief was simply to capture Hackett's performance, to 'embalm' it as Zukor put it. However, Charles Musser argues that the resulting film goes well beyond that and 'shows Porter and Hackett in full control'.[15] It draws upon the stage play and stage performance, but, besides the moat episode, there are also cinematic scenes of Rassendyll on horseback and an elaborate coronation ball with a hundred dancers; sepia stock is used to create effective night scenes. The film closes with another cinematic flourish: back by his fireside in England, Rassendyll sees a vision of Flavia; he picks up the rose she gave him, and the picture fades. An effect that could not have been easily achieved on stage, it show-cases the emotive power of the rival medium.[16]

Zukor's *Zenda* was the first American four-reel feature film to achieve critical and commercial success in the US. It opened on 24 March 1913 at Loew's Theatres in New York, after its first private exhibition on 18 February at, aptly enough, the Lyceum Theatre, where Frohman's *Zenda* had debuted in 1895.[17] It was no doubt helped by a substantial advertising campaign in the trade press, as well as postcards, posters of all sizes, and lobby displays aimed at the general public. Modestly described in copy as 'the greatest artistic achievement ever attained in motion pictures', it promised 'the greatest love story since Romeo and Juliet...and a constant influence of adventure and intrigue'.[18] But even the less partisan press praised it, with the *New York*

Journal dubbing it 'the biggest of all hits in the history of the film play' and the *Morning Telegraph* deeming it 'a piece of artistry'.[19] Its subsequent international career was more chequered: it was banned in Germany and parts of Austria because what was seen as escapist fantasy in the US was perceived to be politically charged on the continent; the idea of an idle, dissolute ruler who could be better replaced by an Englishman was thought in some circles to be seditious.[20]

Its role in the history of the film industry was crucial: along with Bernhardt's *Queen Elizabeth*, O'Neill's *Count of Monte Cristo*, and Maddern Fiske's *Tess of the d'Urbervilles*, *The Prisoner of Zenda* helped to bridge the gap between the audience for the new upstart medium and that of the theatres. The 'embalming' of stage performances may be seen in hindsight as a sort of wrong turn for film as a medium, but during a transitional phase the prestige of these films helped attract not just new audiences but also new capital for the nascent industry. Initially dismissed by many as craze, the 'feature films' produced by Zukor and others began to gain ascendancy over the short, one-reel products of the Motion Picture Patents Company, and the direction of the American film industry was changed irrevocably.[21] In the following years such spectacular multi-reel films as *The Last Days of Pompeii* (Italy, 1913), *Cabiria* (Italy, 1914), and *The Birth of a Nation* (USA, 1915) showed that the feature film was there to stay. The idols of the stage were about to be supplanted by a new generation of idols of the screen, and such figures as Mary Pickford, Douglas Fairbanks, Pola Negri, Rudolf Valentino, and Sessue Hayakawa would enjoy unprecedented transnational success.[22]

Rex Ingram's Zenda

An English version of *Zenda* appeared in 1915 from London Film Productions, who had made rather a business of adapting the hit novels and plays of the previous century, including Charles Dickens's *A Christmas Carol* and Hugh Conway's 1883 thriller about international anarchists, *Called Back*.[23] Like Zukor and Frohman, London Films appreciated that cinema audiences could be wooed with theatre stars: their 1914 version of George du Maurier's *Trilby* featured the original stage Svengali, Herbert Beerbohm Tree, and their *Zenda* starred the Shakespearean actor Henry Ainley, who had played the lead in the 1911 revival of the play at the Lyceum Theatre. The *Times* considered that the screen *Zenda* made for 'a much more dramatic production than the stage could manage, because trick photography introduced the possibility of having the King and Rassendyll before us simultaneously', and the film was successful enough for London Film Productions to produce a version of *Rupert of Hentzau* later that year, again starring Ainley. Hope went to see the latter film and thought it 'very good indeed'.[24]

But by far the most successful version of *Zenda* from the silent era is Rex Ingram's stylish 1922 production for Metro, which featured Alice Terry (who became Mrs Ingram during the filming) as Flavia, Lewis Stone as Rudolf, and Mexican actor Ramon Novarro as Rupert.[25] Ingram was one of the most gifted of the early Hollywood directors, and his own life would make quite a good biopic. The son of an Irish clergyman, he was born Reginald Hitchcock in one of Victorian Dublin's leafier suburbs, Rathmines, but in search of broader horizons he emigrated to America, where he spent some time as a clerk on the New Haven docks, before using a small inheritance to study sculpture at the Yale School of the Fine Arts. Drawn to the early film industry, he adopted his mother's maiden name, and the handsome young Irishman worked first as an actor and then as a writer and director for Vitagraph and Edison. It was as a director that he shone, gradually winning a reputation for his flair for artistic effects.[26] Like his friend Erich von Stroheim, he would eventually be marginalized by the emergent studio system, seen as another creative maverick who spent too much money in the search for perfection; in his later years he partly escaped the Hollywood machine by moving to the Victorine studios in Nice, before giving up film-making altogether with the coming of sound. But in 1922 he was at the peak of his career: the year before *Zenda*, he had directed the enormously successful *Four Horsemen of the Apocalypse* for Metro (later Metro-Goldwyn-Mayer), making a star of Rudolf Valentino and a fortune for the studio, so he was given a relatively free hand for his new project.

The resulting film is a sophisticated piece of work, with opulent sets and a number of Ingram's trademark touches, including complex lighting effects, and comic scenes that undercut the romantic melodrama (see Figures 2.1 and 2.2). While the film largely follows Hope's story, it is less exclusively focalized on Rudolf Rassendyll. For example, the film opens with Rudolf in his ancestral home, where he reads of the forthcoming coronation and muses on his own family's connection to the Elphbergs; but then we cut to Ruritania. Black Michael and his international cast of military henchmen— De Gautet, Bersonin, and Detchard—are introduced in their smoky den,

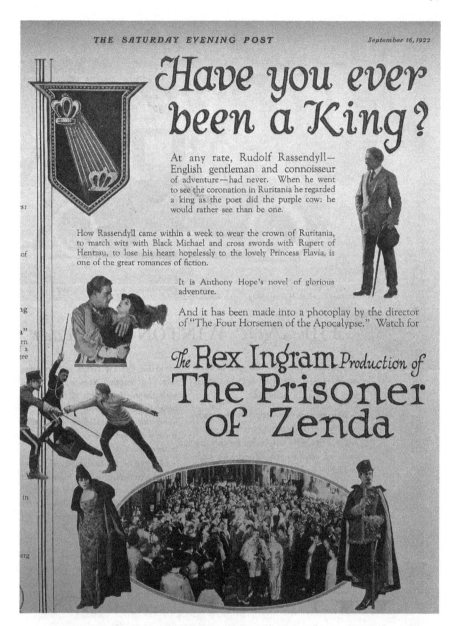

Figure 2.1. Detail from page advertisement for Rex Ingram's *Zenda* from Metro Pictures/*Saturday Evening Post*, 16 September 1922, p. 48, 'Have You Ever Been A King'

Figure 2.2. A (damaged) dustjacket of the 1922 photoplay edition of *Zenda* (Anthony Hope, *The Prisoner of Zenda*, New York: Grosset & Dunlap, 1922. Photoplay edition)

the camera dwelling on each debauched face, before we turn to Rupert of Hentzau, played as a preening hussar by Novarro, complete with monocle and mustache. We then cut to meet the beautiful Flavia in another detailed interior, before we return to Rudolf, whom we see arriving at Strelsau train station; clearly at this point Ruritania has begun to move east in the popular imagination: the Cyrillic signs at the station indicate that we are a long way from the novel's Dresden. Some of the subsequent scenes follow the mise en scène of the stage play: the meeting of Rudolf and his lookalike in the forest, for instance, and the coronation pageantry, for which the sumptuous military uniforms alone cost $80,000. But location shots achieve effects that the stage could not: the coronation scene, for example, is set in what appears to be an actual cathedral. And there are also humorous close-ups that the stage could not achieve: during the ceremony we see a clearly bored Rudolf swinging his sceptre in time to the music before a glare from Sapt (Robert Edeson) reminds him of the solemnity of the occasion.

Scriptwriter Mary O'Hara also created fresh episodes. Rudolf Rassendyll is nearly garotted to death in his room by one of Michael's hired assassins, played by one of Ingram's favorite character actors, the 4'2" Syrian actor John George, born Tufei Filthela. (Ingram's biographer Ruth Barton notes that Ingram delighted in the use of actors who did not look like Hollywood types and had a whole cadre of 'dwarfs, little people, crazies, and eccentrics' [48].) The ending also enlarges the role of the moat around the castle of Zenda, which now poses the extra threat of a powerful current that drags the unwary to a lethal hundred-foot drop. After a struggle Fritz von Tarlenheim (Malcolm McGregor, a former classmate of Ingram's at Yale) manages to cast the scar-faced Bersonin into this deadly stream, and we see him swept to his death; when Rudolf and his team storm the castle and defeat Michael's forces, Rupert leaps into this moat and is seen no more.

Zenda was released to considerable fanfare. It premiered in Los Angeles at Loew's State Theater. As Barton records, 'To emphasize the high-class nature of the evening's entertainment, the picture was preceded by an elaborate musical introduction, with an orchestra playing "Ode to Ruritania", "If Love Were All", and the Zenda waltzes' (109). The waltzes, we might recall, had been around since the first theatre production in 1895. New York, London, and Ingram's native Dublin also had lavish premieres. The author himself, now Sir Anthony Hope Hawkins, attended the London premiere at the Palace Theatre on Shaftesbury Avenue, where Ingram's previous hit, *Four Horseman*, had just finished a run of more than 300 screenings. After some twenty years of adaptations, Hope's personal enthusiasm for another version of his most famous novel may have been somewhat limited, but he nonetheless spoke after the performance in praise of this latest 'veritable triumph of cinematography'.[27] The film did not achieve this triumph unaided, of course: silent film screenings were never actually silent, and the Palace *Zenda* had quite an elaborate sound design. Even after the glamorous premiere, the regular Palace screenings boasted a spoken prologue, two interludes of song, a full orchestra, and a rich variety of sound effects for crucial moments: 'bells…clattering hoofs…murmuring and cheering crowds; guns of honour and clashes of steel'.[28]

Most reviewers seemed to agree with Hope's endorsement of the film. *Picture Play* thought it was 'pure romance and enchantment', while the *New York Sun* felt it was 'easily the peer of all romantic photoplays'.[29] However, in one of the most detailed reviews the *New York Times* complained that, although the film was 'a joy' compared to most cinematic fare and full of delightful visual detail, it was 'needlessly talky" and that "sometimes its action is not clear, its story runs roughly in spots, a number of its efforts at comedy are crude, and at times it lacks the dash and go such a romantic yarn should have'. In undermining the royalist romantic melodrama of a different era, this critic felt that the film had gone too far: while some parts were played seriously, elsewhere the story seemed to have been 'jazzed up for an allegedly democratic country'.[30] But just four years after the pointless industrial carnage of the war, some of the chivalrous sentiments and state pageantry of the Hope/Rose versions perhaps needed a little deflating. (Ingram, whose brother Frank had fought in the trenches in Belgium and France from 1915 to 1918, knew this as well as anyone.)[31] In England, this satirical glint seems to have been lost on most reviewers: the *Pall Mall Gazette*, for instance, lauded the film for 'teeming with scenes of dignified pageantry'—scenes presumably thought to be in keeping with the premiere, which was attended by quite a few titled members of the British establishment, though not the royal family.[32] The London *Times* also admired the 'magnificent' spectacle of the coronation scenes and praised the excellent photography.[33] At any rate, whether or not it had 'jazzed up' its original, Ingram's film generated fresh interest in Hope's novel, and its release was accompanied by the publication of an attractive Photoplay edition, with stills from the production (see Figure 2.2).

Zenda, Selznick, and the Abdication Crisis

None of the sound-era versions is quite as inventive as Ingram's film, though the starry 1937 production directed by John Cromwell for David O. Selznick's International Pictures is a classic in its own right, described by Jeffrey Richards as 'a perfect film'.[34] Selznick (1902–65) is now largely remembered as the producer of *Gone with the Wind* (1939), one of the most successful films of all time, but he had anticipated that success in the 1930s as the wunderkind producer of a string of sophisticated hit films, including *Dinner at Eight* (1933) and *A Star is Born* (1937); he was also executive producer of the very different *King Kong* (1933).[35] Raised as film royalty, he was the son of one of the early East Coast film moguls, Lewis J. Selznick, but the Selznick family empire had come tumbling down in 1923 under the burden of his father's debts. Having learned the business while still in his teens, David made his own way as a producer in Hollywood, working for MGM, Paramount, and RKO before setting up an independent production company in 1935. This rapid ascent was largely fuelled by his insatiable appetite for work, later assisted by Benzedrine, and his intuitive sense of what audiences wanted; it helped, though, that his brother Myron was one of Hollywood's first agents and his wife was Irene Mayer, daughter of Louis B. Mayer of MGM, the former scrap-merchant who had become one of the richest and most powerful men in Hollywood.

While he was clearly a canny businessman, Selznick also felt himself to have an affinity with the literary classics, though his biographer, David Thomson, doubts that he ever had the time to read many of these, given his punishing work schedule, serial infidelity, and ruinous gambling. He had plans at one time to produce versions of, inter alia, *Sister Carrie, Jane Eyre, Tess of the d'Urbervilles*, and even Gertrude Stein's *Three Lives*. While these never made it into production, he did successfully preside over a string of lush literary adaptations, including *The Four Feathers* (1929), *Little Women* (1933), and in one annus mirabilis, 1935, *David Copperfield, Anna Karenina*, and *A Tale of Two Cities*. Whatever his own literary limitations, Selznick took great pains to make these films as convincing as possible, for example securing the services of the bestselling English novelist Hugh Walpole to make the dialogue on *Copperfield* suitably Dickensian (Walpole also plays a cameo part in the film).[36] It is not surprising that his first film as an independent was an adaptation of another nineteenth-century novel, *Little Lord Fauntleroy*, an American novel written by an English-born writer and one that mines upper-class Englishness for all its worth; C. Aubrey Smith, whom we last met as a fledgling actor at the St James's theatre, plays the gruff aristocratic grandfather to the young American heir to an earldom.

The Prisoner of Zenda possessed a particular allure for Selznick. Not only was it by this time another Victorian classic, but in late 1936 and early 1937, as the film entered production, its tale of love versus dynastic duty had acquired a new resonance. The Anglophile producer had been deeply moved by the British abdication crisis, in which the ten-month King Edward VIII gave up the throne in order to marry the American socialite Wallis Simpson. According to screenwriter Ring Lardner Jr., Selznick had burst into tears when he heard the news, lamenting to his assistant, Silvia Schulman, that 'It will wreck the Empire!'[37] Ronald Haver also claims that the producer was spurred to make Zenda because of the excitement created by the abdi-cation, citing his comments that 'the [abdication] had made topical an old problem—that of king and commoner and queen and commoner', though one wonders what actual historical precedents he had in mind; more accur-ately, perhaps, the abdication had made topical some old storylines.[38] The Hollywood studios were apparently reluctant to upset the British market by making a direct treatment of the Edward and Mrs Simpson story, but *The Prisoner of Zenda* offered Selznick an opportunity to rework the dramatic events of 1936 in his own way and to tap into the reserves of popular American interest in the monarchy.[39] As Frank Prochaska has traced, while the British press had steered away from the subject of King Edward VIII's love life, the American newspapers had spent 1936 speculating about the possibility of an American queen: '*King Will Wed Wally*', and '*King Sets June For Wedding To Mrs Simpson*' were two of the more eye-catching headlines of the year. In November, the American Institute of Public Opinion held an opinion poll on whether or not the King should marry his American beloved (he should, was the majority view). Other Hollywood studios also fed the appetite for stories of kings and commoners: Warner Brothers made *The Prince and the Pauper*, and Twentieth Century Fox had *Thin Ice*, in which an incognito prince (Tyrone Power) falls for his skiing instructor, played by Norwegian skating champion Sonja Henie. Nor did American fascin-ation with transatlantic royalty end with Edward's abdication. Denied their American queen, the public moved on to the spectacle of the coronation of George VI and Queen Elizabeth on 12 May 1937, which was the media event of the year. The elaborate ceremony, as it happens, was conducted by the Archbishop of Canterbury, Anthony Hope's old college friend, Cosmo Lang. American radio coverage of the event lasted some seven hours, and there was fierce competition to provide the first newsreel footage; there were even coronation balls and dinners in some US cities.[40] Even while Hollywood was busily manufacturing a new form of celebrity culture, it would appear that the older mystique of bloodlines and titles continued.

The 1937 *Zenda* was to be a major production, lavish enough to do justice to its regal theme (see Figure 2.3). Perhaps the mogul remembered the relatively low-budget version of *Rupert of Hentzau* made in 1923 by his father's failing Selznick Pictures Corporation and wanted to show how far he had come; but it was also an expensive piece because one of Selznick's ways of maintaining creative control was to draft in a whole array of writers and even directors to ensure that the final product would be his vision and not that of any director. The 1937 script was by the combined talents of Wells Root, John Balderston, Donald Ogden Stewart (brought in by Selznick to add more comedy), and playwright Sidney Howard, using Edward Rose's play as well as the novel as their source. As the rewrites piled up, Howard, for

Figure 2.3. Rudolf (Robert Donat) arrives at the coronation, flanked by Zapt (C. Aubrey Smith) and Fritz (David Niven). Publicity still from the 1937 *Zenda*. Everett Collection Inc./Alamy Stock Photo

one, seems to have thought that they were over-egging the pudding: 'Why can't they realize that Anthony Hope wrote that story better than they can'.[41] Cromwell had worked for Selznick at RKO and Paramount and had directed *Little Lord Fauntleroy* for the new production company; the cinematography would be by James Wong Howe, one of the greatest artists in this field. But Cromwell's team was not left alone to shape the film's overall aesthetic. Selznick corralled an old acquaintance, W. S. Van Dyke, to reshoot the storming of the castle and the duel sequences; Van Dyke had directed the then very young producer's first westerns in the 1920s, though he became a reliable all-rounder—that same year he also directed the Ruritanian musical *Rosalie*. More predictably, another Selznick regular—and friend—George Cukor was brought in for further reshoots: he had already directed a number of Selznick's literary adaptations, including *David Copperfield*. This time he was hired to add emotional depth to the renunciation scene in which Rudolf and the Princess Flavia part forever. And quite apart from these other directors, Selznick himself was frequently on set, leading to at least one major fight with Cromwell.[42] He did, however, allow that experts in some areas could probably be left alone: for instance, the former Prince Sigvard of Sweden was an associate technical advisor at the studios and was brought in to coach the stars in royal etiquette; a retired Swedish colonel was hired to make sure that the military uniforms did not resemble those of any particular country too closely.[43] Every effort was made to ensure period authenticity, including the sourcing of newspapers for the year 1898, and suitably Ruritanian uniforms were created by the Austrian designer Ernst Deutsch-Dryden, credited as Ernst Dryden.[44] The full impact of his costumes in *Zenda* is somewhat diminished by the use of black and white film stock, but we can see the uniforms and Flavia's dresses in their dazzling glory in some of the colour production stills, reproduced in Haver's *David O. Selznick's Hollywood*.

In keeping with the film's contemporary royal resonance, the romantic leads for the 1937 film were British. Ronald Colman, who plays the double role of hero and king, had worked as a clerk for the British Steamship Company before joining the army in 1914. A shrapnel injury at Messines ended his military career, and he became an actor, first on stage and then in British films, before moving to New York in 1920. *Beau Geste* (1926) made him a star, and in the sound era his gentlemanly voice as well as his debonair looks led to major roles in numerous films, including two *Bulldog Drummond* films (1929, 1934), *Raffles* (1930), *Clive of India* (1935), and Selznick's *A Tale of*

Two Cities (1935) and *Under Two Flags* (1936). For the Anglophile Selznick, he was an ideal choice to play the triple role: urbanely British, but also rather dashing, and convincing with a sabre in his hand. He had even acted in a double role before, in the 1933 sound version of the much-filmed *The Masquerader*, in which he is both the dissolute MP Sir John Chilcote and his more capable cousin, who impersonates him in the House of Commons when Chilcote is indisposed. The Princess Flavia is played by Madeleine Carroll, in her first major Hollywood role.[45] After a brief stint as a language teacher she took a drama course and soon found stage and then film work in England, beginning with *The Guns of Loos* (1929). Her major break-through came when Hitchcock cast her in *The 39 Steps* (1935), and she left Britain for Hollywood, where she was soon billed with typical industry understatement as 'the most beautiful woman in the world'. She was not Selznick's first thought for Flavia, and other actresses mooted for the part include Jeanette Macdonald and Fay Wray, but Carroll's particular brand of high-caste Englishness (though in fact her father was Irish and her mother French) made her particularly suitable.

On the side of villainy we encounter Raymond Massey as the scheming Michael, Mary Astor as Antoinette de Mauban, and Douglas Fairbanks Jr. as Rupert. (Fairbanks claimed many years later that his father had insisted he accept the part: 'Take it. That role is actor proof. Lassie could play the part.')[46] We can, in fact, discern a clear pattern to the casting: while American and Canadian actors dominate Black Michael's camp, the side of good is decidedly British, made up of members of what Sheridan Morley later termed the 'Hollywood Raj': joining Colman and Carroll are David Niven as Fritz von Tarlenheim and C. Aubrey Smith as Zapt (sic), two more actors associated with a certain brand of upper-class Englishness.[47] The inclusion of the seventy-three-year-old C. Aubrey Smith among the cast also links the film to very first dramatic versions of the novel, since as we have seen he had as a young man replaced W. H. Vernon as Black Michael in the 1896 London stage production and had even for a period worked as the business manager of the St James's. Educated at Charterhouse and Cambridge, his earlier career had included stints as a rancher and broker in South Africa, and he had also been a highly regarded cricketer, captain of the English eleven on tours of Australia and South Africa.[48] After a long career on stage and screen, by the 1930s Smith had become the grand old man of the English commu-nity in Hollywood and was one of America's favorite screen Englishmen, regularly cast in military, aristocratic, and ecclesiastical roles that called for a gentlemanly stiff upper lip or avuncular gruffness. He had already appeared alongside Colman in such films as *Bulldog Drummond Strikes Back* (1934) and *Clive of India* (1935), and he was just what was needed for the part of Colonel Sapt (or Zapt, as his name is rendered in this and some other film versions), another grizzled veteran with a heart of gold.

Selznick, it would appear, saw the film as rewriting the story of Edward and Mrs Simpson, with the roles of King and commoner reversed and duty trumping love. As the crisis gave way to the succession of George VI, the producer even leveraged the film's Britishness to insert himself into the orchestrated spectacle of stability and tradition, masterminding an 'international radio hookup...saluting Britain's new monarch' the night before the 12 May coronation. Douglas Fairbanks Jr. was MC, accompanied by Carroll, Colman, Massey, Niven, and Aubrey Smith. The programme was broadcast nationally by NBC and then 'short-waved to British Broadcasting in London....Selznick greet[ing] London on behalf of Hollywood and the industry'.[49] The British actors were also assembled for a publicity photo 'sending a loyal message of congratulations to Their Majesties'.[50] At one level this was a shameless publicity stunt, but it also seems to testify to Selznick's genuine fascination with royalty, and with the British crown and its traditions in particular, a fascination that was shared by many Americans. The 'hookup' also, of course, shows us the newer form of celebrity culture effortlessly attaching itself to older forms.

Notwithstanding its thinly disguised political fantasies, on the surface the film carefully rejects any affiliation to the present, opening with a prologue that firmly places the action in a more romantic past: 'Towards the end of the last century, when history still wore a rose, and politics had not yet outgrown the waltz, a great royal scandal was whispered in the anterooms of Europe.' The frame of the novel (and of Ingram's version), in which we see Rassendyll in England, is discarded, cut because the film was thought to be too long. Instead we begin with Rassendyll's arrival in Strelsau. This opening sequence also gives us a fair idea of where exactly that is: the camera pans slowly from west to east across a map of Europe; as we come close to Romania the map gradually fades to a shot of a steam train, and as this train pulls into the station of Strelsau we see its itinerary and learn that Strelsau is a stop between Vienna and Bucharest. In a voiceover, our hero reveals that he had decided to take a fishing trip, but as he arrives at the station his future adventures are hinted at: the stern official quickly changes to deference when he thinks he recognizes him, and we see a portrait of the soon-to-be-crowned

King in the background. After this, the film tracks the action of the novel fairly closely. It is all pretty lavish, but the real tour-de-force scenes include a sumptuous version of the coronation (reminding audiences of George VI's coronation in May) and an equally extravagant coronation ball sequence in which Rassendyll and Flavia waltz. The latter is a scene not without its comedy: every time Rudolf stops dancing to ask Flavia a question, the orchestra stops too, as do all the other waltzing couples—nobody dances unless the King dances. The rescue of the real King is perhaps the film's best-known sequence, particularly the extended and athletic duel between Rassendyll and Rupert (see Plate 2.2); if *The Prisoner of Zenda* is still remembered as a swashbuckler by people who have never read the novel, this sequence perhaps explains why. The former US Olympic fencer Ralph Faulkner (who plays Bersonin) was responsible for most of the fine sword-play, coaching the lead actors and doubling for Colman in the more elaborate sections.[51]

When it is clear that the castle must fall to the rescue party, Rupert dives into the moat and escapes: he will live to fight another day, though the planned sequel was never made. Rassendyll returns the royal ring to his now bedbound lookalike, declaring 'my work here is done'; the latter is not so broken down in health that he cannot gamely acknowledge that Rassendyll has taught him how to be a king. Flavia now knows all, and our hero tries to persuade her to leave Ruritania with him, but she recalls her patriotic duty. Tearfully she assures him 'that your heart will always be in my heart; your lips on mine'. After this, Rassendyll literally rides off into the sunset, like a western hero.

Throughout the summer of 1937 the film was heavily promoted in the trade press and in the mainstream media, sometimes with tie-in ads for products such as cigarettes: because films like *Zenda* demand so much of her voice, Madeleine Carroll chooses Lucky Strikes, which are easy on her throat.[52] The official press kit for the film encouraged exhibitors to 'sell the excitement of duelling scenes' by setting up a 'big fencing meet' locally or by displaying swords in the lobby; love letter contests and Madeleine Carroll lookalike contests were also suggested. For the New York premiere at Radio City Music Hall in September, legendary publicist Russell Birdwell came up with an outstanding piece of ballyhoo by flying in the entire population of Zenda, Ontario; this was, in fact, a surprisingly affordable gesture, as the town had only twelve inhabitants.[53] Not to be outdone, the West Coast premiere at Grauman's Chinese Theatre in October saw the film print arrive in a gilded coach flanked by thirty-two men wearing Ruritanian white uniforms.[54] *Time* welcomed Selznick's film as 'the finest treatment' the story had ever had, and the *New York Times* waxed lyrical: 'With all the Graustarkian punctilio this corner can muster up, we rise, click our heels, toast... *The Prisoner of Zenda* and smash the glass.' 'Here', it proclaimed 'is proper, swashbuckling adventure, set in that vast mythical land (of which Zenda is a province) where honor is brighter, villainy unregenerate and beauty incomparable... [H]ere is the most pleasing film that has come along in ages.'[55] The *Brooklyn Daily Eagle* comically imagined its transformative effects on the audience: 'If you see ladies tripping out of Radio City Music Hall this week with the gracious airs of princesses royal and men galloping boldly across Rockefeller Plaza to save fair maidens in distress, it is because they have been momentarily ennobled by contact with *The Prisoner of Zenda*.'[56] The public seems to have agreed with the critics' estimate, and Zenda was among the year's top-grossing films, alongside *Lost Horizon* and *A Star is Born*.[57]

The London premiere was also a grand affair, doubling as the gala charity opening of the new Odeon cinema in Leicester Square, with mounted police controlling the crowds outside. The royal family were represented by the Duke and Duchess of Gloucester. Other titled guests included the Duchess of Rutland, the Lord Chancellor and his wife (Viscount and Viscountess Hailsham), Lord Londonderry, and Lady Iris Mountbatten; actress Valerie Hobson was among the few non-titled celebrities who are mentioned in press accounts. A few of the names might have reminded the audience of Ruritania and Britain's shared Germanic past: the Mountbattens, for instance, were the former Battenbergs.[58] And at least one distinguished guest might have reminded them that royalty was not what it used to be: Prince Vsevolod of Russia, whose father, Prince Ioann, had been killed and thrown down a mineshaft by the Bolsheviks in 1918.[59] Raymond Massey was the visiting star, and Lady Hope Hawkins was there in place of her husband, who had died four years before; she was apparently delighted with the film. Every woman in the audience received a red rose, though this detail may have been lost on those who had never read the novel's ending. As for the film itself, most critics were happy to see the old favourite so splendidly remade, to see English actors in the lead roles, and to see a revival 'of the glories of the romantic school', though the *Times* sniffed that the 'leisurely sophistication' of the original novel had been replaced by melodrama and public-school spirit.[60] Even the caustic James Agate admitted that it was all very well done, singling out for his double-edged praise C. Aubrey Smith as the now very English Sapt: '[I]t is a wonderful performance for an actor so old that his adam's apple looks like it were a bit of the one originally offered by Eve.'[61] As for audiences who had had enough of the romantic spirit of *Zenda*, they could take themselves off to the Vaudeville theatre, where Val Gielgud's satirical *Punch and Judy* imagined how the descendants of the principals might take to 1930s politics: one Bernard Hentzau, a former bank clerk, is dictator of Ruritania and has an American consort. The play was not a success.[62]

From Homage to Parody and Beyond

In retrospect we can see Selznick's film as the peak of *Zenda*'s screen career, and no subsequent adaptation is quite as convincing. The 1952 *Zenda* (MGM, dir. Richard Thorpe) is something of a curiosity, since it is in effect a shot-by-shot Technicolor homage to the 1937 film, even using an adapted version of the original score by Alfred Newman. Like its model, it is a sumptuous affair of sets and costumes, and it was promoted as offering the same kind of grand spectacle as other recent big-budget MGM successes: 'The public which has packed theatres to see the wonders of *Quo Vadis*, the magnitude of *Ivanhoe*, now will revel in the spectacular excitement of the great adventure-romance *The Prisoner of Zenda*.'[63] Again, British actors dominate the cast: Stewart Granger plays the hero/king (see Figure 2.4); Deborah Kerr the Princess; James Mason is Rupert; Robert Douglas is Michael; and Robert Coote is Fritz. Louis Calhern (Zapt) and Jane Greer (de Mauban) are the major Americans, and Lewis Stone, the hero of the 1922 film, reappears here in a cameo role as the Cardinal in the coronation ceremony. Granger and Mason were veterans of the British studio, Gainsborough Pictures, which had produced a whole series of costume melodramas in the 1940s, and Mason had recently whetted his swashbuckling skills in *Scaramouche* (1952).

Nor was Kerr any stranger to costume drama, having starred in the even more extravagant *Quo Vadis* the previous year. No monarchical crisis loomed in 1952, though the British royal family was very much in the news, as George VI died in February of that year, and Elizabeth II was to be crowned queen the following June. Once more the studio could rely on high levels of American Anglophilia, as well as plenty of coronation-themed commercial activity: by early 1953, when the film was playing around the country,

Figure 2.4. Rudolf (Stewart Granger) meets Rudolf in the 1952 *Prisoner Of Zenda*.
Photo 12/Alamy Stock Photo

the media frenzy was already under way, coronation memorabilia was
appearing in the shops, and department stores were gearing up for sales of
British goods to coincide with the June ceremony.[64] Lobby publicity for
Zenda's opening night on 4 November at the Capitol in New York highlighted the coronation connection by featuring a gorgeously attired actor
enthroned as the newly crowned King Rudolf. Spin-offs also emphasized
this aspect of the film: audiences could imagine themselves as royalty in a
Zenda-inspired 'modern version coronation gown' designed by Hollywood
favourite Ceil Chapman.[65] As to the film itself, although it is excessively
loyal to its 1937 predecessor, it is not without its points. James Mason, for
instance, is an interesting Rupert, adding a layer of slightly jaded amusement
to the role. Choreographed by the Belgian fencing master Jean Heremans,
the extended sword fight between Rudolf and Rupert is gripping and even
more spectacular than its predecessors. Bosley Crowther in the *New York Times*
recognized it as the 'dandiest excitement in the film', and even the Catholic
film review *Focus* felt that it was 'one of the longest and most exciting of

screen fights'.[66] But for the most part the film leans heavily on its production values without supplying much in the way of novelty. As *Time* noted, 'Ruritania in this edition is as magnificent a mythical kingdom as MGM money can buy—outsize castles, royal hunting lodges and gargantuan coronation balls.'[67] More form than substance, it remains a shadow of the earlier film. Without being too glib, the same might be said of the 1953 coronation, the extravagance of which belied the extent to which Britain was finished as an empire and too poor to be a superpower: World War II food rationing was to remain in force until 1954. American Anglophilia remained as a powerful aid for the film's publicists, but it was no longer based on the relationship of equals.

For all its lack of originality, the 1952 film did well at the box office, netting some $3 million, having cost roughly half that amount to make. Its success may have been one inspiration for the 1961 Bengali film *Jhinder Bandi* (dir. Tapan Sinha), in which one Gauri Shankar Roy (Uttam Kumar) becomes involved in adventure and romance in the fictional kingdom of Jhind because of his striking resemblance to the King but in the end sacrifices his love for Rani Kasturi Bai (Arundhati Devi) and rides off to let the true King reign.[68] The only significant Anglophone remake after 1952 is the 1979 Peter Sellers parody, which depends for its comedy on the audience's familiarity with the Hollywood *Zenda*s and with romantic adventure conventions more generally. It was not the first lampoon of this sort. *The Great Race* (1965), for instance, includes a *Zenda*-esque parody sequence, set in Carpania, that culminates not in duel but in an epic cream-pie fight, itself a homage to such silent-era comedy battles as Laurel and Hardy's *The Battle of the Century* (1927). Likewise, Richard Lester's 1975 film version of George MacDonald Fraser's comic novel *Royal Flash* (1970) sends up the *Zenda* paradigm with a plot that involves the political scheming of Otto von Bismarck and the resemblance of the rackety Harry Flashman to a crown prince.[69] And that same year the Carry On team made a twenty-five-minute comedy for Thames Television, *The Prisoner of Spenda*, in which Count Yerkackers and Count Yackoff enlist the help of one Arnold Basket (Sid James) to save the throne of Pluritania.

In the 1979 film Peter Sellers plays a triple role: the aged Rudolph (sic) IV, his son Rudolph V, and the latter's lookalike, London cabman Syd Frewin. He is supported by a largely British and continental European cast: Lionel Jeffries appears as Sapt, Simon Williams as Fritz, Lynne Frederick (Mrs Sellers) as the Princess Flavia, Jeremy Kemp as Prince Michael, Stuart Wilson as

Rupert, Catherine Schell as Antoinette, Elke Sommer as a French countess, and Gregory Sierra, the only American, as her jealous husband. (One of the curiosities of a film that is scarcely deferential to the idea of blue blood is that both Sommer and Schell were members of mittel-European titled families: born in Berlin, Sommer had some claim to be called the Baroness von Schletz; and the Hungarian-born Schell's father was the Baron Paul Schell von Bauschlott.) This *Zenda* was above all else, of course, a vehicle for Sellers, who was by this time famous for his multiple-role acting, including his roles in the Ruritanian comedy *The Mouse That Roared* (1959) which we will meet again in chapter 5. The troubled and much-married comedian and actor had first become well known as part of the wildly successful BBC radio comedy *The Goon Show* and moved fairly effortlessly into films, in which his chequered career was bookended by such outstanding successes as *The Ladykillers* (1955) and *Being There* (1979). Beginning in 1963 he struck a seam of gold with the *Pink Panther* films, but other films fared less well, and by 1974 he was facing something of a financial crisis: his last *Pink Panther* film had been in 1964, and his previous seven films had either not been released or done very badly.[70] His agent had signed a three-picture deal with American producer Walter Mirisch in order to raise some money for Sellers, whose deteriorating finances had been further damaged by the 1973–4 financial downturn.[71] It is in this context that the Sellers *Prisoner of Zenda* was made for Universal, with Mirisch producing; it was, in fact, the only one of the three to be made. According to Alexander Walker, Sellers had limited enthusiasm for the project and tried to back out when he saw the 'too broad, too vulgar' script (325). But he had already received some of his fee and was obliged to proceed. Certainly it was not a happy production: Sellers pushed to change the original writers, bringing in Ian La Frenais and Dick Clement, writers of such TV series as *Porridge*, and had Stan Dragoti replaced by Richard Quine as director but then treated the latter badly.[72] Quine had been directing since the 1940s, and his successes included *Bell, Book and Candle* (1958), but at this point he was probably past his creative best; he never made another film.

Filmed on location in Austria at Burg Kreuzenstein, Salzburg Cathedral, and Schönbrunn Palace, as well as at Universal Studios, it is a handsome-looking film (see Figure 2.5), complemented by a good-humoured Henry Mancini soundtrack. Unsurprisingly, the storyline plays fairly fast and loose with its original: the English hero is no longer the younger brother of an English lord but Syd Frewin, a stoic Cockey hansom-cab driver with an

Figure 2.5. Syd (Peter Sellers) and Princess Flavia (Lynne Frederick) at the coronation ball in the 1979 *Zenda*. AF archive/Alamy Stock Photo

uncanny resemblance to the debauched Rudolph V and a great fondness for his horse, Sylvia. Frewin is drafted in by Sapt and Fritz as a decoy, as they fear that Rudolf may be assassinated by Michael's men. But despite their best efforts the King is kidnapped during a drunken evening with his lookalike; Frewin is too engrossed in pornographic stereoscope slides to notice. Sapt persuades the cabman to play the King at the coronation, and the rest of the action tracks the original, if along more slapstick lines, including a long action sequence at the Castle of Zenda in which Frewin wields his cabman's whip rather than a sword.

In the end the doubles escape by diving into the moat, and Michael is defeated. Frewin stays on as King to marry the Princess Flavia, and the real King returns happily to the gambling clubs of London, an ending that may seem to suggest that ability is more important than birth, but any such political resonance is undercut by our earlier discovery that Frewin is probably the King's half-brother. As a comedy it is not overly subtle, leaning heavily on tired double entendres and Sellers' stock-in-trade silly voices: Rudolph of Ruritania, for instance, cannot pronounce the letter 'r'. Sellers was less than impressed with the rough cut and sent in a long list of changes, which Mirisch could not or would not make, and the producer for his part felt that Sellers had sabotaged the film, first by playing Frewin more as a romantic hero than a comic figure and then in his dealings with the media: in a morning talk show interview with Rona Barrett, Sellers actually warned people away from the film.[73] There are, nonetheless, a few genuinely comic moments in the final cut, as when the King's St Bernard, who has taken an instant dislike to Frewin, stops him escaping from the palace. Frewin's midnight assignation with Madame de Mauban turns into one of the best set-pieces of daftness: Frewin and de Mauban are urged by their respective backers to hoot like owls to summon aid, but they can only manage chicken impersonations; a real owl confuses the signalling further, and in the subsequent action ignorant armies hoot and cluck by night.

The film was not a critical success, perhaps not helped by the fact that it emerged into something of a comedy glut.[74] A few reviewers were kind, including Janet Maslin in the *New York Times*, who admired Sellers' 'superb speech defects' and thought that the 'artfully schizoid' balance of Frewin's relative seriousness and the caricatured King worked quite well.[75] But Judith Martin expressed the majority view that this was a remake too many and that the tired formula was not helped by Sellers' impenetrable comedy accents and its broad jokes: 'It's time to let *The Prisoner of Zenda* go. It's wrong to make one novel go through the trial of becoming a movie five times, and the new attempt only creates useless suffering.'[76] In a year marked by the second energy crisis in a decade, it was not difficult for commentators to suggest that *Zenda* was now running on empty. For the *Globe and Mail*, the film's caricature meant that Ruritania was 'done for good'.[77] British reviewers also put the knife in, with the *Daily Mirror* suggesting the film should be marked 'Return to Zenda'.[78] Even so, Mirisch estimated that it made back its $10 million production costs on its US distribution and made money overseas and in 'subsidiary markets' (355).

A property as durable as *The Prisoner of Zenda* is not finished off all at once, and the small screen gave it a stay of execution. Indeed at the same time that Sellers' film was lampooning it, Hope's story was the subject of homage from an unlikely source: *Dr Who*, the long-running science fiction series. The 1978 (Season 16) episode, *The Androids of Tara*, sets the struggle for the crown on a feudal planet on which androids do the hard work. (Its working title was *The Androids of Zenda*.)[79] Hope's lookalikes are updated here with android copies, but the action still culminates in an assault of the castle and a climactic duel between the forces of good and evil, albeit one with electric swords. Television returned to the story in 1984, when a more straightforward

BBC adaptation of the novel appeared on both sides of the Atlantic, with Malcolm Sinclair and Victoria Wicks as the star-crossed commoner and princess (A&E picked it up in the US). This was a scaled-down version, shorn of extensive swashbuckling and expensive Hollywood pageantry. When the series was rebroadcast in 1986, one US reviewer noted that in terms of spectacle it compared very unfavourably not only to the 1937 version but also to the televised royal wedding that had taken place earlier that summer, that of Princess Andrew and Sarah Ferguson.[80] Since then, the only *Zenda*s have been an animated children's film (1988) and a 1996 TV movie with a modern setting, *The Prisoner of Zenda, Inc.*, which borrows the idea of doubles and some names but little else.

The film and television industries endlessly recycle older, 'presold' material, so it would be foolhardy to say that *Zenda* is really 'done for good', but at the time of writing a straightforward big-screen remake seems like a remote possibility. This is not to say that the strain of narrative that was launched by Hope's novel has been forever exhausted: as we will see, there is at least one contemporary popular culture franchise that keeps the flame burning. But before we consider some of the later adventures of the Ruritanian subgenre we must first consider what happened when Hope's formula was Americanized. We leave Ruritania for now and head east to the rocky principality of Graustark and its volatile neighbours, Axphain and Dawsbergen.

3

Graustark

The American Ruritania

Ruritania and the Castle of Zenda live on, even if Anthony Hope is no longer a household name. *The Prisoner of Zenda* has never been out of print and has even made it into the pantheon of Oxford World's Classics; the adjective 'Ruritanian' still has a certain currency, especially on this side of the Atlantic. But who now recalls *Graustark: The Story of a Love Behind a Throne* (1901) and its five sequels, or their author, George Barr McCutcheon (1866–1928)? How often does one hear the term 'Graustarkian'? The answers to those questions may depend on where they are asked. In Europe the imaginary principality of Graustark is long forgotten and was never really that familiar; Vesna Goldsworthy, for instance, makes no mention of it in her account of Balkan Ruritanian fiction. But even in the United States, where McCutcheon's series was first published, the cultural vestiges of Graustark have almost completely vanished.[1]

And yet McCutcheon's bijou Eastern European land was once as well known as Ruritania to American readers. His lively tales of well-to-do American heroes and heroines finding love and adventure in this picturesque principality touched the national imagination and made him a wealthy man. Though there are no towns named for it, there are many other indices of *Graustark*'s fifty-year run of success.[2] At the time of his death, the *New York Times* estimated that the Graustark series had sold some 5 million copies, producing 'one of the largest fortunes ever won by an American writer'; the first volume alone sold in the region of 1.5 million overall, like *Zenda*, remaining popular among younger readers long after its initial heyday.[3] Lucrative stage adaptations toured across the country for years, and musical spin-offs included the *Graustark March* of 1901, the *Beverly of*

Graustark Waltzes of 1909, and a song, *Beverly of Graustark* from 1914 ('You've read the book—you've seen the play—now sing the song').[4] Film versions made the fictional territory familiar to new audiences: *Graustark* (1915 and 1925), *The Prince of Graustark* (1916), and *Beverly of Graustark* (1914 and 1926). McCutcheon's works thus came to impinge upon the lives of some of early Hollywood's most famous figures, including Marion Davies, William Randolph Hearst, and maverick director Erich von Stroheim. As with *Zenda*, these adaptations boosted sales of the original novels: the big-budget adaptations of the 1920s in particular were used to market new 'photoplay' editions, illustrated with film stills and sporting colourful pictorial dust jackets.

But in the 1930s the curtain begins slowly to fall. The novels lost their following after the war, and the last new edition of *Graustark*—outside of the print-on-demand realm—appeared in 1976.[5] Graustark disappears even earlier from the screen: there were no film versions in the sound era, and, tellingly, there has never been a TV adaptation. By the time A. L. Lazarus and Victor H. Jones wrote *Beyond Graustark: George Barr McCutcheon, Playwright Discovered* (1981) to focus attention on McCutcheon's neglected plays, the novels themselves were fading fast in the national memory. At the time of writing it seems fair to say that the novels and their many spin-offs have effectively vanished into the drifting mists of popular cultural history. When McCutcheon is remembered at all, it is probably as the author of *Brewster's Millions* (1902), which has been adapted for the screen eight times, most recently in 2018. The reputation of George Barr's brother, John T. McCutcheon (1870–1949), a war correspondent and celebrated cartoonist for the *Chicago Tribune*, has probably survived more successfully. Here I want to explore some of the reasons for the rapid rise and slow descent of *Graustark* as a popular phenomenon, touching on its visions of heroic New World masculinity, its light-hearted fantasies about affluent Americans marrying European royalty, and the increasingly dark tone of the later novels, in which picturesque Graustark becomes a little too like the United States to offer much in the way of escapism. As with *Zenda*, the fortunes of the series were from the first intertwined with adaptations; and in this case, as we will see, the decline of the novels is anticipated by *Graustark's* failure to ever make it into the sound era of cinema, let alone television.

McCutcheon and Graustark

George Barr McCutcheon grew up at some distance from Ruritanian pageantry. He was born just after the Civil War in a farmhouse 8 miles south of Lafayette, in Tippecanoe County, Indiana, not far from the site of the battle of Tippecanoe. His father, who often spelled the family name McCutchen, came from a family of farmers; invalided home from the Union Army, 'Captain Barr', as he was known, was at various times a drover, the manager of the dining hall at the fledgling Purdue University, a sheriff, and the city treasurer for Lafayette.[6] His mother's family were farmers. Literature and above all drama were taken very seriously in the McCutcheon house, and actors appearing at the Lafayette Opera House were often invited for supper. These included the leading man E. H. Sothern, who as we have seen had his own place in the history of Ruritanian romance.[7] McCutcheon's lifelong passion for the theatre—and an equivalent admiration for such stars as Mary Mannering—was presumably forged in these years. As John T. recollects, though, they were also avid readers of 'The Boys and Girls of New York and the New York Weekly, both adventure publications full of exciting sea stories, pirate tales, trapping and Indian fights and some detective yarns', as well as the work of Horatio Alger and 'Oliver Optic' (William Taylor Adams), tales of plucky and upwardly mobile newsboys and bootblacks.[8] George was already a part-time reporter for the local Lafayette Journal when he enrolled as an undergraduate at Purdue University. Having failed his sophomore year, probably because of his other commitments, he embarked upon a short-lived career as an actor before returning to journalism. He became city editor of the Lafayette Daily Courier, writing plays, stories, and sketches in his spare time, with some of these appearing in the Courier and elsewhere. His circle in this period included two of his brother's old fraternity friends from Purdue: the humorist George Ade, and the novelist and playwright Booth Tarkington, later author of The Magnificent Ambersons (1918).

McCutcheon was by a long chalk the least successful of this group before he penned Graustark in 1901, its succès fou enabling him to quit journalism for a career as a writer. While he continued to write plays, often on more serious themes than his romance novels, it was his fiction that the public wanted. Between 1901 and his death in 1928 he churned out popular novels, sometimes more than one a year, and grew rich on the proceeds. On the advice of George Ade he had accepted a lump sum of $500 for *Graustark* from Herbert S. Stone and Company of Chicago, and thus he profited not at all from the many plays, films, and newspaper serializations of the novel, which were thought to have netted $250,000. (According to his ledger, now in the Beinecke Library at Yale, he did receive an ex-gratia bonus of another $500 from Stone and Company as well as some smaller sums for international editions of the novel.) He learned from this bitter mistake and was a good deal cannier in his subsequent dealings, obtaining a 20 per cent royalty and a $10,000 advance for the first sequel, *Beverly of Graustark*.[9] In fact, as James L. W. West records, McCutcheon became something of an expert at extracting maximum value from his intellectual property, and 'novel after novel was recycled through magazine serial, to clothbound trade edition, to clothbound reprint edition, to movie, dramatic, and second serial versions'.[10] The money that flowed in enabled him and his wife, Marie Van Antwerp Fay, to live in some style in New York, with a chauffeur; paintings on the walls by John Singer Sargent, Jean-Francois Millet, and Jean-Baptiste-Camille Corot; and a peerless library of first editions by Dickens, Thackeray, and Robert Louis Stevenson, among others. While he never achieved the serious critical attention he wanted for his plays and realist novels, he was elected president of the Authors League of America (now the Authors Guild) for 1924–6, and by the time of his death in 1928 he had become a pillar of the literary establishment.

The Graustark series comprises *Graustark: The Story of a Love Behind a Throne* (1901), *Beverly of Graustark* (1904), *Truxton King: A Story of Graustark* (1909), *The Prince of Graustark* (1914), *East of the Setting Sun* (1924), and a prequel, *The Inn of the Hawk and the Raven* (1927). The first tells the story of a well-off but idle American, Grenfall Lorry, whose life changes dramatically when he meets a beautiful young visitor from Europe, a Miss Guggenslocker, on a train journey from Denver to Washington. Very much in the mould of Rudolph Rassendyll, Lorry believes that 'work is becoming to some men...but it does not follow that all men can stand it', and he has been spending his time in Mexico and California, having already 'fished through Norway and hunted in India, and shot everything from grouse on the Scottish moors to the rapids above Assouan' (2).[11] Although he and Miss Guggenslocker are drawn to each other, she has to leave for Europe. Lorry follows eagerly, but, although he knows that she is from Graustark, he has no idea where that is. Eventually, he and his art-student friend in Paris, Harry

Anguish, using Baedeker and the good offices of the French post office, find that Graustark is 'a small principality way off to the east', bordered by Dawsbergen and Axphain. After several days' travel by rail they arrive in Edelweiss, the capital of this remote mountain kingdom. (In one of the novel's many comic touches, they are given the lie of the land by the railway guard, a slangy American named Sitzky.) It is a 'pastoral' city with 'no bustle or strife, no rush, no beggars' (106), though the amiable police chief, Baron Dangloss, is a very prominent figure. The young Americans stand out, since they are 'over six feet tall, broad-shouldered and athletic...like giants among these Graustark men' (107). Soon they discover to their astonishment (if not ours) that Lorry's Miss Guggenslocker is really the Princess Yetive, the much-loved ruler of this pastoral world. Whatever her personal feelings, she cannot marry a commoner, but there is also another hurdle in the path of true love: her country faces ruin unless she marries Prince Lorenz of Axphain. Lorry and Anguish soon prove their worth by thwarting an attempt to kidnap the Princess. (When Anguish hesitates on the brink of this adventure, the formerly idle Lorry encourages him: 'Have you no nerve? What kind of an American are you' [138].) But soon after Prince Lorenz of Axphain arrives in Edelweiss to claim his bride, he is found murdered in his bedroom, and Lorry is the prime suspect. Thanks to the resourceful Harry, Lorry's innocence is established; the real murderer is revealed to be Prince Gabriel of Dawsbergen, and our hero and Yetive finally marry, despite their difference in status. After all, she loves him, 'as a woman, not as a Princess' (393), and is willing to risk her position in order to marry a commoner. Henceforth Grenfall Lorry will be Prince Consort, and their children will rule in due course. While there is initial opposition from some among her council of advisors, most feel that 'the bold, progressive, rich American' will be a good match, and it will be 'the beginning of a new line of princes, new life, new blood, a complete transformation of order' (396).

In its essence, Graustark is an inverted image of America, an imaginary land that is pastoral instead of increasingly urban; hidebound by tradition instead of embracing the new; feudal rather than democratic. But this topsy-turvy world is also a patchwork of contemporary popular fiction. Unencumbered with any personal knowledge of Europe, McCutcheon built his pocket fictional world from the popular adventure novels of the day, including the chivalric adventure romances that topped the newly invented bestseller lists. Such tales were fictional advertisements for the 'strenuous life', the 'higher life, the life of aspiration, of toil, of risk', that President Roosevelt recommended for American men and for America itself in a famous speech of 1899, one consonant with an increasingly imperial vision. But these novels were also in tune with the appetite for social caste among the prosperous at the end of the Gilded Age.[12] Lazarus and Jones adduce as one likely source *When Knighthood Was In Flower* (1898), a romantic Tudorbethan tale based loosely on the life of Mary Tudor; penned by a fellow Hoosier, Charles Major, it was enormously successful as a book, play, and film. There are certainly similarities, including the love between princess and commoner, and court intrigue.[13] Other possible sources include the bestselling novels of Harold McGrath, whose *Arms and the Woman* (1899) and *The Puppet Crown* (1901) pioneered the Americanized Ruritanian novel.[14] But of course, as some contemporary reviewers noted, the most obvious model for *Graustark* was not an American novel at all but the *The Prisoner of Zenda* itself. Grenfall Lorry could be the American cousin of that idler-turned-hero Rudolf Rassendyll, though Lorry is a 29-year-old who does not wish to work in the family's law offices in Washington rather than the 29-year-old younger brother of an English lord. The artist sidekick, Harry Anguish, appears to be modelled on the stage version of *Zenda*'s Bertram Bertrand, who accompanies Rassendyll to Ruritania—the novel's Bertram, it will be remembered, never leaves Paris. Yetive, like Flavia, is a specimen of true womanhood, and her gruff but fiercely loyal protector, Count Halfont, owes a good deal to Ruritania's Colonel Sapt. The most striking resemblance, of course, is that between the lands of Graustark and Ruritania: McCutcheon, like Hope, paints his imaginary country as a place in which the past survives in the present; both countries are a peculiar blend of modernity and the feudal past, and political intrigue is never far from physical violence. However, there are also some significant differences between the two pocket kingdoms. While the intrigues of Ruritania are purely internal, Graustark, which is located a good deal further east, is surrounded by rival territories, its delicate position recalling the contemporary geopolitics of the Balkans in a way that Ruritania does not. The romance plot also runs on different lines. Lorry, like Rassendyll, turns from underemployed sportsman to hero, as American energy and dash outmatches old European scheming, but in McCutcheon's version he is granted a happy ending—there is no Ruritanian King waiting in the wings to spoil things and no need for renunciation. In fact the establishment of an America–Graustark alliance through marriage seems very much the project of the story, and it is essential for the next novel in the series.

Declined by Harper and Bros. and other major houses, *Graustark* was eventually taken by Herbert S. Stone of Chicago. Published on 16 March 1901, it had a slow start, but then, as McCutcheon noted in his ledger, it 'went like a whirlwind'.[15] By June it was on the *New York Times*' city-by-city list of popular titles as one the bestselling books in Chicago and Boston.[16] By September of 1901, ads in the *Publisher's Weekly* were assuring retailers that *Graustark* was 'Nearing its 100th Thousand and Selling Better Every Day' and that it was 'The one "Great Hit" this year by a new writer'.[17] Glowing reviews helped it along. According to the *New York World*, 'never since Anthony Hope's *Prisoner of Zenda* revolutionized romantic literature has a story appeared so replete in blended love and episode, so thrilling and at the same time so tender in its heart passages'. For the *Daily Post* of Houston, the novel's emotional appeal was at its centre: 'A woman is a woman, although she is a princess, is the key note. There are very pretty love scenes, but the love is honest and true, and inspires sympathy.' But readers were also assured that the novel offered a lesson in American manliness: McCutcheon, 'himself an American, has given the reader a noble example of an ideal American as hero'.[18] In later years, as stage adaptations toured the country, Grenfall Lorry would be pictured as 'a brave, handsome, dominant American' whose American pluck earns him the 'willful little Princess'.[19]

A British edition of *Graustark* followed from Grant Richards in 1902 and a German translation in 1903 (*Eine Liebe neben dem Throne*). Swedish, Danish, Norwegian, Italian, and Spanish translations followed later. But perhaps because of its patriotic slant, the novel largely failed to replicate its American success.[20] For London-based trade magazine the *Bookman*, it was just 'another of the numerous tales where a small principality provides the romantic scene and the beautiful princess', though it noted that the hero 'has all the dashing enterprise of his countrymen'.[21] The *Athenaeum* was equally dismissive: 'It is entertaining and not at all ill-constructed, though it makes no pretensions of any sort and is not important.'[22] When a few years later the *Bookman* discussed those authors who were big in America but barely known in Britain, McCutcheon was cited as a prime instance, his Graustark being practically terra incognita there.[23] In the United States, though, McCutcheon's conquest was complete, and *Graustark* reached a new readership among those who did not buy novels when it was serialized in many regional newspapers. Despite, or perhaps because of, this *Graustark* in book form continued to sell steadily, and according to McCutcheon's own carefully kept ledger it had sold 866,208 copies by 1914, considerably more than Hope's *Prisoner of Zenda*.[24]

Literary historians critics have argued that the action-loving protagonists of American romances like *Graustark* offered suitable heroes for an outward-looking nation that was beginning to consider its own future as an empire and its relationship to the territories within its potential sphere of influence (e.g., Puerto Rico and the Philippines). Amy Kaplan offers what is, perhaps, the most sophisticated version of this argument, suggesting that the well-toned heroes of these novels are not so much mirror images for a nation flexing its muscles as compensatory images for the hard-to-picture 'informal empire' of trade and influence that the nation was developing.[25] The heroine of such narratives is there to witness the remasculinization of the American male but is also a composite figure, part New Woman, part future imperial mother. *Graustark* on this model is an image both of a decadent, less muscular Europe and of the more proximate territories that were yet to come under America's imperial wings. It is an argument that explains certain aspects of the novel, including its evocation of the physical stature of Lorry and Harry Anguish. But there are evidently other fantasies at work here as well as those of heroic American masculinity. For instance, as we shall see, *Graustark*'s equally popular sequel follows the adventures of an American woman, the hero being a dashing European prince, hardly a decadent European figure. A recurring aspect of the series—including *Graustark* itself—is the fantasy of the courtship and marriage of a European of royal blood. The territory of Graustark itself, of course, is at the core of the series' appeal. It begins as a heterotopia of modern America, in which life is simpler and adventure is still possible, though as the series goes on it becomes harder and harder to separate out the two countries.

The novel's extraordinary success—from which he earned relatively little, as we have seen—drove McCutcheon to create the 1904 sequel *Beverly of Graustark*. (We might note in passing that John T. McCutcheon had also been capitalizing on European court pomp with his cartoons of the visit of Prince Henry of Prussia to the United States in 1902.)[26] Where his first novel had appeared from a relatively minor Chicago house, *Beverly* was contracted to Dodd, Mead and Company of New York, a sign of McCutcheon's greater bargaining power in the publishing world. An attractive hardback book, it featured a pasted-on *en grisaille* illustration of Beverly as a Gibson Girl type and internal colour illustrations by one of the most successful magazine artists of the day, Harrison Fisher (see Plate 3.1).

Beverly of Graustark introduces an important variation to the Ruritanian theme, replacing the idler hero with a self-reliant American heroine. (The adventuring heroine of Anthony Hope's *Sophy of Kravonia* does not appear until 1906.) Set two years after the events of the first novel, the story opens with a description of Graustark, that 'serene relic of rare old feudal days', and a summary of the events of the previous novel.[27] Grenfall and Yetive, we learn, now spend most of their time in Washington, though they spend a few months every year in Edelweiss. Our protagonist, Beverly Calhoun, the daughter of a southern member of Congress, is a firm friend of Yetive's. Though she is an 'absolutely healthy' modern young woman, her southern background hints that she might be a suitable candidate for the chivalric world of Graustark, since in Beverly's veins run the 'warm, eager impulses of the south'; she possesses a 'hereditary love of ease and luxury' and the expectation of 'chivalry and homage' (7). When Prince Gabriel of Dawsbergen escapes from captivity in Edelweiss and displaces his half-brother, Prince Dantan, on the throne, Grenfall and Yetive have to return at once to their now unsettled principality. Beverly, who was originally meant to accompany them, resolves to follow despite the political upheaval. But en route to Graustark she is abandoned by her escort and falls in with a band of ragged mountain men who mistake her for Princess Yetive, a role she decides to embrace. Baldos, their leader, is a dashing and romantic figure who fortunately speaks fluent English, and she is immediately drawn to him. After a series of adventures, including an attack by a mountain lion, they reach Graustark, where, still pretending to be the Princess, she finds Baldos employment as her personal bodyguard. The handsome vagabond-leader is clearly not what he seems, and she secretly hopes that he is the fugitive Prince Dantan, displaced from the throne by Gabriel. A complication exists in the form of the lecherous military chief, Count Marlanx, who has designs on Beverly and plots to kill Baldos. But after various twists, Marlanx is disgraced and exiled, Baldos pledges his love, and he and Beverly are to marry. In the final pages it is revealed that he is, indeed, Prince Dantan of Dawsbergen, now restored to his kingdom. As with *Graustark*, the reader is treated to a heady cocktail of derring-do and what the reviews liked to call 'heart interest'. Here, for instance, is Dantan revealing his passionate love to Beverly:

> 'Beverly, dearest one, you never can know how much I love you,' he whispered into her ear. 'It is a deathless love, unconquerable, unalterable. It is in my blood to love forever. Listen to me, dear one:
>
> I come of a race whose love is hot and enduring. My people from time immemorial have loved as no other people have loved. They have killed and slaughtered for the sake of the glorious passion. Love is the religion of my people. You must, you shall believe me when I say that I will love you better than my soul so long as that soul exists. I loved you the day I met you. It has been worship since that time.'

This fevered passion is reciprocated by Beverly, with her warm Southern temperament:

> His passion carried her resistlessly away as the great waves sweep the deck of a ship at sea. She was out in the ocean of love, far from all else that was dear to her, far from all harbors save the mysterious one to which his passion was piloting her through a storm of emotion.   (341–2)

Such tempestuous love interest was evidently a key ingredient of the novel's success, an intimate complement to its high adventure. But McCutcheon was careful to counterbalance these grand romantic flourishes with comic interludes. Indeed when they reach Edelweiss the relationship between Baldos/Dantan and Beverly comes close to farce at times: she is a commoner pretending to be a Princess; he is a Prince pretending to be a commoner; and Princess Yetive herself pretends for a time to be Beverly's maid. (Less amusing to latter-day readers are the comic accounts of Beverly's excitable African-American maid, Aunt Fanny.) There are also a few sly jokes about the exact location of Graustark, as when Beverly has to fend off her father's worried letters: "'Father says the United States papers are full of awful war scares from the Balkans. Are we part of the Balkans, Yetive?" she asked of Yetive, with a puzzled frown' (322); she concludes that they are not. These lighter touches also serve as reminders that we are in a particular kind of narrative universe, one in which nothing really bad is going to be allowed to happen to our central character and in which everything will turn out well in the end. It is a tone that McCutcheon does not always maintain in some of the later novels, as we shall see.

Like *Graustark, Beverly* was a bestseller, the sixth most popular title that year in the United States, and serialization followed in various national newspapers. [28] The *New York Times*, among others, enthusiastically welcomed the new Graustark novel, which it preferred 'for all its tinsel and unreality' to McCutcheon's more sombre realist novel of 1903, *The Sherrods*: 'In Graustark things happen just as in a comic opera, and the story is about as convincing as one, but for all that it is entertaining... One can't be too particular in this cunning little kingdom of Graustark, and so long as Mr McCutcheon holds his reader's attention, and keeps events at full gallop from the first page of the book until the end, who wants to quarrel with him[?]'[29] According to his own later account, though, McCutcheon had been bored by the sequel as a writing project. Glossing over any financial motives, he claimed that 'letters from my readers forced me into it' and that *Beverly* was 'literally manufactured'.[30] (In a hostile review, the *San Francisco Sunday Call* lends credence to this view, listing some of the popular sources from which McCutcheon could have taken the dramatic situations, from James Fenimore Cooper to the Nick Carter dime novels.)[31]

In a rather disparaging review, the English *Athenaeum* described Beverly as a Gibson Girl: the book is 'illustrated on the lines of a popular weekly journal, with far-away suggestions of "Gibson Girls" and intimate hints of American fashion-plates'.[32] The 'Gibson Girl' was the young woman of the period as she appears in the illustrations of Charles Dana Gibson, whom we encountered earlier as the illustrator of *Rupert of Hentzau*: she is part athletic and independent New Woman, part idealized American beauty. Despite its hostility, there is indeed some truth in the *Athenaeum*'s assessment, as part of Beverly's charm is that, despite her supposed hereditary love of ease and luxury, and her susceptible Southern heart, she is an attractively formidable and resourceful heroine, decidedly more New Woman than Angel in the House. She does not stand idly by but uses her silver-handled revolver on an attacking mountain lion (63)—though unfortunately she also wings Baldos—and later she takes a shot at the predatory Count Marlanx. On both occasions we are reminded of the ethnic stock she comes from: she has 'fighting blood in her veins' (63) and is animated by 'the valor of the South' (286). In this respect the novel, like its predecessor, uses Graustark as a sort of proving ground for American identity; but this time it is the feisty and athletic American Girl who is put through her paces rather than the manly hero. She is a go-getting American type who *earns* her Prince.

Our heroine is implicitly contrasted here with the actual young American women who were marrying into aristocratic European families in this period, the 'Dollar Princesses', who are an important context for the novel and one clue to its popular appeal. They included such heiresses as Mary Leiter, who married George, Lord Curzon (Anthony Hawkins's Balliol contemporary), and Consuelo Vanderbilt, who married the Duke of Marlborough.[33] Such marriages took place against the backdrop of a more general shift in elite American attitudes to aristocracy and its trappings. The vogue for the importation of European medieval buildings came a little later, but in the 1890s and 1900s the so-called robber barons were already creating their own medieval and renaissance America in the form of Loire-style chateaux, Gothic Revival castles, and Tudor Revival mansions.[34] In the early 1900s some thirty young American women were presented at the British court each year, as America's most powerful families courted feudal prestige to add to their financial might.[35] Dollar-princess matches between Old World prestige and New World money inspired cultural phenomena as diverse as the 'annually revised' *Titled Americans: A List of American Ladies Who Have Married Foreigners of Rank* (1890); several of Henry James's works, including *The Golden Bowl* (1904); and even an operetta, *Die Dollarprinzessin* (1907), with this last the basis of the 1909 transatlantic musical comedy hit *The Dollar Princess*. McCutcheon is tapping into this contemporary American fascination with Old-World prestige, 'blood', and fairy-tale matches while also celebrating the modern companionate marriage of equals. Importantly, Beverly chooses to marry her beloved *before* she finds out he is a Prince, just as Grenfall Lorry falls for Yetive when she is just plain Miss Guggenslocker. Tuft-hunting Dollar Princesses are in fact explicitly invoked and criticized in the novel, not because they want to marry European aristocrats but because they are not, like Beverly, marrying for love: she sternly warns us that 'the American girl who marries the titled foreigner without love ... is a fool' (343).[36]

The next in the series, *Truxton King: A Story of Graustark* (1909), also made it to number 6 on the nation's list of bestsellers for the year, but it marks a departure from the adventure-filled but largely comic-operatic world of the previous novels: not only does the adventure plot overshadow the love interest, but murder and mayhem are described in a naturalistic way that seems at odds with romantic escapism.[37] We have moved on a few more years, and Yetive and Grenfall are no more, tragically killed in a railway accident; their only child, the young Prince Robin, reigns with a cabinet of powerful Graustarkians and under the tutelage of one John Tullis ('Uncle Jack'), an American plutocrat. The scheming Count Marlanx of *Beverly* is still in exile. Truxton King is the new Grenfall Lorry, 'a tall, rawboned, rangy young fellow' with devil-may-care eyes, the bored, footloose scion of a rich American family turned 'globe-trotter and searcher after the treasure of Romance' (1)—his surname suggests, presumably, his natural aristocracy. He associates Graustark with such Romance, but when he arrives he finds it disappointingly prosaic, as the modern world continues to chip away at its feudal and pastoral anachronisms: the railways are making inroads into the country, and Cook's tourists swarm over Edelweiss (a Mr Hobbs, a Cook's tours agent, becomes his own guide).[38] He is more impressed with a local beauty who works for her uncle in an antique shop near the castle, despite her attempts to warn him off. A chat with Baron Dangloss, the chief of police introduced in *Graustark*, reveals that she is not a local but one Olga Platanova, the daughter of an executed Polish anarchist. Happily, Truxton finds a safer romantic object when he trespasses in the Castle grounds and meets the young Prince and his lovely Aunt Loraine. Meanwhile the theme of anarchism reappears in the form of a plot to assassinate the young Prince. Olga Platanova, her Uncle Spantz, and a Committee of Ten, including an American anarchist Anna Cromer and her husband, are the conspirators, supported by an éminence grise, none other than Count Marlanx, who plans to take over the country once the Prince is dead. Truxton and Loraine are kidnapped by the conspirators and kept in the cellar beneath the antique shop, where Loraine is revealed to be a fellow American, John Tullis's sister. The conspirators plan to use her as a decoy before handing her over to the lecherous Marlanx, but Truxton and Loraine manage to escape and foil the assassination attempt: the Prince is saved, though the bomb goes off, killing and maiming many. Marlanx disposes of his anarchist allies and lays siege to the Castle, before Truxton manages to bring support from Dawsbergen. Marlanx is killed in a final assault on the Castle, our hero is made a baron, and he and Loraine plan to marry before they return to New York.

In *Truxton King* we see the Ruritanian formula under severe strain: Graustark's feudal isolation appears no longer to keep at bay the pressures of the present. Russia wishes to have more influence over the principality through the railway; the unions are restless; and Prince Robin's life is threatened by anarchist 'Reds'. The latter group are represented as an international menace, a danger to America as well as to Graustark. Anna Cromer is a 'rabid Red lecturer, who had been driven from the United States, together with her amiable husband: an assassin of some distinction and many aliases' (86). When a strike is called by the 'ugly looking crowd' who are building

the railway, Truxton exclaims, 'A strike? Gad, it's positively homelike' (140).
Even Marlanx comments on the Red threat to America:

> We cannot harbor dynamiters and assassins...They are a dangerous element
> in any town. Those whom I do not kill I shall transport to the United States
> in exchange for the Americans who have managed to lose themselves over
> here...Moreover, I hear that the United States Government welcomes the
> Reds if they are white instead of yellow.   (276)[39]

Why should the 'Reds' be such a preoccupation in what is meant to be a
novel of romantic escapism? McCutcheon was meant, after all, to be the
'leading literary confectioner of the day...indispensable to Summer
vacations, ocean and railway travel, and in all other exigencies where the
sweet tooth asserts itself'.[40] It could be argued that this aspect of the novel
is shaped by contemporary awareness of the political volatility of Eastern
Europe. But I would suggest that the answer lies less in Europe than in the
class warfare of the United States at the turn of the century, a struggle that
was particularly bitter in Chicago, where McCutcheon lived for some years
before his major success. The Midwestern metropolis had mushroomed
during the nineteenth century, driven by, inter alia, meatpacking, heavy
industry, and the city's central place in the nation's railway networks.
Unsurprisingly, it had also become a flashpoint for clashes between labor
unions and business interests. The latter usually came out on top, abetted by
the police force and an anti-union press (John T. McCutcheon worked for
the *Chicago Tribune*, a bastion of anti-union opinion).[41] Chicago was the site
of the infamous Haymarket Affair of May, 1886, in which locked-out workers were shot and police were killed by a bomb blast; the subsequent trial of
the supposed bombers was dominated by the United States' first 'Red Scare'.
Chicago was also ground zero for the nationwide Pullman Strike of 1894,
organized by the American Railway Union under Eugene V. Debs (born,
like McCutcheon, in Indiana). Nor was is it a coincidence that in 1905 the
city was the birthplace of the most radical of the American unions, the
International Workers of the World, alias the "Wobblies'.

   McCutcheon, though, was emplotting national as well as local tensions.
The fevered public imagination increasingly lumped together trade unionists,
anarchists, and Eastern and Southern European immigrants as the enemies
of American prosperity. Labour and America's captains of industry clashed
many times between the Haymarket affair and the First World War, and
business interests liked to assume that much of this unrest was stirred up by

outsiders. Hostility to what were perceived to be dangerous alien elements was given fresh impetus by the shooting of President McKinley in September 1901, even though his assassin, Leon Czolgosz, was American-born and had fairly tenuous of ties to anarchist groups. This new Red Scare issued in the Immigration Act of 1903, which, inter alia, allowed for the exclusion and deportation of anarchists—Anna Cromer is presumably meant to have been packed off under this new legislation. The Russian Revolution of 1905 further heightened concerns about the growth of the left. In these years, of course, socialism in America had some real political force: few years after the appearance of *Truxton King*, Eugene Debs ran as a socialist candidate in the 1912 Presidential Election, attracting close to a million votes, in a year that Woodrow Wilson won with around 6 million.

Into Graustark bleed elements of non-Ruritanian realities, and McCutcheon's anxious Red-baiting is rooted not in Eastern Europe but in contemporary America. In fact, his evil anarchists are probably based on some real figures: Anna Cromer and her assassin husband recall the actual anarchist couple of Emma Goldman and Alexander Berkman, the latter of whom had been jailed in 1892 for attempting to assassinate the industrialist Henry Clay Frick during the Homestead Steel Strike. The depiction of Cromer and her husband is curiously prescient, since Goldman and Berkman *were* subsequently deported from the United States, aboard the *Buford*, the 'Soviet Ark', in December 1919, along with a couple of hundred of other personae who had been deemed non gratae by an increasingly paranoid federal government.[42]

The novel's Ruritanian world struggles to contain these dark energies. Ultimately McCutcheon portrays his anarchists as deluded pawns in a larger game: they are all rounded up and shot by Marlanx when he has no further use for them. (This idea that anarchists and socialists are in the end mere puppets in complex power struggles is one that appears in other popular fiction of the period, notably in the thrillers of John Buchan.) But their bomb attack on the young Prince and its aftermath are evoked more vividly than anything else in the novel: 'A score of men and horses lay writhing in the street; others crept away screaming with pain; human flesh and that of animals lay in the path of the frenzied, panic-stricken crowd; blood mingled with the soft mud of Regengetz circus, slimy, slippery, ugly!' (263). It is hard to imagine anything like this in Hope's Ruritania; swashbuckling has given way to something more akin to industrial slaughter. Any hopes that the reader may have entertained that the beautiful Olga Platanova would be rehabilitated in the novel are quite literally blasted, as it is she who throws the fatal bomb, blowing herself to smithereens in the process: 'We draw a veil across the picture of Olga Platanova after the bomb left her hand; no one may look upon the quivering, shattered thing that once was a living, beautiful woman' (263). Again, we seem some way here from cardboard kingdoms. A further element that seems at odds with the good-humoured fantasy world of the earlier novels is sexual violence: we are left with little doubt of what Marlanx has 'in store for her' when Loraine is to be brought to him (206). In some ways we are closer here to the visceral world of the dime novel than to light romantic fiction; the last two novels of the series, *East of the Setting Sun* and *The Inn of the Hawk and the Raven* are even more explicit in this respect.[43]

Notwithstanding the intrusions of real-world politics, industrial carnage, and sexual menace into Graustark, in the end the forces of darkness are effectively vanquished. Prince Robin's reign is preserved, and the happy couple return—suitably ennobled—to the United States. However, the story's conservatism is evident in this ending too: there is no exotic exogamy here, as Truxton has come halfway around the world to marry another New Yorker, and they plan to live quietly in the US, retreating from the strenuous life. Despite its darker elements, the novel was well received and sold briskly.[44] The *Literary Digest* assured readers that it would be 'welcomed by all those who have made the acquaintance of that stirring principality', and the *New York Times* promised that there would be 'plots and counterplots, love-making and fighting, the scurry of hooves, the crack of rifles, the clash of swords...with all the rush and go which McCutcheon has trained his readers to expect'.[45] Reviewers seemed to agree that it was 'just as exciting as its predecessors', as the previously hostile *San Francisco Call* put it. Echoing the earlier response to *Zenda*, this reviewer emphasized that the thrilling 'love stories...are clean and sweet, too, proving that criticism, psychology and problems are not necessary to hold the interest of the reading public'. Even McCutcheon's slang is a 'clean, healthy form of slang'. For the *Evening Star*, McCutcheon had by now 'established a sort of cult for the mythical kingdom where modern adventurers find a fertile field for their imaginings and an opportunity for their heroic endeavours'.[46]

We meet Truxton and Loraine again in the next in the series, where they briefly play host to Robin, the eponymous *Prince of Graustark* (1914) (see Figure 3.1). The series was losing some ground, and this title only just made the top 10 bestsellers list.[47] *Prince of Graustark* marks a return to lighter

Figure 3.1. A. I. Keller's cover for *Prince of Graustark* (George Barr McCutcheon, *Prince of Graustark*, New York: Dodd, Mead & Company, 1914)

shades of romantic comedy after the relatively somber tones of *Truxton King*, and political violence features not at all. Its sunniness, perhaps, relates to its setting: we barely see Graustark, and instead we spend time among the well-to-do residents of the Catskills (where Truxton and Loraine live), on board a transatlantic passenger ship, and in Paris and Interlaken, before finally arriving in Edelweiss. By now Prince Robin is grown up—"as good-looking a chap as one would see in a week's journey (14)—and he visits America to raise money to pay off Graustark's major creditor, Russia: huge sums have been spent restoring the damage done by Marlanx's revolt and in modernizing the principality's transport infrastructure. The action is focalized at first not through him but through William W. Blithers, a bumptious steel magnate, who schemes to marry off his lovely daughter, Maud, to the young Prince and who buys up Graustark's debts to strengthen his hand. The young Prince, though, has been long officially affianced to the daughter of Beverly and Prince Dantan, the Crown Princess Bevra of Dawsbergen, whom he has never seen. The romantic farce of *Beverly of Graustark* is revisited when the Prince, crossing the Atlantic incognito as R. Schmidt, falls in love with a beautiful young woman travelling under the name Bedelia Guile, whom he suspects is really Maud Blithers. After various adventures together, including a high-speed car chase in Paris, he follows her to Graustark, where he discovers that she is not Maud but the Crown Princess Bevra of Dawsbergen, something that the reader has long suspected.

In effect *The Prince of Graustark* is a second-generation love story: the child of a Graustarkian-American marriage falls for the child of a Dawsbergenian-American marriage. Despite or because of the 'independent American blood in the two young people' (21), they end up inadvertently following the path that was laid down for them; personal choice and the interests of statecraft are aligned. The geopolitical and financial affairs that are behind the Prince's American tour—the dominant role of Russia in particular and the possibilities of a European war—are kept firmly in the background. As one reviewer noted: 'There [is] something in the first chapter of Austria and Servia and Russia—but only a hint in prescience of present events, for the war was not on when this story was written, and the story is not of war—at least of the military sort'. Instead we have a love story that 'will give us as many million hours of thorough enjoyment as *Graustark* and *Beverly of Graustark* did in their time.'[48]

After a break of ten years or so, McCutcheon returned twice more to Graustark. *East of the Setting Sun* (1924) imagines the principality in the aftermath of the First World War. While it failed to make the top 10 bestsellers list for year, serialization in the *Saturday Evening Post* guaranteed it a wide readership. It is in many ways a reprise of *Truxton King*, with the Red spectre again haunting the tiny European principality. Pendennis 'Pen' Yorke is the latest avatar of Grenfall Lorry, an American war correspondent, sent to see what has become of Graustark during the war. 'Jugo-Slavia swallowed up a lot of those little states and Czechoslovakia gobbled up a lot more,' an unnamed Publisher notes in the opening chapter.[49] It is not Pen's first visit to Eastern Europe, since we learn that he was in Budapest in 1919, during the formation of the Hungarian Soviet Republic led by Béla Kun, described in the novel as a violent chaos, and he married and then promptly divorced a young woman who needed an American passport to flee the country. When the reporter arrives in Graustark he is amazed at his warm reception, but he soon discovers that this is because his ex-wife is in fact the Princess Virginia of Dawsbergen; she is thus the sister of Bevra, heroine of *The Prince of Graustark*, and daughter of Beverly and Dantan from *Beverly of Graustark*. Pen is watched over by Hobbs, the former Cook's Tours agent, now working for the secret police, but he has a dangerous rival in Prince Hubert of Axphain. Hubert is the exiled heir to the throne of Axphain, which has, like Hungary, been overrun by socialists. It turns out, though, that Graustark has its own resident Reds, including (again) an American, one Michael Rodkin, who turns out to be one of Pendennis's own Harvard classmates. Something of a comedy of errors ensues: Virginia is not sure if Pendennis cares for her, and vice versa, and much play is made of the fact that they may still be married. But, as in *Truxton King*, the romantic comedy is at times overshadowed by the political material, and a note of menace runs through the narrative. The crisis comes when the socialists of Axphain invade. Although they are soon beaten back, being half-starved, Rodkin takes advantage of the confusion to kidnap Virginia, having long lusted after her from afar. But Pendennis races to the rescue and saves Virginia from rape. Rodkin is killed by his own communist henchmen, and Pen and Virginia return safely to Edelweiss, where her family think it is best for her to marry Pen, even though he is a commoner, and to leave Graustark for America. A weary Duchess notes that 'Civilization . . . goes forever towards the West', away from those who live to the East of the Setting Sun. Better, then, to follow the 'strain of clean, fresh, virile blood that came out of the veins of strong people from across the sea, the beat of a free heart, glow of renewed vitality' (158). Old Europe, it would appear, is doomed.

Not only is this a strange note for a Ruritanian romance to end upon, but the action that leads up to it is much too close to the American anxieties of these years to make for escapist reading. Again, it is difficult to understand the failure of fantasy here without some sense of the politics of the post-war years. As we saw in *Truxton King*, McCutcheon had long been wary of 'Red' elements in the United States. In the immediate aftermath of the Bolshevik Revolution in Russia, such views were widely held, and the Red Scare of 1919–20 was probably the most intense until the McCarthyism of the 1950s. Nor, of course, was the US unique in its concerns about the threat of socialism, and European newspapers and politicians also painted a lurid picture of life under Bolshevism. Winston Churchill's account of Russia in a 1918 election speech is particularly vivid but not atypical: 'Civilisation is being completely extinguished over gigantic areas, while Bolsheviks hop and caper like troops of ferocious baboons amid the ruins of cities and the corpses of their victims.'[50] In parts of continental Europe, counter-socialist political and paramilitary movements ultimately led to the rise of fascism. In the United States, as historian Robert K. Murray (no partisan of socialism) describes, the Red Scare was marked by a sort of national hysteria that saw the rule of law blithely ignored by self-styled patriots, in the pursuit of virulent campaigns against anything that smacked of anarchism, socialism, or Bolshevism.[51] Attorney General A. Mitchell Palmer sponsored the federal witch-hunt, using the all-new General Investigation Division of his office. In charge was a very young J. Edgar Hoover, who quickly put his experience at the Library of Congress to good use by compiling an elaborate filing system for the tracking of supposed enemies of the state. But there was also a flourishing clutch of amateur bodies that were keen to sniff out anarchy and scotch socialism. These included the American Defense Society, the American Protection League, the National Civic Federation, and later such minor groups as the Fred Marvin's Key Men of America. Other bodies, like the American Legion and even the Ku Klux Klan, also positioned themselves as the defenders of America and 'Americanism' in the face of radicals and dangerous aliens.[52]

Against this phobic background it is easy to see how Graustark had become so bedeviled by socialism, though it is harder to see how returning to America is going to make life appreciably safer for Pen and Virginia. Given the strain that his escapist fantasy was under by this time, as McCutcheon made his Ruritania more and more like a miniature America and less like its pastoral refraction, it is not surprising that for the last novel in the series the author decided to write a prequel. *The Inn of the Hawk and the Raven: A Tale of Old Graustark* (1927) takes us back into the safer territory of the nineteenth century: Yetive is a mere child, Count Halfont is Regent, and the country is still a sort of landlocked feudal island. (Like its predecessor, this novel failed to make the top 10, suggesting that the appetite for Graustark, at least in book form, was not what it once was.) The setting is not Edelweiss and the court but a hidden valley in the forest, home to a band of robbers, and the story turns on the love affair between Gerane, daughter of the robber-king, Jonifer, and one of the soldiers who undertakes to capture him, the English-born Colonel Starcourt. Of course, this being a Graustark novel, Jonifer is from a disgraced and exiled branch of the royal family, and Gerane's mother was a kidnapped noblewoman, so our heroine has 'gentle blood in her veins' on both sides.[53] With its hidden valley of robbers, and its romance plot, *The Inn of the Hawk and the Raven* brings to mind R. D Blackmore's stirring historical yarn *Lorna Doone* (1869), though there are also echoes of E. M. Hull's desert romance *The Sheik* (1919, filmed 1921) and Sigmund Romberg's 1926 operetta *The Desert Song*, in which kidnapping similarly leads to romance. Going back in time allows McCutcheon even more scope to indulge in his fascination with 'blood' and nobility. This time the nearest thing to a can-do American hero is Colonel Starcourt, who is said to have the 'bulldog' virtues of the English, but even he belongs to a titled family, and Gerane will be Lady Starcourt upon her marriage. It was to be the last of the *Graustark* novels, though by no means the last of Graustark, which had by then moved to new media.

Graustark on Stage

Like *The Prisoner of Zenda*, *Graustark*'s popularity was boosted first by stage and then by film productions. On stage, the visual and romantic appeal of the narrative was accentuated, and action played a lesser role, though it was far from being an insignificant part of the entertainment. The first novel in the series had a complex history of production on its way to becoming one of the most lucrative plays of the period. New York producer and director Frank McKee obtained the rights from Herbert S. Stone and Company, and with the pioneering female journalist Jeanette L. Gilder he planned to make the adaptation a vehicle for leading lady Mary Mannering.[54] But this project seems to have been delayed, and in the meantime actress and playwright

Grace Hayward wrote and staged her own version of the play. (In this five-act version, copyrighted by Hayward on 10 March 1902, Lorry pays off Graustark's debts, thwarting one Prince Boloroz, who tries to buy the Princess's hand in marriage.) Hayward was married to theatrical manager Dick Ferris, and for the next few years *Graustark* toured minor houses, mostly in the Midwest, with Grace herself appearing as Yetive and Ferris at times playing Lorry. The play eventually had its first New York outing on 20 January 1908, when Hayward's version was played at the Keith and Proctor Harlem Opera House to a packed auditorium; the *New York Clipper* singled out for praise its elaborate sets, 'pretty love scenes', and 'considerable suspense'.[55] The path of true love did not run quite as smoothly off stage as on, and by the end of the decade Ferris and Hayward were divorced. Ferris continued to stage the play on his own, though Hayward (by then married to George Gatts of the United Play Company) obtained a judgment against him in 1911 for box office earnings of $51,200—a figure that gives some idea of the play's profitability.[56]

The year 1908 also saw the appearance of a series of better-capitalized touring productions under the management of George Duane Baker and James W. Castle. (Castle was already a well-known figure, with productions of *Quo Vadis* and *When Johnny Comes Marching Home* under his belt; Baker later went on to a career in the cinema and was involved in the first film version of *Graustark*.) *The New York Dramatic Mirror* reported that by 1911 Baker and Castle were running three (McCutcheon's ledger says four) different *Graustark* road companies, covering the Eastern, Central, and Southern circuits (see Figure 3.2).[57] According to McCutcheon, Mary Mannering now refused to appear in a play that had already toured the minor houses, so less well-known figures played the part of Yetive, including the German-born Eda von Luke, Isabel Macgregor, and Gertrude Perry.

Using 'elaborate scenic production, picturesque costumes and electrical innovations', these versions of the play added spectacle to McCutcheon's idealistic scenes of love and valour, with their lavish realizations of the throne room and Edelweiss by night coming in for particular praise.[58] We have, in fact, a good sense of the costly staging of this production, because one of the Grosset and Dunlap editions of the novel is illustrated with photographs from the play (see Figure 3.3)—it should not be confused with the later 'photoplay' edition, a tie-in with stills from the 1925 film.[59]

Much of the novel's strenuous-life ethos came through, and Lorry was seen to 'override the old world traditions' and win the fair lady through

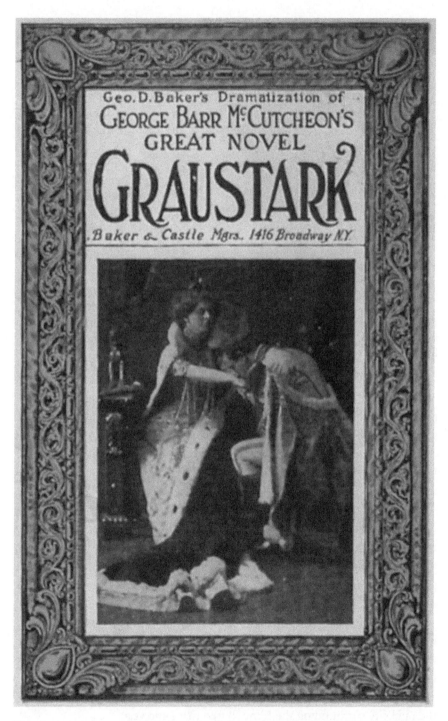

Figure 3.2. A postcard advertising the Baker and Castle production of Graustark, 1910

"HE IS MY PRISONER! HE DIES WHO DARES TO TOUCH HIM!"

Figure 3.3. Lorry is accused of murder. A scene from the play, reproduced in the illustrated *Graustark* (George Barr McCutcheon, *Beverly of Graustark*, New York: Dodd, Grosset & Dunlap, 1910, between pp. 372 and 373)

'sheer force of character and manly attributes'.[60] Press releases stressed that the play was 'clean and wholesome'.[61] At the same time, the photographed scenes from the play make it clear that much of the attraction of the production was its use of costumes and elaborate sets. Republican America, while embracing the strenuous life, appeared to be just as susceptible to fine uniforms and the trappings of royalty as Britain was.

Versions of *Graustark, Beverly of Graustark*, and *Truxton King* (also adapted by Grace Hayward) toured until at least 1916, though at less and less prestigious venues and with ever more vivid advertising. The United Play Company of Chicago, for example, a theatrical syndicate, kept *Graustark* on the road by promising audiences a 'Blood-bubbling, Heart-leaping Story of Love and Adventure, An American's Fight for a Kingdom in the Balkans'.[62] But by May, 1913, the company felt that they had extracted their money's worth out of the rocky principality, and the plays were released for stock production, where they staggered on for several more years; in smaller towns, early film productions regularly competed with these lingering stage versions.[63] As late as 1925, a musical version of *Graustark* went on tour, presumably taking advantage of the publicity surrounding the film released that same year.[64]

Graustark on the Screen

The first film versions tended to replicate the relatively static stage adaptations, but by the 1920s directors were more willing to exploit the scope of their medium to create heroic action in imaginary space. Gorgeous uniforms and elaborate representations of the Graustarkian court continued to be a mainstay of the films, which also mined the comedy of the originals. The first *Graustark* film appeared in 1914, a three-reel version of the second novel of the series, *Beverly of Graustark*.[65] As with *The Prisoner of Zenda*, its origins tell us a lot about the relationship between the theatre and the cinema in these years. *Beverly* was produced by the Protective Amusement Company, formed by the powerful theatre production and booking agency Klaw and Erlanger (part of the Theatrical Syndicate) and the film company Biograph.[66] Klaw and Erlanger controlled hundreds of American theatres, particularly in the southern states, and they had ventured into cinema as early as 1897, when they exhibited a filmed version of a Passion Play, that of the village of Horitz in Bohemia.[67] As John C. Tibbetts notes, they were probably inspired by Famous Players to put their own theatrical assets to use rather than simply losing audiences to the new medium: they would present 'Famous Plays in Pictures'. *Beverly of Graustark* was one of a series of these famous plays, which also included *The Billionaire*, a version of McCutcheon's *Brewster's Millions*. They already owned the rights to a stage version of *Beverly*; they had the costumes; and they had actors readily available.[68] Biograph was home in this period to the great pioneering director D. W. Griffith, though he does not seem to have been involved in *Beverly*.[69] His wife, Linda Arvidson, starred, however; Charles Perley played Dantan; and Gertrude Robinson appeared as Candace, Dantan's sister. Subtitled 'A Modern Romantic Comedy Drama from George Barr McCutcheon's Novel of the Same Name', it follows the play rather than the novel in some details: for example, as in the play, the mountain lion scene disappears, and instead Beverly helps to fight off Prince Gabriel's spies, using Dantan's pistol to good effect.

Scene 67—*Exterior of cave*—Dantan and soldiers enter, firing.
Scene 68—*Hills, near cave*—Gabriel's spies go toward cave.
Scene 69—*Exterior of cave*—Dantan wounded drops pistol. Beverly enters; takes pistol, fires.

Scene 70—*Hills*—Gabriel's spies fighting.
(Sub Title) The Graustark Forces to the Rescue.[70]

The Klaw and Erlanger films are not usually seen as marking any great advance upon the Famous Players in Famous Plays approach that we considered in chapter 1. However, even this brief segment displays an understanding of the grammar of cinema, and clearly this is not simply a filmed play. Partly because of their limited distribution, few of these films received any critical attention, and *Beverly of Graustark* does not seem to have been an exception. On its rerelease by Biograph in 1916, *Moving Picture World* considered that *Beverly* retained 'all of the fine flavor of romance beloved by readers of this writer of novels'; but it attracted little notice elsewhere.[71]

Far more of a splash was created by the Chicago-based Essanay company's six-reel version of *Graustark* itself (April, 1915), directed by Fred E. Wright and starring established matinee idol Francis X. Bushman as Grenfall Lorry and Beverly Bayne (later Mrs Bushman) as the Princess Yetive.[72] This is classed as a 'lost film', but the summaries we have suggest that it again closely followed the original story, or more likely the stage version, and romance takes precedence over the action elements. A number of stills survive, as does a delightful chromolithographic poster showing the marriage of Yetive and Grenfall Lorry.[73] It strongly suggests the costume-drama aspect of the film: Yetive is wearing a white wedding dress, though also her crown, while Lorry, who wears a dress sword, is in a white hussar's uniform, with yellow frogging and scarlet cuffs, set off by a cream cape. In stills we sometimes see Bushman as Lorry looking more the action hero, wearing thigh-high leather boots. This was a relatively costly production for the time: most of the film was shot in Chicago, unsurprisingly, but a few scenes were filmed in New York, Washington DC, and California, which suggests an ambition to get away from simply filming the stage version and to make some use of the potential of the camera to create its own fictional world.[74] Heavily promoted, the film seems to have been one of the hits of the season, praised for its thrilling episodes and visual appeal, even if we discount some of the press releases masquerading as reviews ('*Graustark* Heralded As One Of The World's Greatest Dramas').[75] *Motography*, for instance, described it as photographically 'a gem' and felt that Graustark was convincingly evoked.[76] We can only speculate as to what recent immigrants from Eastern Europe made of that imaginary country, but we know that at least some audience members felt that Essanay had given them characters who were 'even more thrilling and more lovable than our imagination-pictured heroes', while Bushman himself noted that the feature contained the romance, fairy-tale elements, and 'brass buttons and gold braid' that his public demanded.[77] In 1916, *Motion Picture Magazine* included it in its list of 'Photoplay Classics' that would last, though it admitted that the war in the Balkans showed up the 'absurdities of such a plot'.[78]

Essanay followed up the success of the 1915 film with *The Prince of Graustark* (November, 1916), a five-act photoplay with Bryant Washburn (Prince Lorenz in the earlier film) and Marguerite Clayton, again directed by Fred E. Wright. The plot is that of the novel, including the twist in the tale that reveals that the Prince has been pursuing his own fiancée all along. This too was an expensive production, featuring an appearance by members of the Russian ballet and location shots, including 'a beautiful estate on Chicago's North Shore'.[79] The good humour of the novel was retained, and reviews praised its 'snap and brilliancy [and] typical Americanisms'.[80] Even the hard-bitten *Variety* was impressed: *The Prince of Graustark* was 'not a sick-ening love story, but holds the interest... Washburn [is] a fair representative of a dashing prince and Miss Clayton is youthful and attractive.' The film was, *Variety* concludes, the 'best done by Essanay in some time'.[81]

These three films arrived at a choppy period in the international film industry, which was far from immune to the effects of the war. The outbreak of conflict had in general given a considerable edge to the American film business, as production was disrupted in Europe. But for films like *Graustark* there was an unexpected difficulty with the British market. As *Variety*'s London correspondent explained: 'Nothing German, or sounding like German, will get by here... For instance the M.P. Sales Agency has been holding up *Beverly of Graustark* for the last 6 months as there are too many German helmets [sc. Pickelhaube] shown in this Klaw and Erlanger produc-tion for it to get by. Essanay will likely be forced to do the same with their *Graustark* pictures.'[82] A German-sounding company name like Klaw and Erlanger was a further liability, as the article notes.

With the European industry still recovering, the post-war years were prosperous ones for American film companies, who once again turned to McCutcheon's popular work for content. A film now thought to be lost, *Truxton King*, was released by Fox in 1923 as a romantic drama, featuring rising star John Gilbert in the lead, Ruth Clifford as Lorraine, and Mickey

Moore as the young Prince Robin. The attack on the castle by Marlanx's forces was singled out by reviewers for praise for its shots of cavalry horses leaping over the audience's point of view, but the script also played up the humour of the original, with the Cook's tour guide, Hobbs (Otis Harlan), providing many of the laughs. The spectre of communism disappears completely, and Prince Robin's enemies are simply an opposing Graustarkian faction.[83] The film was not heavily promoted, but we might note in passing that it was hoped that such films-from-books would create opportunities for cross-medium advertising, with publishers Grosset and Dunlap listing *Truxton King* in their page ad in the trade paper the *Exhibitors Herald*, urging cinema owners to 'Link up your publicity with your local bookseller'.[84]

By far the most elaborate screen treatments of McCutcheon's work were the 1925 version of *Graustark* and the 1926 version of *Beverly of Graustark*. *Graustark*, subtitled 'A Modern Romance by George Barr McCutcheon', was a Joseph M. Schenck production for First National, adapted for the screen by Frances Marion and directed by Dimitri Buchowetzki, with Norma Talmadge and Eugene O'Brien in the lead roles (see Figure 3.4). Talmadge was at this point at the height of her career, a name synonymous with screen glamour, and Schenck a powerful figure in Hollywood production. The resulting film was a big-budget seven-reel feature, though only five of these have survived.[85] Not all of the spectacle in this expensive production cost dear, though: shooting was moved to the MGM lot in Culver City, to take advantage of the elaborate sets left over from Erich von Stroheim's *The Merry Widow*. There, as Schenck himself was tied up with other projects, the extremely capable Irving Thalberg oversaw the production.[86] Frances Marion, a gifted screenwriter, reworked the original story, so that Princess Yetive acquires a father, King Ferdinand (Frank Currier), and Lorry is helped in Graustark by the American ambassador rather than his sidekick, Harry; Dangloss is now a villain. As with earlier film versions, the accent is on romance more than adventure. As *Photoplay* put it, 'Love conquers all [in this film], even our good sense.'[87] In the best Ruritanian tradition, a starring role is given to the spectacular costumes and settings, under art director William Cameron Menzies. Talmadge's gowns were singled out for praise, *Variety* describing them in its own distinctive argot as 'all creations, and eye-smashing', while the settings were 'heavy, impressive and artistically done...the whole thing...as handsome as the Kohinoor diamond'.[88] A tie-in Gross and Dunlap photoplay edition of the novel features some of the more elaborately realized scenes, in which Talmadge's

Figure 3.4. Princess Yetive (Norma Talmadge) and Lorry (Eugene O'Brien) in the wedding scene of First National's Graustark, 1925. Granger Historical Picture Archive/Alamy Stock Photo

gowns are carefully lit for full effect. With its mixture of star power, glamour, and royal love interest, *Graustark* charmed the public. After its premiere at the Capitol, New York, on 6 September it had to do battle with such box-office draws as Lon Chaney's *The Phantom of the Opera* and Charles Chaplin's *The Gold Rush*, but it held its own and was one of First National's hits of the season.

McCutcheon, of course, received nothing from *Graustark*'s screen success, as he had sold the rights outright in 1899. On the other hand, he did very well from the 1926 *Beverly of Graustark*; after litigation, McCutcheon had retrieved the film rights of *Beverly* from Biograph, and in 1924 he had sold them again for $30,000.[89] The resulting MGM film, directed by Sidney Franklin, starred Marion Davies and Antonio Moreno, supported by Roy D'Arcy (General Marlanax [sic]) and Irish actor Creighton Hale (Prince Oscar). Davies was a former 'Ziegfeld girl' turned screen comedienne; her presence in the leading role is scarcely surprising, since this was a Cosmopolitan picture, produced under the aegis of newspaper magnate William Randolph Hearst, Davies' partner. The *Citizen Kane* version of Hearst's life suggests that he entered the film business to bolster Davies' career, but the film industry was in fact a very natural complement to his newspaper and newsreel interests. By controlling much of the publicity market, Hearst could make or break films, and he certainly pushed *Beverly*, using his newspapers to full effect.[90] The Spanish-born Moreno had come to prominence as a matinee idol of the 'Latin Lover' stamp, but he was a good complement for Davies and a talented comic actor in his own right, as he would show to even greater effect the following year in the enormously successful romantic comedy *It*, opposite Clara Bow.

Agnes Christine Johnston's script plays fairly fast and loose with the original plot, adding some *Twelfth Night*–style transvestism to the plot complications of the novel. This was presumably to trade on Davies' reputation for cross-dressing roles, which she had played in her film debut *Runaway Romany* (1917), in *When Knighthood was in Flower* (1922), and in *Little Old New York* (1923).[91] Beverly is visiting her cousin Prince Oscar, ruler of Graustark, when he is injured in a skiing accident, and she impersonates him in order to foil a political plot—shades of *The Prisoner of Zenda*, as well as McCutcheon's novel. Dressed as Oscar (see Plate 3.2), she is protected from her enemies by Dantan (Moreno), leader of a band of shepherds. She is attracted to the handsome shepherd and reappears as Beverly in order to win him, but, although Dantan is suitably smitten, he now believes that Beverly-as-Oscar is his rival in love and challenges him to a duel. All such complications are dissolved in the end, the plotters thwarted, and Dantan revealed to be a Prince in disguise. With imposing art direction by Richard Day and Cedric Gibbons, splendid costumes for Davies, and an expensive colour sequence at the end, the film was a visual treat as well as a successful comedy.[92] Pre-release publicity highlighted *Beverly*'s romantic, dramatic, and comic strengths: 'A Girl Alone In A World of Men!' 'The ravishing girl who had all men at her feet – The dashing young Prince, the ladies all fell for. One and the same! What possibilities for surprising twists, gales of laughter, a different love story, in this great starring triumph of adorable Marion Davies! Miss Davies impersonates a boy so cleverly you will be amazed to see her performance.'[93] Elsewhere, film gossip columns celebrated Davies' severe 'Beverly Bob' haircut and noted the resemblance between the close-cropped actress and the Prince of Wales, whose 1919 and 1924 visits to the United States had been widely covered.[94] Upon its release, the Hearst press dutifully trumpeted the film.[95] The trade papers were also used to boost it, with elaborate page ads in *The Moving Picture World, The Film Daily*, and elsewhere assuring exhibitors that *Beverly* was a surefire hit and Davies a comic sensation. But the film also drew positive reviews from the less partisan press. The *New York Times* singled out the 'stunning uniforms and costumes... and elaborate settings', while among the trade papers *Motion Picture News* asserted that this was a 'snappy entertainment... with tremendous vim'; although *Variety* was less enthusiastic than some, it admired Davies' slapsticky comic performance and the production values, noting that 'the film rides into its happy ending done on a massive scale in colors'.[96] The public was equally impressed, and *Beverly* was one of the *Exhibitor's Herald's* 'Biggest Money Makers of 1926'.[97]

In the 1926 *Beverly of Graustark*, then, McCutcheon's pocket kingdom reaches something of a peak as a fantastic American heterotopia, not just a land of lavish costume spectacle and cross-class romance but a licensed comic space of fluid gender identities. Sadly, in this same period what might have been the greatest—and oddest—*Graustark* film was never made. In 1924 and 1925, the trade papers advertised that First National was making a sequel to *Graustark* and *Beverly*, a version of McCutcheon's *East of the Setting Sun*, which had recently been serialized in the *Saturday Evening Post*. Joseph Schenck had bought the rights to the story as a vehicle for Constance Talmadge, younger sister of Norma, and had lined up the gifted but wayward Erich von Stroheim to direct, play the villain, and write the script; newcomer Walter Pidgeon was to be the hero.[98] Born in Vienna, von Stroheim had come to directing via acting, specializing in what might be described as 'filthy hun' roles during and after the war: he was 'the man you love to hate'. But as a filmmaker he was a pioneering auteur in terms of cinematography and editing, obsessive about visual detail, and a creator of many of silent cinema's most memorable scenes.[99] His keen interest in psychology led him to explore sexual and other forms of obsession, edgy material for the increasingly corporate studios. According to his friend Don Ryan, 'His penchant is Freud, with trimmings by Havelock Ellis and sauce by Krafft-Ebing.'[100] Even worse from the studios' point of view, the director's almost pathological perfectionism could lead to ruinous overruns of his shooting schedules, producing endless footage that had to be cut down for exhibition. The most infamous instance of this was *Greed* (1924), his eight-hour version of Frank Norris's novel *McTeague*, which MGM insisted be edited radically. The butchered *Greed* drew hostile reviews, but in 1925 von Stroheim had a commercial hit with *The Merry Widow* (see chapter 4), based loosely on Franz Lehar's opera. Another lavish European drama seemed like a natural step, for him, and *East of the Setting Sun* was ideal for this purpose.

Von Stroheim rewrote the script extensively, removing the communist menace and making other key changes. As Richard Koszarksi explains:

> The hero journalist had become the representative of a Ford agency, and the invasion of Graustark by the neighboring communist state . . . was completely omitted. In the place of this climax, von Stroheim substituted the abduction of the Princess Milena by the dissolute Prince Vladimir and a last minute rescue by the U.S. marines.[101]

In keeping with the style of lecherous villainy he had honed in such films as *Foolish Wives*, von Stroheim would himself play the debauched Prince Vladimir, a composite of two of the novel's characters: Prince Hubert and the scheming socialist Rodkin. Having first horsewhipped and then tortured the hero with a hornet's nest, the wicked Prince finally gets his just deserts: run to ground at an inn, *The Sign of the Devil*, he jumps from a window only to impale himself on the inn's sign, a giant pitchfork. In the end, alas, Schenck had second thoughts, and this extraordinary film never entered production. All that survives are von Stroheim's elaborate costume designs and a few trade-paper ads.[102]

There were to be no more screen excursions to Edelweiss. Presumably hoping to repeat the success of the 1925 *Graustark*, a sound version was mooted in 1938. Screenwriter Howard Estabrook, who had won an Oscar for his 1931 film *Cimarron*, worked on the script in April and May of 1938, with the assistance of Lillian Hellman, among others.[103] However, like many scripts, it went no further, and the *Graustark* series' romance and pageantry never made it into the sound era.

Graustark in Decline

The *Graustark* novels sold steadily through the 1930s, abetted by memories of the previous decade's film versions. We can track the residual power of the series not just through sales but also through articles in such pedagogical publications as the *English Journal* (published by the National Council of Teachers of English) and the *School Review*. These magazines published articles every few years on what high school students were reading outside of set texts, and as late as the 1940s the *Graustark* novels are cited as staples of juvenile fiction, alongside various older classics and more recent tales aimed at the younger reader (including *Pollyanna, A Girl of the Limberlost*, and Joan Clark's *Penny Nichols* detective novels).[104] When the studies factor in gender, the *Graustark* series are seen to be most popular among girls. Playful echoes can also be heard in the films of the period: the crime serial *Secret Agent X–9* (1937), for instance, features a character named Shara Graustark (Jean Rogers) in a story in which X-9 (Scott Kolk) must recover the stolen crown jewels of Belgravia.[105]

In the post-war years the novels fell out of favour, even among younger readers. If we take the most renowned 'newspaper of record' in the United States, the *New York Times*, we can see that in the 1950s and 1960s Graustark is still referenced from time to time, to describe small, old-fashioned countries, to evoke a past era of popular fiction, or in the obituaries of the actors of the 1920s (Marion Davies died in 1961; Eugene O'Brien and Francis X. Bushman died in 1966). An article of 1959, for example, describes Monaco as Graustark-like, noting that it was enjoying a boom in the wake of Grace Kelly's marriage to Prince Rainier; presumably readers were meant to be familiar with the reference, even if not all of them would remember that Beverly of Graustark was an American princess.[106] (As we will see, the Kelly–Grimaldi match also evoked a flurry of references to Ruritania.) In 1955 Cambodia is described as a version of Graustark; in 1960 Laos is 'a kind of Oriental Graustark'.[107] But, for the most part, from 1960 on the name Graustark appears in the sports pages, as a horse of that name enjoyed considerable success. When A. L. Lazarus and Victor H. Jones's *Beyond Graustark* appeared in 1981, reviews suggested that McCutcheon's novels had fallen into complete oblivion.[108] We might take as one index of their obscurity that in 1999 the famously difficult John Ashbery published a poem entitled 'Beverly of Graustark' in the *American Poetry Review*.[109] For Ashbery

(1927–2017), the rocky principality was clearly still a point of reference at that point, but one suspects that the vast majority of his readers must have found it a typically opaque one (the her/him hesitation in the poem suggests that it is the 1926 film version, with its cross-dressing, that is being evoked rather than the original novel). Graustark also lives on in academia, but less so in English departments than in the social sciences, where the name is sometimes used, like Ruritania, to sketch out theoretical international scenarios and issues in economics and political science.

McCutcheon himself died on 23 October 1928. His fine collection of first editions, paid for by the Graustark treasury, had been sold off in April 1925. His brother, John T., long outlived him, and his cartoons are now probably better known than George Barr's work; curiously, he even ended up owning his own tiny kingdom, an island in the Bahamas rather than a landlocked European principality. And yet, while Hope's Ruritania has in most ways proved to be a more durable creation than McCutcheon's Graustark, the latter's fantasies of American royalty in Europe have not been without imitators on the page and screen.

But now it is a time for a musical interlude. The period of McCutcheon's greatest success also witnessed the flourishing of colourful pocket kingdoms on the musical stage. In Ruritanian operettas and musicals, star-crossed lovers, gorgeous costumes, and royal intrigue are also de rigueur, even if there is more waltzing than duelling. In some of the most successful examples, though, Ruritania represents less an escapist fantasy land than the tradition-bound world from which the protagonists are trying to escape.

4

Ruritania in Waltz Time

From Operetta to the Film Musical

If Ruritania has a national time signature, it is 3/4. When Daniel Frohman first produced *The Prisoner of Zenda* at the Lyceum in New York in 1895, you could not only see the story brought to life but also go out on the town afterwards and dance to Frank M. Witmark's *Zenda Waltzes*. Ever since, the waltz has featured in stage and film productions as the marker of pocket-kingdom elegance and romance. In 1925 Hope's imaginary land was more fully scored, through Sigmund Romberg's operetta version, *Princess Flavia*. That the statelet had musical leanings should not surprise us too much, since the chocolate-box principalities of operetta were one likely source of inspiration for Anthony Hope, as we have seen. And in turn, long before Romberg's direct treatment, a whole chorus line of operettas and musical comedies borrowed plot and mise en scène elements from *Zenda*. Germanic at first, these tuneful Ruritanias tended to drift further east in the twentieth century, like their siblings in other cultural forms. There was a swing back towards Germany after the success of Sigmund Romberg's *The Student Prince* (1924), but the *Stage* could claim with some justice in 1949 that 'every Englishman who can write a musical comedy or light opera turns sooner or later...to the territory of those Balkan nations that were once rather uneasy kingdoms'.[1] That same year J. C. Trewin recalled the generic 'theatrical Balkans' that took shape in show after show between the wars as centring on 'toy state[s] in the mountains...where the eagle has two heads...loud with bells, polychromatic with uniforms, bushy with beards'. This, he suggested, was a musical stage of 'Ruritanian fabrication'.[2]

Musical Ruritania, as it developed in the early twentieth century as an amalgam of *Zenda* and earlier operatic material, offered spectacle and pageantry as well as an opportunity to exploit the lingering public interest in royal families, even as these began to be forced out of European politics. As with the Ruritanian novel and play, it explored a range of contemporary themes, including the competing pulls of the nation and the self, duty and pleasure, tradition and modernity. However, on the musical stage the swashing of bucklers is a good deal less important, and the pocket kingdoms are sometimes less lands of adventure than homes of the reality principal, from which the protagonists sometimes escape to the bright lights of Paris, London, or even Heidelberg. Lushly orchestrated songs and melodies express the longing they feel not just for love but for some other kind of life, and romantic fulfillment tends to win out over the duties of rank and nation. Royalty itself, indeed, is not always taken so very seriously. However, one aspect of the fantasy remains the same: musical Ruritania, like that of the novel, is a land of arrested time in which the trappings of modernity, where they exist at all, thinly drape more traditional social mores, gender roles, codes of honour, and forms of power. As we shall see, Sigmund Romberg in the United States and Ivor Novello in Britain were the most prolific exponents of the pocket-kingdom musical stage, but many others played supporting roles, from Jacques Offenbach to the Marx brothers to Ian Fleming.

Operetta and Musical Comedy

Any survey of musical Ruritania must begin with operetta, a combination of operatic singing, spoken dialogue, dance, and romantic and comic plot. While the work of Gilbert and Sullivan retains a certain currency, this form of light opera has been largely moribund for some time: writing almost forty years ago, the American scholar Gerald Bordman begins his survey of American operetta with the line 'I'm well aware that operetta has become almost a dirty word'.[3] Yet from the 1850s until the 1950s the form enjoyed immense popularity. The last screen versions of such 1920s operettas as *The Desert Song* (1953) and *The Student Prince* (1954) could still draw large audiences, and formally trained singers like Kathryn Grayson and Mario Lanza were major film stars. Operetta's origins as a form are complex and beyond the scope of a study like this, since, as Richard Traubner details, among its ancestors are French *opéra comique* and vaudeville (short farcical sketches with songs), English ballad operas, and German Singspiel.[4] More immediately, operetta grew directly out of the short, farcical musical plays that began to appear in Paris in the 1840s in the theatres of the boulevard du Temple.

Hervé's *Don Quichotte et Sancho Panza*, which appeared at Adolphe Adam's Théâtre National in 1848, is sometimes cited as the first real operetta.[5] But it was in fact a young German whose work made the greatest mark in these years, the cellist turned composer Jacques (Jakob) Offenbach.[6] At his theatre on the Champs-Élysées Offenbach developed operetta into a whole evening's entertainment in such popular successes as *Orphée aux enfers* (1858), and *La belle Hélène* (1864). *Orphée*, for instance, was a rollicking two-act parody of Gluck's revered treatment of the Orpheus and Eurydice legend, the Greek myth transformed into a vehicle for topical references and comic views of the relations of the sexes; the *galop infernal* from Act 2, a sensation in 1858, later provided the music of the *cancan*. Writing in the 1930s, Siegfried Kracauer argued that the appearance of operetta at this time and place was due to an affinity between the new cultural form and the phantasmagoric world of the Second Empire, which he saw as 'living in a dreamworld', and driven by empty spectacle, not unlike the Germany of his own period.[7] Whether or not this was the case, Offenbach's music certainly seemed to capture something of the spirit of the times, and the Parisian public responded eagerly, though his work also appealed to audiences far from the dreamworld of Paris.

Offenbach produced what is probably the first Ruritanian operetta in *La Grande-Duchesse de Gérolstein*, a hit in April 1867 (see Figure 4.1) at the Théâtre des Variétés in Paris, where it charmed the crowds that had flocked to the city for that year's Exposition Universelle, as well as the Emperor himself and the visiting Czar of Russia.[8]

With a libretto by Henri Meilhac and Ludovic Halévy, this operetta is set in the ersatz Germanic Duchy of Gérolstein, a name presumably borrowed from Eugène Sue's *Mystères de Paris*, in which the incognito hero is the Grand Duke of that territory.[9] The comic plot features a rather spoilt young Grand Duchess who turns the tiny country upside down because of her unrequited infatuation with one of her soldiers, Fritz. When a London production followed that November at Covent Garden, the *Era* in its warm review opined that 'the main idea, of course, is to satirise the small German states of the last century, and their political pretensions'.[10] Offenbach's Gérolstein is a possible ancestor of Hope's Germanic Ruritania, and it is a probable source for one of his more immediate models, Grünewald, in Robert Louis Stevenson's *Prince Otto: A Romance* (1885). Stevenson's imaginary principality, we are told, is bordered by the oxymoronic 'Maritime Bohemia' and by Gerolstein (sic), 'an extinct grand duchy'.[11]

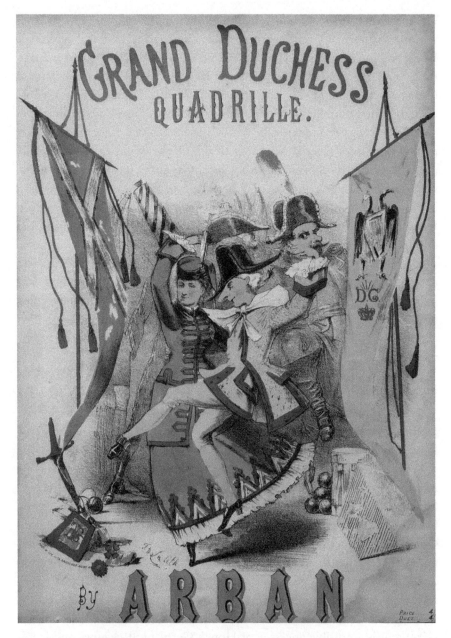

Figure 4.1. T. W. Lee's chromolithographic cover for Jean-Baptiste Arban's *Grand Duchess Quadrille* (London: Boosey & Co., 1867), a popular dance based on Jacques Offenbach's *Grand Duchess of Gérolstein*

In turn *Zenda,* and later *Graustark,* proved to be very useful sources for the musical stage of the early 1900s, a period in which operetta and less vocally demanding forms of modern musical comedy competed and overlapped. The United States seems to have been to the fore in this trend.[12] Pixley and Luder's musical comedy *The Prince of Pilsen,* for instance, a considerable hit in Boston and New York in 1902–3, features a brewer and Alderman from Cincinnati, Hans Wagner, who is taken to be the Prince of the title while on holiday in Nice; the real Prince goes along with this as he has designs on young Nellie Wagner. The most popular numbers included the choruses by the Prince's fellow students from Heidelberg, anticipating the later success of *The Student Prince.*[13] Similarly, in George Broadhust and Max Witt's thin musical farce *The Duke of Duluth* (1905), Nat Wills plays a hobo who is taken for a duke in Wot, a land largely populated by attractive female singers and dancers. Such shows were at best second cousins to Hope and McCutcheon's work, but in 1905 there also appeared one of the first musical shows to take us to Ruritania itself, with more than a hint of Graustark. This was *It Happened in Nordland* (Lew Fields Theatre, 5 December 1905), an operetta by the Irish-born Victor Herbert, better known for his *Babes in Toyland* (1903) and *Naughty Marietta* (1910). The Mitteleuropean Nordland is ruled by Queen Elsa, but, when the Queen vanishes on the eve of an arranged marriage, she is replaced by her lookalike, American diplomat Katherine Peepfogle, who in the best Ruritanian tradition makes as good a fist of ruling as her noble double. This show was a huge success, running for some 254 performances in New York.[14]

In the meantime another strain of Ruritanian musical theatre was shooting up in Europe. The topical and risqué work of Offenbach had at this point long been eclipsed by a new style of Viennese operetta, one of the first of which was Johann Strauss II's *Die Fledermaus* (1874). As Traubner describes, these evolved into 'modern operettas in which the waltz was used for romantic, psychological plot purposes, and danced as much as sung'.[15] As in the US, these new operettas converged to some extent with musical comedy; romantic love plots dominated, and elaborate sets and costumes were the norm. The new breed also found Ruritania to be a useful territory, as we see in the greatest success of this kind in the Edwardian years, Franz Lehár's *The Merry Widow.* In its original production as *Die lustige Witwe* (Vienna 1905, with scenario and lyrics by Leo Stein and Victor Leon), Pontevedro is the name of the fictional pocket state.[16] In the English version, produced by impresario George Edwardes at Daly's Theatre on 8 June 1907, it is renamed

Marsovia, and that is the name I will use here.[17] In both versions, in fact, all of the action takes place in Paris, though Marsovian affairs dominate, the plot centring on a scheme to keep the rich Marsovian widow of the title, Sonia (Lily Elsie in the London production), from marrying an outsider and thus preventing her vast wealth—and loans she has made to the state—from leaving the country. The First Secretary of the embassy, Prince Danilo (Joseph Coyne), Sonia's lover when she was a peasant girl back in Marsovia, is urged by the ambassador, Baron Popoff, to court the widow in the interests of the nation. After various complications Sonia and Danilo realize that they still love one another, and their personal happiness as well as the prosperity of the nation is secured when they come together in the final act, set in Maxim's. The main attraction, was, of course, not the blini-thin romantic plot, nor even the lavish spectacle, but the music, which included a Parisian can-can, 'Marsovian' folk music, and, of course, its signature piece, the syrupy Merry Widow Waltz, which draws Danilo and Sonia together. The central place this operetta accords to romance and to dance also makes it an important transitional piece, looking forward to the dance-centred romantic musicals of Astaire and Rogers as much as it harks back to *Die Fledermaus* and other Viennese operettas; film versions of *The Merry Widow* by Erich von Stroheim and Ernst Lubitsch further developed this dance-as-courtship aspect of the operetta.[18]

   Act 1 is arguably set in Marsovia itself, insofar as the action takes place at its embassy in Paris, technically Marsovian soil. But we derive a clearer sense of what the distant principality itself may be like from such lines as these sung by Sonia:

> I'm always saying something wrong,
> I'm so Marsovian.
> For when a man would wed a girl,
> In my own native land,
> He doesn't call her star or pearl,
> And want to kiss her hand.
> Says, he, 'Let us get married now,
> We are both growing big,
> My father has a cow,
> And your mother has a pig.'[19]

Marsovia, we learn, is an old-fashioned and stern land, where adulterous men are shot, and straying wives are beaten black and blue. It is, in short, the very opposite of fleshpotted Paris, where the Marsovian ambassador spends

MR. GEORGE ALEXANDER

As Rudolf Rassendyll.

Plate 1.1. From the 100th souvenir programme of *The Prisoner of Zenda*: George Alexander as Rassendyll in full military pomp

Plate 1.2. Evelyn Millard as Princess Flavia, from *The Sketch*, 19 February 1896, 159

Plate 2.1. James K. Hackett in a publicity still from the 1913 *Prisoner of Zenda*. Famous Players Film Company

Plate 2.2. Rudolf and Rupert (Douglas Fairbanks Jr.) duel. Publicity still from the 1937 *Zenda*. AF archive/Alamy Stock Photo

"I hated you to-night, I thought," she cried,
taking his face in her hands.

Plate 3.1. Beverly and Dantan. One of Harrison Fisher's illustrations for *Beverly of Graustark* (George Barr McCutcheon, *Beverly of Graustark*, New York: Dodd, Mead & Company, 1904, between pp. 345 and 355.)

Plate 3.2. Publicity still from the MGM *Beverly of Graustark* (1926), with Marion Davies (a former Zeigfield Follies dancer) as Oscar. The Hollywood Archive/age fotostock

Plate 4.1. Robert Helpman as the Vulgarian Child Catcher in *Chitty Chitty Bang Bang* (dir. Ken Hughes, 1968). AF archive/Alamy Stock Photo

Plate 5.1. Tully leads the Grand Fenwickian invasion of New York, in the 1959 film version of *The Mouse that Roared* (dir. Jack Arnold). United Archives GmbH/ Alamy Stock Photo

much of his time at Maxim's, having champagne suppers with a whole chorus of French beauties: Lo-Lo, Do-Do, Jou-Jou, Frou-Frou, Clo-Clo, Margot, To-To, Zo-zo, and Fi-Fi. The trope of the refugee from provincial life going off the rails in Paris was already a familiar one in this period. Readers of Henry James, for example, will recognize some faint echoes of *The Ambassadors* (1903), in which the fictional town of Woollett, Massachusetts, plays the part of the joyless and anachronous Marsovia, in contrast with the sophistication of Paris. William Everett suggests that the Viennese original offered metropolitan audiences a chance to imagine their own superiority compared to the provincials of the Austro-Hungarian empire, but this does not altogether explain the operetta's international appeal.[20] In Britain, it is more likely that *The Merry Widow* evoked an image of the self-denying Victorian past being replaced by the Edwardian present, the virtues of work, duty, and saving yielding to the joys of leisure, spending, and greater personal freedom. Mourning could be cast off, and widows could be merry. In other words, for British audiences Marsovia does not represent the Balkans so much as the older Britain they hoped to leave behind, with its Sabbatarianism and Evangelical piety. Ronald Pearsall argues that 'the Edwardians were apprehensive about the future, and escaped into a never-never world represented by *The Merry Widow* and other operettas and musical comedies', but it seems at least as plausible that the pleasure-filled world of the operetta *was* the bright future they saw before them.[21] Not everyone in the audience fully approved of this cultural shift, of course. For the young Osbert Sitwell, 'Mammon underlay the smudgy softness and superficial prettiness of the whole performance, as the skull supports the lineaments of even the youngest and freshest face.' And for Arnold Bennett, it was '[a]ll about drinking, whoring and money...Names of tarts on the lips of characters all the time. Dances lascivious, especially one'.[22] But for most people this superficial prettiness and lasciviousness was rather the point. Edward VII saw it four times, and even the young Adolf Hitler was a frequent visitor to the Vienna production.[23] Lehár's operetta was just as popular on Broadway, helping to confirm the American image of Paris as a place of sensuous enjoyment, but also, perhaps, creating an expectation that such pleasures might be had more locally and suggesting that the Puritan values of such places as Woollett, Mass., had had their day.[24]

This frothy vision of emigré Ruritanians cutting capers in Paris charmed Europe and America for years, and its best-known tune became absolutely inescapable. In New York it ran for 416 performances. In Britain alone, some

200,000 copies of the sheet music were sold, and more than 1 million people went to see it; at the height of its success the *Widow* could be seen at 400 theatres around Europe. As one contemporary newspaper put it, the treacly signature waltz had 'almost driven Europe crazy' in 1907 and 1908.[25] An Edison short comic film *The Merry Widow Waltz Craze* (1908), directed by Edwin S. Porter, poked fun at the new trend: Mr Lightfoot becomes obsessed with the music, dancing his way through several comic scenes until he is eventually waltzed right into jail. Even the burgeoning field of psychology was drawn to the *Widow*: in 1914, Dr Stefan Deliya of the Clinical Hospital in Vienna published a pamphlet in which he tried to explain the psychological appeal of the music. The operetta also left its mark upon contemporary fashion on both sides of the Atlantic, with the broad-brimmed 'Merry Widow' hat, laden with flowers and feathers, leading the way.[26] Not only did Lehár's work represent a life of consumer pleasure, then, but it also helped to foster it directly, and wherever the operetta played a whole array of spin-off merchandise sprang up, from gloves to cigars to cocktails. Sometimes consumers were a little too eager to embrace the *Widow* life-style: a near-riot broke out at the New Amsterdam Theatre in New York on 13 June 1908 when free 'Merry Widow' hats were offered to theatre-goers to mark the 275th performance of the operetta.[27]

While the Marsovians never leave Paris, subsequent musical plays take us to Ruritania itself, giving more scope for picturesque backdrops, peasant and court costumes, and, perhaps above all, sumptuous military uniforms. Another Viennese waltz vehicle, for example, Oscar Straus's operetta *Ein Walzertraum* (Carltheater, Vienna, 2 March 1907; *A Waltz Dream*, Hicks's, London, 28 March 1908), takes us to Rurislavenstein, or Flausenthurn in the original version. Like *Graustark* it imagines what would happen if a commoner really did marry a Ruritanian Princess, and it reverses the scenario of *The Merry Widow*: Austrian Lieutenant Niki marries the Princess Helene and becomes Prince Consort, but he spends his time in Rurislavenstein pining for the lost fleshpots of Vienna, including its waltzes. Later Ruritanian hits were often more musical comedy than operetta and included *The King of Cadonia* (Prince of Wales, 3 September 1908), *The Balkan Princess* (Prince of Wales, 19 February 1910), and *Princess Caprice* (Shaftesbury Theatre, 11 May 1912). *The King of Cadonia* was the product of the combined talents of Frederick Lonsdale (book), Adrian Ross and Arthur Wimperis (lyrics), and Sidney Jones and Frederick Rosse (music). The King of a fictional and politically volatile territory flees his burdensome role and, incognito, falls in love with the Princess Marie, daughter of the next in line to the throne, the Duke of Alasia. He crosses paths with a group of anti-royalist conspirators, who, when they discover what a nice chap he is, are content for him to rule, and he and the Princess can now live happily ever after. The threadbare story led one critic to proclaim that he 'liked it very much. But then I always have. I liked it when it was *The Prisoner of Zenda*.'[28] But, however derivative, *Cadonia* was a considerable success, inspiring Lonsdale to return to Ruritania just two years later with *The Balkan Princess* (Prince of Wales, 19 February 1910), in which the title character, Princess Stephanie of Balaria (Isabel Jay), is to choose from various official suitors, one of whom fails to appear. This is the socialistic Grand Duke Sergius (Bertram Wallis), whom she tracks down incognito and falls for, though when he proposes a toast to her downfall she has him arrested. She decides to abdicate the throne to avoid marrying one of the other suitors, but Sergius decides to renounce his socialistic ways, stops her abdication, and they are united. A review from the *Playgoer and Society Illustrated* gives us a fair idea of what audiences had come to expect from such plays: 'An exquisite mounting, tuneful music, pretty girls and pretty frocks.'[29] Leo Fall's *Princess Caprice* (Shaftesbury Theatre, 11 May 1912), starring Clara Evelyn and Harry Welchman, is cut from the same shiny fabric and features extravagant court spectacle, comic intrigue, and mistaken identities in the Kingdom of Thessalia, presumably a name meant to recall the actual Greek area of Thessaly (see Figure 5.2). (Fall was also the author of the 1907 hit, *Die Dollarprinzessin*, produced in English in 1909 as *The Dollar Princess*, which we encountered in chapter 3). The reluctant Princess Helen turns out to have been switched at birth and so can, without a qualm for duty, marry the music teacher she loves, leaving her maid of honour, Anna, the real Princess, to marry Nicola, the Prince of Micholics.[30]

In the 1890s and early 1900s, such plays as these offered a sort of compromise between the exotic escapism of such pieces as *The Geisha* (1896), *San Toy* (1899), and *Florodora* (1899) and the more 'realistic' London-set musical comedies: *A Gaiety Girl* (1893), *The Shop Girl* (1894), *A Country Girl* (1902), *The Girl from Kay's* (1902), and *The Quaker Girl* (1910), for instance. This second group featured hard-working young women falling for millionaires in disguise, lost heiresses working in department stores, and other infrequently encountered urban fauna.[31] All three varieties, of course, tended to share the same motifs of disguise, love's tangles, and conflicts between duty and self-fulfilment and usually allowed for at least one spectacular set.

Figure 4.2. A postcard promoting the Shaftesbury Theatre production of *Princess Caprice*, 1912

During the war years, Mitteleuropean uniforms may have savoured too much of the Hun for British tastes, and Germany and the Balkans were forsaken for other romantic territories, including the fantasy Orient of *Chu Chin Chow* (His Majesty's Theatre, 31 August 1916) and the stage Italy of *The Maid of the Mountains* (Daly's Theatre, London, 10 February 1917), both of which ran and ran.[32] In the United States, even the term operetta fell into temporary disfavour.[33] But, despite lingering anti-German feeling and stiff competition in the form of imported American jazz revues, the post-war years saw another efflorescence of Ruritanian operetta and musical comedy. The great hit of the Armistice period in Paris was Charles Cuvillier's *La Reine joyeuse*, billed as an 'opéra bouffe', which Londoners enjoyed two years later as *The Naughty Princess* (Adelphi, 7 October 1920).[34] It is another plot of the clash between duty and individualism, tradition and modern personal and sexual freedoms, in this case centring on the Princess Sophia of Panoplia (Lily St John), a slang-slinging flapper with cropped hair, who rejects an arranged marriage and wants to live a bohemian life: she is 'fed up with the court'.[35] Other interwar Ruritanian fare included *Princess Charming*, the 1926 anglophone version of a Hungarian operetta by Albert Szirmai, first performed in English in 1926; *Lucky Girl* (1928), a musical comedy version of Reginald Berkeley's 1926 play *Mr Abdulla* (more on this later); and three years later *The White Camellia*, based on a play by Laura Leycester, and with music by Pat Thayer. Set in Villinia, capital of Passidinia, the action of this last turns on the attempts of the White Camellia revolutionaries to oust King Alexis and to crown Prince Adolphe in his stead. This may seem like an attempt to engage at some level with the political instability of the Balkans, but the real appeal of the piece, as Herbert Farjeon described in the *Graphic*, was standard Daly's musical comedy fare: tenor Harry Welchman in his hussar's costume, complete with boots and spurs; ringing manly choruses in the messroom; girls in peasant costume, other girls in evening dress; and above all, the waltz that 'wells and swells with boundless passion'.[36] Passidinia, in other words, was a colourful land of romance, intrigue, and frogging that would have been entirely recognizable thirty years earlier to Hope's generation.

Ruritania's pre-eminence on the musical stage in the interwar period owed a great deal to Austro-Hungarian composer Sigmund Romberg, who created three pocket-kingdom operettas in less than four years, swimming gamely against the tide of increasingly jazz-tinged musical comedy. The first of these was the enormously successful *The Student Prince* (1924), based on

Wilhelm Meyer-Förster's novel *Karl Heinrich* (1899) or, more accurately, on the popular stage version of that novel, *Alt-Heidelberg* (1901). As *Old Heidelberg*, this was first produced in London at none other than the St James's Theatre in London in March 1903, with our old friend George Alexander in the lead role of Karl Heinrich, the young Prince of the imaginary kingdom of Sachsen-Karlsburg. The action is divided between the royal court at Karlsburg and the university town of Heidelberg. The strictly raised Karl Heinrich and his tutor leave Karlsburg for Heidelberg, where the repressed young Prince finds tender young love with the innkeeper's daughter, Kathie, and more boisterous pleasure in the all-male world of the student societies. He has to leave all this when the King falls ill, but in the last act, set two years later, he returns to Heidelberg, only to find that the past is a country that is not easily re-entered: now that he is the ruler of Sachsen-Karlsburg, Kathie tells him that they must part, and even his old student companions treat him with a new formality. The *Era* remarked that the play's charm resided in its representation of 'joyous, exuberant animal life'; the life of Heidelberg and youth are contrasted with the court at Karlsburg, capital of a 'petty German state'.[37] This version of Ruritania, then, closely resembles Marsovia as it is described in *The Merry Widow*: it is the land of the reality principal rather than the place of romantic daydreams, even if one is the King. *Old Heidelberg* proved a box-office hit for the St James's and drew crowds to King Street well into 1904. America had already seen two versions of the play when the success of Alexander's production led to a third New York *Old Heidelberg* (Lyric Theatre, 12 October 1903), with Richard Mansfield (then 46) as the not-so-studious Prince and Grace Elliston as Kathie.[38]

Romberg's 1924 operetta, produced by the Shubert brothers, adheres to its theatrical original, contrasting the singing, drinking, and courtship of Heidelberg with the path of duty and self-abnegation in Karlsburg, or Karlsberg as it sometimes appears. (There had already been a number of film versions of the play, including a 1915 production with Wallace Reid, Dorothy Gish, and Erich von Stroheim.)[39] Featuring a libretto by Dorothy Donnelly, its best-known songs include the rousing 'Drinking Song' and 'Gaudeamus Igitur'. If the singing looked back to the nineteenth century, the treatment of the romance between the leads, Howard Marsh and Ilse Marvenga, was given a more modern, physical aspect, at least according to George Jean Nathan in the *American Mercury*, who claimed that 'the Prince goes at Kathi [sic] on all occasions like a hobo after a free lunch, while Kathi meets his advances all too often like an Elinor Glyn book advertisement'.[40] The Shuberts' initial anxieties about lingering anti-German feeling proved groundless and audiences were all too happy to see a peaceful, pre-war Europe evoked.[41] *Variety* hailed the operetta as 'a musical smash, colorful, gorgeous and beautiful', and at Jolson's 59th Street Theatre it ran for 608 performances, the longest Broadway run of the 1920s; there were nine touring productions.[42] Interestingly, the London production at His Majesty's Theatre of this 'spectacular light opera' fell a bit flat, running for an unremarkable 97 performances, despite the presence of Marvenga as Kathie, lavish sets of the Karlsburg court, and fine Hussar uniforms that reminded the *Stage* of Alexander's *Prisoner of Zenda*. Whether its limited success was because of the production itself or some other factor is hard to establish. Later critics have sometimes suggested that Germany may have been still unpopular with British audiences, but the more hostile contemporary reviews focus on the operetta's Americanism and its lack of humour compared to the original play, which had been recently revived.[43] Nevertheless, on both sides of the Atlantic *The Student Prince* enjoyed a long afterlife in touring productions, and Marvenga played Kathie some 3,000 times.[44] The operetta is probably most familiar now through the lavish 1954 MGM film version, to which we will return.

In the meantime, Romberg and the Shuberts returned to Hope country with *Princess Flavia*, an operetta version of *The Prisoner of Zenda* itself. After a trial run under the name *The Royal Pretender*, *Princess Flavia* opened at the Century Theatre on 2 November 1925. Romberg's was a name to conjure with at this point, and no expense was spared on the production, the tour de force being the sumptuous coronation scene, supposedly based on the 1910 ceremony for King Nicholas I of Montenegro and described by one reviewer as 'an orgy of beauty and luxuriousness'.[45] The cast was enormous, running to 150 men and women, and the uniforms and sets were as extravagant as any that had been seen on the New York stage. In the dual role it featured the English star, Harry Welchman, then making his Broadway debut, and the young American soprano Evelyn Herbert played Princess Flavia (see Figure 4.3); both of them seemed to have performed with distinction. But the score itself was weak, with few memorable songs or melodies. *Variety* admitted that 'no operetta has ever been presented in New York with the same huge cast, the sumptuousness and the grand éclat which marked the premiere [and]...had it a score commensurate with its production, it would pack the Century for a year's run'.[46] But it did not have

Strauss-Peyton

EVELYN HERBERT

In the Title-Rôle of "Princess Flavia," the Shuberts' Superb Production of Romberg's Operetta

Figure 4.3. Evelyn Herbert as the title character in Sigmund Romberg's operetta *Princess Flavia*, from the *Theatre Magazine*, January 1926

such a score, and it closed after 165 performances, a mediocre result for such a costly production. When compared to other recent hits—*Rose-Marie* (1924) and *No, No, Nanette* (1925), as well as Romberg's own *Student Prince*—it lacked a certain sparkle. *Princess Flavia* enjoyed mixed fortunes on tour, with sold-out shows in some locations and limited interest in others, suggesting, perhaps, that while there was still a provincial appetite for Ruritanian spectacle, Romberg's operetta did not meet it.[47] No London production followed.

Nothing daunted, Romberg returned to the same well with *Rosalie* (1928), co-written with George Gershwin, with a plot by William Anthony McGuire and the prolific Guy Bolton and with lyrics by Ira Gershwin and P. G. Wodehouse. It was produced by the legendary Florenz Ziegfeld, who felt that Wodehouse and Romberg would bring to the project a sense of old Europe; Wodehouse, of course, was no stranger to the *Zenda* formula, having written *The Prince and Betty* in 1912. The story is a blend of material from the newspapers and McCutcheon's *Graustark* novels. American West Point cadet pilot Lieutenant Richard 'Dick' Fay, played by Australian tenor Oliver McLennan, falls for a beautiful peasant girl (Marilyn Miller), and he flies solo to Romanza to court her, only to discover she is really the Princess Rosalie. A royal visit to the United States allows the lovers to meet again at a West Point dance, but the queen (Margaret Dale) opposes their marriage. In the end all obstacles are removed when Dick's friend Bill (Jack Donahue) suggests that they spark a revolution that will force the Romanzan royal family to abdicate. There are many of the usual *Zenda* staples—royalty, disguise, hussar uniforms and gorgeous dresses—but there is also an attempt here to be topical: the 1926 visit of Queen Marie of Romania to the US is evoked, as is Charles Lindbergh's 1927 solo flight from New York to Paris. Unlike *The Student Prince* and *Princess Flavia*, *Rosalie* sees rank and hierarchy overcome by love: the modern American world, with its airplanes and companionate marriages, defies the gravity of old European duty and rank. Modernity also creeps into the music, of course, with the ebullient tones of the Rombergian male choruses ('The Hussar March', 'West Point March') sounding rather dated next to Gershwin's jazz- and blues-inflected songs, with their flatted fifths ('How Long Has This Been Going On', for instance, originally written for *Funny Face*).[48] The public seemed to enjoy this mixture of something old and something blue, and, splendidly produced at the New Amsterdam Theatre, *Rosalie* ran for 327 performances. (We will return to the film remake, which also involved Wodehouse.)

Ivor Novello's Ruritania

In Britain too by the mid-1930s, operetta and operetta-flavoured musical comedy were ceding territory to new American trends, but they continued as viable forms. The British composer who did most to keep the Ruritanian line going was the Cardiff-born David Ivor Davies (1893–1951), better known to the public as Ivor Novello and to the theatrical world as just Ivor.[49] Once enormously successful, a rival to his friend Noel Coward, he is now largely remembered not so much for his own work as for the Ivor Novello Awards for composition and songwriting. Of his own vast output as a composer, only a handful of melodies are still familiar, including two of his sentimental war songs: "Till the Boys Come Home (Keep the Home Fires Burning)' (1914, lyrics by Lena Guilbert Ford), a veritable national anthem during the First World War; and 'We'll Gather Lilacs' (1945), which performed a similar role in the next. As one newspaper noted in the year of his centenary, he had not 'enjoyed the rediscovery, reappraisal and renais-sance that are customary on such occasions'.[50] This is something of an understatement. A few of Novello's plays are occasionally revived, but usu-ally by amateur groups, and his hit musical plays have followed the path of most operetta into deep obscurity. Once voted Britain's best film actor, his films too are forgotten outside specialist circles. It is a curious fate for someone who enjoyed extraordinary popularity across four decades as a composer, actor, and playwright.

Buoyed by the enormous vogue of *Keep the Home Fires Burning*, Novello worked as a composer through the 1910s and 1920s, contributing steadily to popular musicals and revues. But his matinee-idol looks also helped to make him a sought-after actor, on screen and then on stage. First spotted by Louis Mercanton, director of the very first of Zukor's Famous Players films, his early roles included the lead in *The Bohemian Girl* (1922), a film that also featured *Zenda* veteran C. Aubrey Smith. He starred in two of Alfred Hitchcock's early films—*The Lodger* (1926), and *Downhill* (1927), the latter adapted from Ivor's own play of the same name—while stage roles in these years included the part of Prince Karl Heinrich in a 1925 revival of *Old Heidelberg*, in which he appeared, according to James Agate, in 'a uniform reminiscent of a municipal bandsman from Southend'.[51] His success on Broadway with *The Truth Game* led to an offer to come to Hollywood, where his new circle of friends included Tallulah Bankhead and Greta Garbo. However, MGM could not decide what to do with him as an actor, and Ivor ended up working primarily on scripts, including the dialogue for *Tarzan the Ape Man* (1932). Johnny Weissmuller's famous line 'Me Tarzan, you Jane' was apparently written by him. Unsurprisingly, perhaps, he decided to return to London, where he began to write the musical plays that brought him fresh fame and also created a fresh image of Ruritania.

Novello scored his first great stage hit with *Glamorous Night*, a romantic extravaganza, which opened at Drury Lane on 2 May 1935. Having grown up on a diet of *The Merry Widow* and other rich Edwardian fare, his bedroom decorated with pictures of Lily Elsie as Sonia, his own version of Ruritania was clearly at some level a nostalgic project, an attempt to recapture the spell of the operettas and musical comedies of his Edwardian youth; his heroine, Militza, even borrows her name from the Princess's maid in *The King of Cadonia*.[52] There would be scope for Mitteleuropean royal pageantry, romance a-plenty, and affect-freighted arias; there would, in short, be glamour, something that audiences craved in a Britain still feeling the effects of the Great Depression. *Glamorous Night's* troubled kingdom is Krasnia, ruled by King Stefan (Barry Jones) and his prima donna lover, Militza Hajos (American soprano Mary Ellis), who is of Gypsy origin. However, we enter the world of Krasnia not through them but in the company of our hero, an Englishman, Anthony Allen (Novello himself), who has invented 'a system of television which can bring any desired scene before the eyes of the public'.[53] This was topical stuff: the BBC began television broadcasting only the following year. Offered £500 and two months' leave by his employer, Lord Radio (Clifford Heatherley), to develop his new device—or possibly to suppress it—Allen travels to Krasnia, where naturally he becomes involved in the affairs of the nation (see Figure 4.4). Baron Lydyeff (Lyn Harding, a regular Drury Lane villain) is plotting against King Stefan, and he plans to get rid of Militza, in whom he recognizes the power behind the throne. Allen saves Militza from assassination outside the opera house and is rewarded by the King. Militza and Allen end up aboard the same ship, and, after he saves her from another attempt on her life, they fall in love; Lydyeff's men sink the ship, but Militza and Allen survive, and ashore they go through a sort of Gypsy betrothal ceremony. However, Militza realizes that she also has a duty to her king and country, and she rallies her people to help the King, who has fallen into Lydyeff's clutches. In (another) climactic scene, Allen saves the day again when he shoots Lydyeff as he threatens to kill the King. But King Stefan will only reign with Militza at his side, and the lovers must part, despite their Gypsy vows. The King rewards Allen for his services with financial backing for his invention, and our hero returns home to London to perfect the technology at Actual Vision Studio. Sore of heart, he watches his first broadcast, which shows the wedding of the King and Militza. It is quite a prescient ending: two years later, the coronation of George VI and Queen Elizabeth would be seen as 'the first formidable demonstration of television in the coverage of outdoor news events'.[54]

Part of Novello's charm for his contemporaries was that he revitalized formulae with which they were already more than familiar. The action opens not in the forest of Zenda but on a suburban street in London, complete with a Wall's Ice Cream tricycle, and our hero is not an aristocratic Guards officer but an inventor, the son of an electrician: this is a democratized Ruritanian fantasy. The next scene takes us to the modernist interior of Lord Radio's office in Superhet House, before we are finally whisked off to the exotic yet familiar Krasnia.[55] Even there there are surprises—sinking ships are not part of the usual Ruritanian subgenre, most such territories being landlocked; this is the author's little joke, as well as a show-stopping spectacle. The final scene recalls the renunciation at the end of Anthony Hope's novel, returning us to the hero's everyday world, in which he contemplates what might have been. But this too is updated: at Actual Vision Studio we see distant Krasnia through Allen's television invention, a stage innovation presumably accomplished using a projector and scrim.[56]

Krasnia itself is a typically out-of-time land in which uniforms are dazzling, passions run high, the peasants are fickle, and political scheming is rife; but there are a few original touches in the way Novello handled it musically. There is, for instance, some mise en abyme fun in the form of the opera within the play, also called *Glamorous Night*, which Allen goes to see in Krasnia; in Act 1.6 we see the final scene of this opera, which also features a ballet sequence.[57] As Traubner notes, the device of the operetta within a more contemporary musical play allowed him to 'have his Schmalz-covered cake and eat it too'—the more old-fashioned numbers could be cordoned off and enjoyed by the audience at one remove, as it were.[58] The same tongue-in-cheekiness carries over into the dialogue, as in this exchange between Militza and Anthony Allen:

> ANTHONY: Aren't these things always happening in this little musical com-
> edy country?
> MILITZA: Musical comedy? Aren't you being rather insolent?
> ANTHONY: I don't mean to be. But it is, let's face it. Pure musical comedy,
> and as such completely out of date. (Act 2.1, p. 26)

Figure 4.4. Anthony Allen (Ivor Novello) at the Krasnian court in *Glamorous Night* from the *Playgoer*, May 1935

But the audience did not come for irony only, and the main draw remained the array of melodic songs by Novello, with lyrics by Christopher Hassall. These do not stray too far from romantic cliché, as in the title song, sung by Militza, in which she evokes a glamorous and magical night, a voice recalling moments of love while the moon shone above. Shorn of Novello's rising melody and the spectacular staging, the lyrics can seem trite, but in context they worked their magic. And fond though he was of the 'out of date', Novello was happy to incorporate more current musical numbers, however tenuous their tie to the action. When Anthony and Militza set sail on the Silver Star, they are treated to shipboard entertainment in the form of the jazzy 'Shanty Town', sung by the stowaway Cleo Wellington (played by the African-American singer Elisabeth Welch).

Glamorous Night also works by drawing its energy from the political events of the day. The opening Guards chorus both acknowledges the present and deems it irrelevant: there may be rumours of war from Berlin, but the audience should not worry, as we (the Guards, Krasnia, the musical itself) will not be joining in. This rejection of the world of politics is somewhat disingenuous, though, since Novello's pocket kingdom draws heavily on contemporary media accounts of the 'playboy King', Carol II of Romania (1893–1953), and his lover, Elena, or Helena, Lupescu (1895–1977), known in the press of the time as Magda Lupescu.[59] Divorced from her army-officer husband, in 1925 she became Carol's public consort and the focus of the hostility of Romania's ruling families; that Lupescu's father had been Jewish made her an easy target in a country in which anti-Semitism was rife.[60] Carol was forced from his position as Crown Prince, and under the name Carol Caraiman he lived in exile with Lupescu in France, divorcing Princess Helen in 1928. But in 1930, three years after the death of King Ferdinand, he flew back to Romania from Munich and claimed the throne as King Carol II, replacing his own young son, Mihai, while skywriting planes wrote 'Carol' over Bucharest.[61] The playboy King was acclaimed as something of a modernizer, promoting education, youth movements (the Straja Tarii), agricultural reform, and air links to the rest of the world while retaining a taste for Ruritianian uniforms and royal pageantry.[62] However, the country's independence was undermined as Germany extended its sphere of influence in the region, Romanian oil and grain making it a very desirable satellite. In *Glamorous Night*, then, we see an artfully refracted version of Romania in the early 1930s. (John Buchan's *Castle Gay* and *The House of the Four Winds* also recycle some of this history.) King Stefan and Militza are, like King Carol and Elena Lupescu, on the cusp between a traditional world, in which the prestige of royalty was more or less taken for granted, and one in which the crown has to contend with democratic and fascistic forces. Lydyeff, with his black military uniform, is some kind of proto-fascist, not unlike the Romanian Iron Guard leader Corneliu Codreanu. Here, though, the exotic Militza, rather than being a target for anti-Semitic hostility like Lupescu, is the conduit between King Stefan and the people, and she forsakes her own true love to stand by him.

This musical tale of kings and commoners seems to have also anticipated events a little closer to home. Among those who came to see the exotic but unhappy land of Krasnia in 1935 was one of King Carol's distant cousins, King George, who died later that year just after *Glamorous Night* had prematurely finished its long run. Edward VIII was crowned on 20 January 1936, and within days the American press was already discussing the American socialite Mrs Wallis Simpson as his 'Friend No. 1', though the British press was rather more circumspect.[63] (See chapter 2 for the abdication's other

Zenda resonances.) England, in other words, had its own Militza. Edward abdicated that December when it became apparent that the political establishment would not tolerate the twice-divorced Simpson as his consort. It is quite tempting to speculate that Ivor, with his wide circle of well-connected friends, had some inkling of Prince Edward's relationship with Simpson, which had begun in 1934. At any rate, *Glamorous Night* was a success not only for Novello and Hassall but also for Drury Lane, which had not seen such crowds since Coward's *Cavalcade* four years earlier.[64]

After the war Novello produced *King's Rhapsody* (Palace Theatre, 15 September 1949), another piece that seems to echo the life of the Duke of Windsor as well as that of Carol of Romania, though it is set firmly in the late-Victorian past.[65] Our protagonist this time is Nikki (Novello), the exiled heir to the Muranian throne, who is supposed to have left because of a love affair with an actress, Marta Karillos (Phyllis Dare), though it was really because he is a thwarted reformer. Upon the death of the King, Nikki is visited in Paris by his worldly mother (Zena Dare), who urges him to return to Murania so that he can marry the young Princess Cristiane of Norseland (Vanessa Lee) and thus provide a royal heir. Cristiane has something of a reputation in the popular press as an icy 'snow Princess', but she has long held a torch for the rebellious Nikki and yields to his seduction when he mistakes her for one of her own retinue. When an heir is born Nikki is prevailed upon to abdicate, as his reformist charter has created powerful enemies. By this point Nikki realizes that he loves his young wife, but, as in Anthony Hope's Ruritania, personal feelings come second to patriotic duty, and he leaves Murania once more. Ten years later the former monarch attends his young son's coronation incognito, and in the final scene we see him alone in the cathedral after the ceremony, clutching a white rose dropped for him by the Queen. *King's Rhapsody* is, in effect, old-school romantic melodrama given a new lease of life—in the Dare sisters Novello was even casting two Edwardian stars. The elaborately created settings include a room in the Summer Palace of the Royal Family of Norseland; the exterior of the Palace at Bledz, Murania, and the ballroom of same; a box at the Paris Opera; and, most dramatically, the interior of the Cathedral of Bledz. Special effects play a lesser role than in *Glamorous Night*, but again there is a performance within the performance, this time a Muranian Rhapsody Ballet.

The lyrics conjure up a romantic world of sincere and ideal transformative love, as with Cristiane's soaring opening song, 'Some Day My Heart Will Awake', which promises that music will open her eyes and her heart to a world of rapture. But there are also some nice comic lines, as when the formidable Queen Elana hears of Cristiane's embroidered trousseau: 'Embroidery! Does that still go on?' (Act 1.4, p. 16). Other more contemporary touches include a parade of human mannequins in negligees and gowns in Act 1.5, a scene that would not be out of place in a Hollywood musical. *King's Rhapsody* was a major success, running for 841 performances and outliving Novello himself, who died in March 1951. While some critics felt that it was a bit too familiar, others approved of this return to 'Ruritanian gaiety and romance' and to 'Ruritanian splendour'. J. C. Trewin in the *Illustrated London News* felt that a little escapism was welcome: the post-war 'theatrical Balkans', now 'less sinister than of old [are]...an area off any normal map, and one where currency regulations and atomic bombs [mean] nothing whatsoever'.[66] Some even saw Novello's nostalgic turn as Britain's answer to the increasing hegemony of the American musical: Ivor Brown in the *Observer* proclaimed that Novello could 'with his tranquility stand up to all the bounding Oklahomans and Brigadooners in the world', while Harold Hobson in the *Sunday Times* viewed it as 'a better musical than *South Pacific*'.[67] Few would now agree.

In his final musical, *Gay's the Word* (Palace Theatre, Manchester, 17 October 1950), Novello paid his last respects to the old formula by making Ruritania the title of a flop show, his trademark operetta within a musical play. In this knowing backstage musical he pokes fun at the cult of American musical 'vitality', as well as at his own retro style, with such songs as '(We'll Gather Strength in) Ruritania'.[68] When he died the following year, he was mourned as a national treasure by enormous crowds of fans—his funeral was even broadcast on the radio. But Ivor's particular brand of whimsy and escapism seems to have held its power only while he was on stage himself to bring it to life: the film versions of *Glamorous Night* (1937) and *King's Rhapsody* (1955) failed to please. *Glamorous Night* was last revived briefly in 1975 and *King's Rhapsody* in 1988; neither production resembled the big-budget originals, and neither was a success. Novello's musical Ruritania was essentially a more colourful heterotopia to the Britain he knew. In 1951 he claimed that he would like to write a realist play but found he could not: 'Prewar is forgotten, the war years are too miserable, the present is so dreary. Escape lies in imagination and romance', but the same could have been said of *Glamorous Night* in the 1930s.[69] However saturated it was in the social and political changes of its time, his Ruritania always offered audiences a glimpse of something better, a brighter, more passionate, and more melodic reality, a place of transfiguring romantic love; in this, of course, it doubled the stage itself. For Novello himself, a gay man living in a homophobic society, its vision of powerful but always stymied romance may have also had a more personal dimension.

Novello's work, already backward-looking at the time, effectively marked the end of Ruritania on the musical stage. There have been a few exceptions, such as Noël Coward's *The Girl Who Came to Supper* (Broadway Theatre, 8 December 1963), which emplots the involvement of an American showgirl, Mary Morgan (Florence Henderson), with the Prince Regent of Carpathia (José Ferrer) and his son, the young King Nicholas III (Sean Scully). It was not a great success, closing after 112 performances.[70] And while such pieces as *The Merry Widow* and *The Student Prince* are regularly revived, there have been few new Ruritanias to add to the pre-war list. American 'folk' musicals like *Oklahoma* (1943), with their self-assured rendering of ordinary people and their athletic dance sequences, seem to have largely finished off an older form preoccupied with waltzing royalty.

The Ruritanian Film Musical

The novels of Hope and McCutcheon were early candidates for screen adaptation, as we have seen, and the first decades of the new medium also saw a swathe of films that deploy Ruritanian motifs without following the originals too faithfully. As Charles Morrow describes, this is a motley group that includes, for example: Douglas Fairbanks in *Reaching for the Moon* (Vulgaria, 1917) and *His Majesty the American* (Alaine, 1919); Wallace Reid in *Hawthorne of the USA* (Bovinia, 1919); Harold Lloyd in *His Royal Slyness* (Thermosa, 1920); Jackie Coogan in *Long Live the King* (Livonia, 1923); Pola Negri in Lubitsch's *Forbidden Paradise* (nameless European territory, 1924); Gloria Swanson in *Her Love Story* (Viatavia, 1924); and Harry Langdon in *Soldier Man* (Bomania, 1926).[71] While some of these are tales of adventure and high passion, many, as one can guess from the talents involved, were comedies. *Reaching for the Moon*, for instance, is a short comedy in which Douglas Fairbanks, an American who finds himself King of Vulgaria, has to escape a whole series of assassination attempts; he eventually wakes to discover it was only a dream and settles down happily to life in New Jersey. In the comedy short *His Royal Slyness*, Harold Lloyd's character goes to Thermosa to fill in for a Prince who is busy living it up in the United States; accidentally caught up in a revolution, he finds himself installed as President. Ruritanian settings continued to be in vogue through the 1930s, from romantic comedies to Westerns, including *The Princess and the Plumber* (Daritizia, 1930); *The Last of the Lone Wolf* (Saxonia, 1930); *Million Dollar Legs* (Klopstokia, 1932), starring W. C. Fields; *My Pal the King* (Alvonia, 1932), with Tom Mix and Mickey Rooney; *The King's Vacation* (unnamed territory, 1933); *King Kelly of the USA* (Belgardia, 1934); *I'll Tell the World* (1934, Ruritania); and *Fit for a King* (unnamed territory, 1937).

Given the popularity of the *Zenda* formula, and the tsunami of film musicals after the development of synchronized sound, Ruritanian musicals were bound to follow. Like their predecessors on the stage, these films often accentuated the spectacular, making a virtue of the static qualities of court-bound romance narratives, and they could also use song, dance, and background music to orchestrate emotion and to create a sense of Ruritania as a place apart from the everyday. In the interwar years this waltz-centred material was popular on both sides of the Atlantic, though it seems to have had a particular vogue in Britain. Whether made in Hollywood or Pinewood, in many cases the directors of these films were continental emigrés, such figures as Erich von Stroheim (Austrian) and Ernst Lubitsch (German) in the United States and Paul Ludwig Stein (Austrian) and Hanns Schwarz (Austrian) in Britain.

Even before the arrival of sound we encounter a sort of pre-sound musical in the form of Erich von Stroheim's quirky version of *The Merry Widow* for MGM, released in 1925 (see Figure 4.5).[72] Immediately after the disaster of *Greed*, Stroheim made *The Merry Widow* as part of his three-picture deal with the studio, and it would become his most commercially successful film.

This was not, of course, a 'musical' in the usual sense, since synchronized sound was not to arrive until 1927. Nonetheless, David Mendoza and William Axt composed a score for the film based on the operetta, and major theatres had small orchestras to play this music, including the ineluctable title waltz; even minor theatres would have had a pianist or some other basic form of musical accompaniment. As one might anticipate, given Stroheim's aesthetic, the film is anything but a straightforward adaptation of the operetta, and plot, setting, characters, and themes are all reshaped by the director. Much of the action is set in the fictional territory of Monteblanco before we move to Paris; as Richard Koszarski notes, in the shooting script 308 of the 477 scenes precede the action of the operetta. Set pieces thus include the expected waltz scene at Maxim's but also episodes at the court of

Figure 4.5. Mae Murray as Sally O'Hara and John Gilbert as Prince Danilo in a scene from Erich von Stroheim's 1925 film *The Merry Widow*. Photo 12/Alamy Stock Photo

Monteblanco, bacchanalian revelry at a Monteblancan brothel, and a duel in the Bois de Boulogne.[73] Mae Murray is the female lead: a former Ziegfeld Follies dancer who became an actress and producer, she was promoted as the 'girl with the bee-stung lips', and by this time she was a major MGM star. In Stroheim's treatment she is not a Monteblancan beauty but an American, Sally O'Hara, 'première danseuse' with the Manhattan Follies troupe, which is touring the mountainous principality. After her love affair with Prince Danilo (John Gilbert) is derailed by his family, she marries the elderly, debauched, but enormously wealthy Baron Sadoja (Tully Marshall, a Stroheim regular), who dies shortly after. Stroheim's most striking change at the level of character, as Koszarski notes, is to split Danilo in two: we meet the spoilt but charming Prince Danilo at the same time we meet his cousin who also covets Sally, the sneering Crown Prince Mirko. The latter is played by newcomer Roy D'Arcy, who became something of a specialist in sneering villains; the following year he appeared as the villainous General Marlanx, in *Beverly of Graustark*. Like Rex Ingram, von Stroheim delighted in strong contrasts and grotesque details, and the glamour of the Ruritanian scenes is undercut by glimpses of the pocket kingdom's backwardness: opulent scenes of Monteblanco's royal court are immediately followed by shots of pigs in the street. Perhaps the most striking scenes are those that show the sexual decadence of the court itself. The film explicitly shows the drooling foot fetishism of the Baron, though the scene in which he dies in a pile of Sally O'Hara's shoes did not make it into the final cut. The *New York Times* reviewer, Mordaunt Hall, noted of the gala screening that it had the usual von Stroheim touch, which he describes as 'an Emile Zola–Elinor Glyn complex. He is strong for violent love, but delights in having a little convenient mud somewhere in the vicinity.'[74] However, the film's happy ending returns us to a more uncomplicated picture of affluence; shot in Technicolor, it offered a glimpse of, as Hall describes, 'the colored uniforms, the glittering gems, the pearls and the ermine in the gold crown'. While the film earned considerable sums for MGM—estimates of gross receipts vary from MGM's $996,000 to Stroheim's $4.5 million—its director earned nothing, as MGM offset his share of the profits against losses on *Greed*. But his vision of Ruritania, or perhaps, rather, Graustark, remains a memorable one. Stroheim's Monteblanco is a melange of Austro-Hungarian feudalism and Prussian militarism, but it was also a distorted picture of America, one in which a predatory ruling class was free to do pretty much what it wanted, the court's sexual decadence evoking a more general corruption. Danilo redeems himself through his love for Sally, but it is the grotesque Baron and Mirko who linger in the memory.

The first 'real' Ruritanian musical, using the new sound technology, was by another continental wanderer, Ernst Lubitsch, whose *The Love Parade* (1929) pairs French singer Maurice Chevalier with Jeanette MacDonald in a plot that owes a good deal to *The Merry Widow*. Chevalier plays the philandering Count Alfred Renard, the Sylvanian military attaché in Paris, who takes full advantage of the relaxed sexual morality of that city until he is recalled to Sylvania. Intrigued by his dubious reputation, the Queen (MacDonald) decides to marry him, but Renard does not take to his new role as Prince consort, a role with no real power; their marriage—and the country—goes through a crisis before the Queen makes him her equal, and the couple are reconciled. The film possesses Lubitsch's trademark sophistication, and, like the *Merry Widow*, it is typical of the kind of romantic comedy that as Rick Altman describes becomes a staple of the film musical: the obstacles to the lovers' happiness lie within themselves rather than in some external authority figures. But there is also a broader form of comedy at work in the parallel comic love plot involving Renard's Parisian valet, Jacques (Lupino Lane), and the surprisingly worldly—and tall—Sylvanian maid, Lulu (Lillian Roth). One of the film's most delightful slapstick scenes shows the latter pair throwing each other about and mauling each other while singing the syncopated comic duet 'Let's Be Common', which celebrates the physical freedoms of being plebeian rather than royal lovers. As the song ends Jacques follows Lulu indoors, and we see a light come on in an upstairs room, but just as we are assuming that the couple are consummating their plebeian passion, Jacques is thrown through the window, head first, and Lulu sings, modifying the song, that he'd better not do it again. If the film's main plot focuses on the post-marital tensions that follow an interclass marriage, then, it also offers a glimpse of a world that is classless because everyone is at the bottom. With such earthy material we are a long way from the aristo-military fantasies of Anthony Hope.

Lubitsch also directed *The Smiling Lieutenant* (1931), a version of the 1907 operetta *Ein Walzertraum* (*A Waltz Dream*, discussed earlier in this chapter), before turning to the first sound production of *The Merry Widow* (1934), again starring Maurice Chevalier and Jeanette MacDonald. This sticks closer to the stage original than von Stroheim's wildly idiosyncratic take and features Lubitsch's famous light touch. It was a decided hit critically, the

New York Times praising it as 'in the excellent Lubitsch manner, heady as the foam on champagne, fragile as mist and as delicately gay as a good-natured censor will permit'. Lubitsch's triumph was to shape 'the sheerest of butterfly-wing embroidery out of the bustles and gas-lamp period of the operetta'.[75] This lush production (it cost $1.6 million) won an Oscar for Cedric Gibbons and Fredric Hope for Art Direction, but Lubitsch resists the temptations of endless spectacle and keeps the action moving, playing up the humorous aspects of Marshovia's (sic) plight. Edward Everett Horton turns in a fine comic performance as Ambassador Popoff, asking Danilo in one scene, 'Have you ever had diplomatic relations with a woman[?]'; other minor characters also work to undercut the seriousness of the love plot.

Romberg's *Rosalie* took a tortuous route to the screen that involved a Marion Davies film that was never produced and an MGM-commissioned treatment by P. G. Wodehouse that was never published or used. When MGM finally made a film version in 1937 (dir. W. S. Van Dyke), starring Nelson Eddy and Eleanor Powell, songs by Cole Porter (including *In the Still of the Night*) replaced those by Romberg and Gershwin—a sign of changing tastes.[76] The film allowed Powell (see Figure 4.6) to wear some extravagant costumes but also to show off her extraordinary dancing abilities, another indication that waltz-driven operetta was on the way out. In the elaborate Romanzan festival sequence, Powell, dressed as Pierrette, tap-dances her way along an array of giant tin drums and then through a series of what appear to be plastic scrims held up by Pierrots. It is a show-stopping piece that spotlights individual kineticism and seems to belong to a different musical and emotional world than that of the original operetta.

Not all visits to musical Ruritania worked as well. The financially precarious Fox Film Corporation tried its hand at the form with *My Lips Betray* (1933), adapted from a Hungarian play, Attila Orbók's *A Tuenemeny* (1922), and with songs by William Kernell. Set in Ruthania, the whimsical plot deals with a romance between a popular singer, Lili Wieler (Lilian Harvey), and King Rupert (John Boles), who is more interested in songwriting than in the country's parlous finances. Much of the comedy turns on Lili's not recognizing Rupert, who poses as the songwriting Captain von Linden. In the end the discovery of oil in the plains of Malu saves the nation from bankruptcy, Rupert's arranged engagement to Princess Isabella of Moravia collapses, and the King can marry Lili—now to be the Countess Malu. Despite the heavy promotion of its Anglo-German star, Harvey, the film failed to please. *Screenland*'s dismissal of it as 'a charming bit of fluff—mythical kingdom-Cinderella stuff' was one of the more positive reviews. *The New Movie Magazine* was much less

Figure 4.6. The Princess (Eleanor Powell) in the 1937 film version of *Rosalie*. PictureLux/The Hollywood Archive/Alamy Stock Photo

kind: 'The plot of this film is laid in the mythical kingdom of Ruritania, which would have been a very good place to leave it lying.'[77]

But perhaps the greatest Ruritanian musical of this period, or indeed of any, is *Duck Soup* (1933), a film that is not always thought of as a musical at all.[78] Original songs by Bert Kalmar and Harry Ruby include the Freedonian national anthem 'Hail, Hail Freedonia' and the big production number 'This Country's Going to War', though there are also musical snippets of everything from Suppé to the blackface minstrel song 'I Wish I Was in Dixie's Land'. *Duck Soup* is a sort of reductio ad absurdum of musical Ruritania, containing a hodge-podge of McCutcheon and *Merry Widow* elements, as well as farce, slapstick, and something approaching narrative anarchy. Margaret Dumont plays Mrs Teasdale, a rich widow who is bankrolling the bankrupt country of Freedonia and who appoints Rufus T. Firefly (Groucho Marx) as its leader. Firefly attempts to defeat the schemes of neighboring Sylvania, while also vying with its ambassador to marry Mrs Teasdale, but he ends up declaring war on Sylvania. As with other Marx Brothers vehicles, the plot is easily overwhelmed by the freewheeling visual and verbal antics. The elaborate 'This Country's Going to War' sequence, for example, marries Busby Berkeley–style crowd spectacle to minstrel revue. Ruritania's uniform fetish is sent up by having the brothers play on the Freedonian guards' helmets like drums and snip off their plumes, while Firefly's own rapidly alternating military uniforms evoke everything from the American Civil War to the American Boy Scouts. The film was released in the same year that Adolf Hitler became Chancellor of Germany, and it is tempting to see *Duck Soup* as an attack on fascism and national socialism, but it would be more accurate to say that, in the rivalry of Freedonia and Sylvania, nationalism of every kind is lampooned, together with its complement, military heroism. Like Lubitsch's work, *Duck Soup* suggests a certain impatience, to say the least, with the romantic world view of Ruritania. Curiously, while now viewed as a classic, it was not particularly successful at the time, and it ended the Marx Brothers' relationship with Paramount.

On the other side of the Atlantic, too, the coming of film sound ushered in a boom in musicals, and by 1936 they accounted for roughly one third of all films made in Britain.[79] Their production was partly underwritten by the 'quota' system, which Britain adopted in 1927 to allow native film production to survive in the face of Hollywood's dominance. Exhibitors were required to show a certain percentage of British films, and national production increased as a result. The resulting cinema has been variously seen as a largely conservative 'cinema of reassurance' (in Stephen Shafer's phrase); as being too dependent on other media, such as the stage; or as an uncertain attempt to offer a new 'middlebrow' aesthetic for a society in transition.[80] At any rate, it is certainly true that the musicals treated here are often stage-derived and that they strike a shaky balance between respect for tradition and rank and the idea that true love is more important than caste.

Ruritanian musical comedies appeared alongside their close kin, Viennese romances, with both varieties summoning up 'a historical world of magical kingdoms furnished with cafés, and inhabited by waltzing, singing, champagne-drinking aristocrats for whom the quest for true love over-rode questions of class and matters of taste'.[81] Love-children of *The Merry Widow* and *The Prisoner of Zenda*, these films were in part aimed at the continental market while also being popular at home. As in the United States, some were the work of expatriate Austrian and German film-makers, though even Alfred Hitchcock tried his hand in this market with *Waltzes from Vienna* (1934). There were, in fact, so many of these ersatz productions that critics began to call for a cinema that dealt more directly with modern British life.[82] Tuneful Ruritanias featured in such offerings as *Lucky Girl* (British International Pictures, 1932), *Prince of Arcadia* (Nettlefold, 1932), *The Queen's Affair* (Herbert Wilcox, 1934), *Princess Charming* (Gainsborough, 1934), *Heat Wave* (Gainsborough, 1935), and *Everything is Rhythm* (Joe Rock, 1936).

Princess Charming (US title *Alexandra*), for example, was a film version of the 1926 operetta by Albert Szirmai and a classic comedy of youth versus age.[83] The Princess Elaine (Evelyn Laye) of the diminutive Novia is betrothed to the elderly and impecunious King Christian (comic actor George Grossmith Jr.) of neighbouring Aufland, who sends his envoy, the tall and handsome Captain André Launa (Henry Wilcoxon), to escort her to him. When revolution breaks out, the only way she can cross the border is for the Captain to marry her, 'pro tem', as in McCutcheon's *East of the Setting Sun*, but of course they fall in love and stay married, and the King is paired off with his old amour, Countess Annette, played by French singer and actress Yvonne Arnaud. Additional comedy is provided by one of the variety stars of the period, Max Miller, in drag, as an escaped lunatic who promises the King an answer to his financial problems. One gets a sense of the generally chipper tone of the film from the following exchange between Elaine and her ladies in waiting: the shots and explosions of the revolution are heard outside, but they continue to serve her morning cup of tea, as she reclines in her enormous bed with her cuddly toy:

PRINCESS ELAINE: What is that?
LADY IN WAITING: I'm sorry your highness: that is the revolution.
PRINCESS ELAINE: It's too early—so inconsiderate.

There are distant echoes here of the less comic fate of Europe's royal families. It was not so very long since the demise of the Habsburgs, Hohenzollerns, and Romanovs, and audiences would have been reminded that October of the continuing political instability of the Balkans by newsreel footage of the assassination of King Alexander of Yugoslavia in Marseilles. But for the most part the film eschews such realities, and its Ruritanian territory is a place in which love conquers the divisions of class. As in many of these productions, royalty is shown to be in fact little different to the rest of the population: the blue bloods may be better dressed and have nicer manners, but they are still looking for true love and more money.

Sometimes, as in *Lucky Girl*, the Ruritanians visit Britain. Based on an earlier stage musical, the film was essentially a vehicle for the comic talents of Gene Gerrard (the stage name of Eugene O'Sullivan), who starred and directed; the female lead was played by Molly Lamont, a South-African dance teacher turned musical star. Gerrard appears as the English-raised Stephan Gregorovitch, who accedes to the throne of the impoverished Karaslavia. On the advice of his American efficiency expert he returns to England to raise money on the crown jewels. After a good deal of singing and dancing, and a comic episode in which the royal party is mistaken for a gang of jewel thieves, Stephan and the heroine, Lady Moira, are united, her wealth suggesting a solution to Karaslavia's financial problems. Posters dubbed Gerrard the 'Monarch of Mirth and Crowned Prince of Laughter Land', but as one might guess it is not a film that is deferential to ideas of blood. The *Motion Picture Herald* opined that it was the kind of film that Lubitsch would have liked to make, as the story of royal misadventures was of the kind 'dear to his democratic heart'.[84] The fascination with the feudal past lingers on but in increasingly less deferential forms.

Britain had its own royal crisis in the 1930s, of course, and, trading on the real-life drama of the abdication, a film version of *Glamorous Night* appeared in 1937. Directed by the Belfast-born Brian Desmond Hurst, it featured Mary Ellis reprising her stage performance as Militza, Otto Kruger as the King, Victor Jory as the Prime Minister, Barry Mackay as Anthony Allan, and the veteran Maire O'Neill (Molly Allgood) as the servant, Phoebe. The action of the stage play is changed around considerably, and the rising political tensions of the 1930s feed more obviously into Krasnia: Prime Minister Lyadeff (sic) is now presented as the leader of a blackshirt fascist group—eventually overthrown by a band of gypsies, led by Militza. *Variety* noted that the recent abdication gave it a certain timeliness: when it appeared at Drury Lane 'it bore a resemblance to the story of King Carol of Rumania and Mme Lupescu, but present-day audiences will conjure up the later romance'.[85]

By the end of the 1930s, the deluge of Ruritanian and Vienna-waltz films had receded in Britain and the USA; tastes were changing, the industry was changing, and the rise of Nazi Germany made it difficult to sustain the idea of Mitteleurope as a location of idyllic escapism.[86] In the post-war years, however, Novello's fantasy world clearly still had some appeal, as we have seen from the stage longevity of *King's Rhapsody*. In 1955 the hit play was brought to the screen by British producer/director Herbert Wilcox, with Errol Flynn playing Nikki and Anna Neagle (Mrs Herbert Wilcox) as Marta Karillos.[87] Flynn had once been the dashing swashbuckler par excellence, but by this period his career and his health were in decline, and the second-string British film industry offered him the kind of work that he could no longer find in Hollywood. As a further incentive, his third wife, Patrice Wymore, was offered the part of the young Princess Kristiane.[88] The Murania of the play has for some reason been changed to Laurentia, which is described in a superimposed title as being 'guarded by immemorial mountain peaks, gaunt and forbidding'; it is 'a country of strange contrasts...romance, and the venom of intrigue'. Partly shot on location in Catalonia, and using the cathedral at Sitges for the coronation scene, the film presents Laurentia as more Mediterranean than the Germanic/Eastern European territory one might expect, though the costumes are as colourful as anything in the screen *Prisoner of Zenda* of three years earlier. It is not entirely a copy of the original: for instance, there is extensive use of flashback to fill in Nikki and Marta's love story; an elaborate dream sequence is added for Kristiane's lonely wedding night; and there is a rather pointless duel between Nikki and the Prince of Murania, the latter's title a playful reference to the play. Most significantly, perhaps, the ending is made more upbeat: as Nikki stands alone at the cathedral altar, Kristiane comes to stand beside him, and their hands join as the titles roll. But despite the relatively plush Cinemascope production, and Flynn's fading star-power, the film failed to recapture the success of the stage play. One of Flynn's biographers claims that 'after 93 minutes the end credits are a welcome relief', but this is a little unfair.[89] Certainly, the implausibility of the original is all the more obvious on screen, but the film also has its strengths, not least the chemistry between Flynn—a very convincing ageing rake—and his actual young wife. Martita Hunt is an effective Queen Mother of the Lady Bracknell school, with Francis De Wolff quite menacing enough as Lombardo, the Prime Minister. If the film is largely forgotten, it is perhaps because Novello's songs have not aged well.

Two of the most successful Ruritanian features of the post-war period were big-budget colour remakes of earlier hits. *The Merry Widow* was remade by MGM in Technicolor in 1952 with Lana Turner in the lead role. And if the songs of *The Student Prince* still linger in our international popular culture, it is probably because of the highly successful MGM Ansocolor film version of 1954, directed by Richard Thorpe, who made the Technicolor *Prisoner of Zenda* for the same studio. One of the film's attractions was to be Mario Lanza in the part of the tuneful Prince, but, because of a dispute between Lanza and MGM, he was replaced by Edward Purdom, who lip-syncs the songs to the voice of Lanza. Ann Blyth plays Kathie, and other roles are taken by a whole array of well-known character actors, including S. Z. Sakall, billed as S. Z. 'Cuddles' Sakall, as Kathie's innkeeper father; Louis Calhern as Karl Heinrich's grandfather, the King of Carlsburg; and Edmund Gwenn as Prof. Juttner.

Some of the reviews of the 1954 *Student Prince* accurately predicted that operetta was on the way out. Musicals more generally, however, continued to draw large audiences until the end of the 1960s. The last great Ruritanian example appeared in 1968, the children's fantasy film *Chittty Chitty Bang Bang*, adapted loosely from Ian Fleming's *Chitty Chitty Bang Bang: The Magical Car*. This had been serialized in the *Daily Express* in 1964 and was published as three separate volumes from Jonathan Cape in 1964-5.[90] Fleming had seen Count Louis Zborowski race one of his two Chitty-Bang-Bang cars at Brooklands in the 1920s, and his stories of the Potts family and their magical car are 'dedicated to the memory of the original Chitty-Chitty-Bang-Bang, built in 1920 by Count Zborowski'.[91] The Potts are explorer and inventor Commander Caractacus Pott, R.N. (Retired), his wife, Mimsie, and their eight-year old twins, Jemima and Jeremy. They save an old racing car from scrapping, and Caractacus restores it, only to find that it has magical powers; the three episodes recount the family's adventures in it, including their trip to France, where they clash with a gang of ruthless robbers led by Joe the Monster.

Chitty Chitty was produced for the screen by Albert R. 'Cubby' Broccoli, who was also behind most of the James Bond films between 1962 and 1989. Scripted by Ken Hughes, Roald Dahl, and the uncredited Richard Maibaum, the musical's catchy songs were written by the Sherman brothers. Dick Van Dyke turns in a characteristically lively performance as Caractacus Potts, who is now a widower so that a love interest can be found for him in the form of Truly Scrumptious (Sally Ann Howes), daughter of a local sweet manufacturer. In place of the family's French adventures, the film offers an extended Ruritanian sequence, which begins when Potts tells the children a story about the scheming Baron Bomburst, who covets their magical car. This story then comes to life, as it were, and the Baron's comical secret agents appear. The German actor Gert Fröbe, who had played Goldfinger in the eponymous Bond film, plays the unscrupulous Baron, who uses an airship to kidnap the eccentric Grandpa Potts (Lionel Jeffries), mistaking him for his inventor son. Potts senior is carried off to the Baron's castle in Vulgaria, a Ruritanian land dominated by an extraordinary castle, actually Neuschwanstein in Bavaria. Children are forbidden in Vulgaria, by order of the Baroness (Anna Quayle), so that the townspeople secret them away underground. The magical car brings the rest of the family and Truly Scrumptious in hot pursuit of Grandpa, but Jemima and Jeremy are captured by the sinister Child Catcher, brilliantly played by the Australian ballet dancer and choreographer Robert Helpmann. Eventually Caractacus and Truly save the day, with the help of the locals, and the wicked Baron and Baroness are overthrown; the children of Vulgaria roam free once more, and the Potts family and Truly fly back to a happy ending in England.[92]

Vulgaria, filmed on location at Neuschwanstein and the picturesque town of Rothenburg ob der Tauber in Bavaria, returns Ruritania to its Germanic roots—there is nothing Balkan about it. It is at first glance a comic territory, more Fredonia than Ruritania, but life in Vulgaria also has a curiously violent edge. The ludicrous Baron Bomburst and the Baroness sing a cloying duet of lovers' baby-talk, 'Chu-Chi Face'. But while they sing he tries to kill her in various slapstick ways. Likewise, the banning of children, and the activities of the Child Catcher, are more than a little creepy. The film's German locations have their own disturbing resonances. Neuschwanstein is a castle associated with the eccentric King Ludwig II, who was deposed after a team of psychiatrists deemed him unfit to rule, and it is, perhaps, a suitable location for a flight of fancy. But Rothenburg's recent history at this point was much darker. A well-preserved medieval town, and a popular tourist destination since the nineteenth century, in the 1930s it came to be regarded by the Nazis as the epitome of pure German identity—their *Kraft durch Freude* [sc. strength through joy] organization subsidized group vacations in the town for working-class Germans and for ethnic Germans from recently annexed territories.[93] As Joshua Hagen records, Hitler Youth rallies became a 'new high point for Rothenburg's tourist season', and the town's distant anti-Semitic past was proudly celebrated as a mark of its exemplary racial unity. Rothenburg was increasingly purged of what were perceived to be non-German elements, from its Jewish citizens to its 'foreign' architectural details. Children were never forbidden in Rothenburg as they are in Vulgaria, but Jews effectively were, with the last of the town's small Jewish population being driven out by orchestrated mobs in October of 1938, anticipating the pogroms of Kristallnacht in the rest of Germany. The concealment of children from the authorities was something that was also fairly fresh in people's memories in 1968, not least through the 1959 film version of *The Diary of Anne Frank* (1947). *Chitty Chitty Bang Bang* takes us back to a Germanic Ruritania, then, but just beneath its surface, and sometimes poking through, are recent historical traumas that are incommensurate with both the cosy adventure tradition and the film's own musical frothiness (see Plate 4.1). Perhaps it is this curious texture as much as its hummable songs that make it such a memorable piece of popular culture.

The film was heavily promoted, playfully billed in newspaper ads as 'the most fantasmagorical musical in the history of everything'.[94] As the *Daily Mirror* noted in November 1968, the publicity campaign would comprise 'balloons by the million; enough Chitty tee-shirts to cover the entire Soviet armed forces (what a thought); Chitty wall paper. Chitty paper cups, plates, saucers, jigsaws, dolls, cars, paperback and LP Records... [W]e are obviously only a couple of bangs away from the Chitty Chitty Bomb.'[95] The exclusive charity premiere at the Odeon in Leicester Square was attended by, appropriately enough, members of one of Europe's surviving royal families, the Windsors, their own Germanic origins now more or less forgotten. Attracting mixed reviews, it nonetheless performed well at the box office, and it has lingered long in the popular imagination, a staple of Christmas television schedules before the long-touring West End stage version (2002) gave it a further lease of life.[96] Indeed, Vulgaria, land of the slapstick sinister, may now be better known to younger audiences than Ruritania itself.

From *La Grande-Duchesse de Gérolstein* to *The Student Prince* to *Chitty Chitty Bang Bang*, musical Ruritania covers an extraordinary range. Its territories have been less the swashbuckling realms of Hope's imagination than places of pure pageantry and romance, even though ceremony and tradition are often what the hero and heroine actively fight against. It is unlikely that we have seen the last of this musical dynasty. Meg Cabot's *Princess Diaries* series (chapter 6) continues the Ruritanian line, and in a recent interview Cabot said that she hopes one day to see a Broadway musical version of the popular novels: 'I think a *Princess Diaries* musical would be hilarious. For [the heroine's cat] I think they should adopt a stray cat from an animal shelter and train it like they did with Sandy the Dog from *Annie*...I'm so looking forward to seeing that one day.'[97] One suspects that she may not have too long to wait, though it seems unlikely that the waltz will feature as prominently as it did in previous musical Ruritanias. We will return to Cabot's Ruritania redux and its Disney adaptation, but first we must see what became of the pocket-kingdom formula during the Cold War, when the world itself seemed to become a smaller and very breakable place.

5

Pocket Kingdoms, the Cold War, and the Bomb

In the early 1950s the tiny and backwards duchy of Grand Fenwick (pop. 6,000), located somewhere in the French Alps, begins to run into financial trouble. Its leaders hatch a desperate plan: they will declare war on the United States, and when they are inevitably defeated they will be able to apply to the victors for Marshall Plan funds. But their scheme goes awry. When the Grand Fenwickian archers arrive in New York a nuclear drill is under way, and, with everyone hiding out in underground shelters, the European invaders encounter almost no resistance. They also stumble across a deadly weapon, a Q-Bomb, based on a new element, Quadium, which they take back with them to Grand Fenwick. Soon the superpowers come calling, offering their assistance and protection, but instead the duchy uses its new status to form a League of Little Nations, securing world peace. This is the whimsical plot of Leonard Wibberley's *The Mouse That Roared*, which was first a *Saturday Evening Post* serial (1954–5), then a bestselling novel (1955), and then a film starring Peter Sellers (1959). Here is Ruritania for the Cold War years.

The social and political backdrop against which this new variant appeared was very different not only to that of 1894 but also to that of the 1920s and 1930s, and it will be useful to sketch in some of its features. The atomic bombs dropped on Hiroshima and Nagasaki in August 1945 had made the world seem a smaller, more frangible place for one thing. But that shrunken world was also divided along new political lines. The map of Europe had already been radically redrawn in the earlier twentieth century, with the disintegration of the Austro-Hungarian Empire, the transfer of German territory to its neighbours under the terms of the Versailles Treaty, and the formation of larger nation states, such as Yugoslavia, from smaller kingdoms.

In this second carve-up, Europe was effectively split in two. On 5 March 1946, Winston Churchill was visiting Westminster College in Missouri to accept an honorary doctorate when he gave his 'Iron Curtain' speech, offering a powerful metaphor to describe the new geopolitics:

> I have a strong admiration and regard for the valiant Russian people and for my wartime comrade, Marshal Stalin. There is deep sympathy and goodwill in Britain—and I doubt not here also—toward the peoples of all the Russias and a resolve to persevere through many differences and rebuffs in establishing lasting friendships... It is my duty, however... to place before you certain facts about the present position in Europe. From Stettin in the Baltic to Trieste in the Adriatic an iron curtain has descended across the Continent. Behind that line lie all the capitals of the ancient states of Central and Eastern Europe. Warsaw, Berlin, Prague, Vienna, Budapest, Belgrade, Bucharest and Sofia; all these famous cities and the populations around them lie in what I must call the Soviet sphere, and all are subject, in one form or another, not only to Soviet influence but to a very high and in some cases increasing measure of control from Moscow.[1]

If the Soviet Union held sway on one side of that curtain, the United States easily dominated the other. Britain, once a global power, still had an enormous army and navy, but the war had cost it roughly a quarter of its national wealth. Rationing continued into the 1950s, and the rebuilding of Britain's cities was slow work. With its own economic problems to deal with at home, and faced with increasingly powerful anti-colonial forces, over the next few decades it would reluctantly have to give up its overseas empire, piece by piece.[2] It was no longer a superpower, as was made clear by the Suez Crisis of 1956.

For decades to come the binary division demarcated by the iron curtain would elide older national and imperial alignments, and not just in Europe, shaping the fates of nations as well as the minutiae of everyday life for countless individuals. It was a tense stalemate. By 1949 the United States had lost its monopoly on the new weapons of mass destruction, and the Cold War became an atomic arms race between the superpowers. Partly inspired by the views of diplomat George Kennan, US foreign policy came to revolve around the checking and countering of Soviet influence. In his famous 'Long Telegram' from Moscow of 22 February 1946, Kennan had urged the United States not only to strengthen its own body politic against the 'malignant parasite' of communism but also to offer security to Europe to stop the spread of communism there:

It is not enough to urge people to develop political processes similar to our own. Many foreign peoples, in Europe at least, are tired and frightened by experiences of past, and are less interested in abstract freedom than in security. They are seeking guidance rather than responsibilities. We should be better able than Russians to give them this. And unless we do, Russians certainly will.[3]

This approach of 'containment' became Truman's policy and underlay the Truman Doctrine of support for 'free peoples'. The resulting war of position bled into local conflicts around the globe, sustaining a whole series of proxy 'hot' wars, coups, revolutions, and invasions: e.g., Iran (1952, CIA-backed coup d'état); Bolivia (1964, CIA-backed coup); the Dominican Republic (1965, invasion by the United States); Angola (1975, civil war with Cuban involvement); Vietnam (1955–75, proxy war); Grenada (1983, US invasion).[4] But containment also came to underwrite some less obviously military endeavours, notably the postwar European Recovery Program (aka the Marshall Plan), and its successors, the programs run by the Mutual Security Agency from 1951 and the Agency for International Development (USAID) from 1961 that pumped billions of dollars into countries which, it was perceived, might otherwise succumb to the evil of communism.

The space race between the United States and the USSR was not only part of this Cold War competition but sometimes explicitly military. In 1958 Project Defender was put in place to harness science to defend against Soviet missile attacks, and one of the ideas advanced was Bambi (Ballistic Missile Boost Intercepts): missile stations were to be stationed in space, and these would be used to blast Soviet missiles out of the firmament as they powered towards the United States.[5] By 1959 the Advanced Research Projects Agency at the Pentagon was envisaging the use of orbiting battle-stations mounted with lasers for the same purpose: all of this was long before Ronald Reagan's much-derided 'Star Wars' program.[6]

In the cultural realm too war was waged. The Soviet Union strategic-ally deployed the Kirov and Bolshoi ballets, and its virtuoso classical solo-ists, on Western tours. The US Central Intelligence Agency financially supported an array of cultural activities that it was felt would help in the fight against communism, bankrolling such literary magazines as *Encounter* in Britain and supporting all kinds of flag-flying, from tours by the Boston Pops orchestra to the 'New American Painting' exhibitions in 1958–9. Books critical of communism—or simply indifferent to its values—were smuggled into the Soviet Union, most famously Boris Pasternak's *Doctor Zhivago* (1957), and George Orwell's later works became a critical part of the CIA's armoury.[7] In the UK the Information Research Department (IRD) performed a similar role, if on a smaller scale, influencing the BBC's Overseas Services and bankrolling such volumes as Bertrand Russell's *What is Freedom* (1952) and translations and even a cartoon strip version of Orwell's *Animal Farm* for use in Malaya, India, Burma, and elsewhere.[8]

Unsurprisingly, fears of communist subversion and nuclear annihilation vied for space in the popular culture of the period. Ruritanian fantasies that conjured up romantic adventure in the exotic, semi-feudal corners of Europe could scarcely hope to thrive against such a geopolitical backdrop, except as pure nostalgia. In fact Hope's book did continue to sell, with at least a dozen different British and US editions being available in the 1950s and 1960s. But from a story with broad appeal, *The Prisoner of Zenda* had become a children's classic, with, for example, the first Classics Illustrated comic book edition appearing in October 1950; an abridged 'World-Famous Books' edition from Hart in 1960; a Blackie 'Chosen Books' edition in 1961; and a Dent's Children's Illustrated Classics edition in 1962. As we have seen, screen adaptations of the story continued to attract audiences, though, of the two post-war versions of *Zenda*, one (1952) was a gorgeous but backward-looking shot-by-shot Technicolor remake of the 1937 film, and the other (1979) a parodic Peter Sellers vehicle. It was *Graustark's* fate to be all but forgotten; by the end of the 1960s, people were more likely to be familiar with the American racehorse Graustark (1963–88) than with the novels, plays, and films which inspired his name.

However, the 1950s also saw the creation of a new breed of Ruritanian fantasy, a curious mutant strain born, like Godzilla, of the atomic age. *The Mouse That Roared* is in fact just one of a whole series of Cold War Ruritanian novels, films, and plays, from the 1940s through to the 1980s, that offer a glimpse into the anxieties, fears, and longings of those fraught years, when nuclear armageddon seemed like a very real possibility. As we shall see, as the old formula was reimagined for new geopolitical and technological realities, and for a new affective landscape, the chocolate-box kingdom came to represent an imaginary territory just outside of the spheres of influence of the twin superpowers. Escapist stories of romantic adventure gave way to political satire and uneasy atomic-age comedy, blending Ruritania and radiation.

Bombs and Curtains

If the Cold War was the major defining factor for the post-war world, the arrival of the atomic bomb was the other, and it has a significant off-stage presence in all of the Ruritanian narratives we will consider here. As Paul Boyer has shown in *By the Bomb's Early Light* (1985), the initial reaction to the destruction of Hiroshima and Nagasaki had been a sense of momentous political change, captured in Anne O'Hare McCormick's comment that the bomb had created 'an explosion in men's minds as shattering as the obliteration of Hiroshima'.[9] Writers, broadcasters, and scientists alike called for the creation of some form of world state as the only way effectively to prevent a future war that could destroy all human life. But such utopian impulses quickly faded during the paranoid years of the Cold War; especially after August 1949, when the USSR conducted its own atomic tests. In the United States there were fears of Reds at home, stoked by, for instance, Truman's Employees Loyalty Program from 1947 and the renewed vigour of the infamous House Un-American Activities Committee, though as we saw in chapter 3 these were only the latest in a long series of Red Scares. The war in Korea (1950–3) further exacerbated American fears of socialist world domination, with the Chinese army entering the conflict on the side of North Korea and the USSR offering support. (The term Bamboo Curtain emerged to describe the political divisions of Asia.) When the war broke out, US politicians, such as Lloyd Bentsen (D., Texas), actually called for the atomic bomb to be used to fight the red menace in Korea, and President Truman himself threatened to use it if necessary.[10] Nor were these politicians out of step with military views: in December of 1950 General Macarthur requested permission to use atomic bombs on Korean targets at his own discretion, arguing that the resulting 'belt of radioactive cobalt' would end the war quickly and stave off further incursions from China for decades to come.[11] Truman and his cabinet regarded atomic weapons as acceptable options, and later Eisenhower took a similar view.

The new weapon of mass destruction was absorbed swiftly into popular culture, and bomb-themed products popped up in some unlikely places. In July 1946 the Bikini Atoll in the Marshall Islands was used for the first time as a site of atomic testing by the United States, the islanders having been evacuated, and pigs, goats, and other animals brought in as human substitutes aboard the target fleet, which included Japanese and German warships.[12] Within days of the first test, Bikini lent its name to the new two-piece swimwear developed by French engineer Louis Réard; an earlier version, the 'atome', had failed to find favour.[13] The bikini's name was presumably meant to connote its explosive and cutting-edge nature, while simultaneously drawing on some pre-war idea of Pacific island sensuality. Younger consumers could also tap into the bomb's aura: for instance, in the late 1940s American children could play with the Lone Ranger Kix Atomic Bomb Ring and head off to school armed with their bomb-shaped Atomic Crayon Sharpener.[14]

However, atmospheric testing from the early 1950s on spread a second wave of terror, and the bomb's sinister character came more clearly into focus in the West. People began to realize that they might survive a nuclear blast only to succumb to the radioactive fallout that would linger long after. One of the things that changed their minds was the Castle Bravo test of 1954 at Bikini Atoll, which used a hydrogen bomb, or H-bomb (i.e. based on nuclear fission), ash from which reached a Japanese fishing boat the *Lucky Dragon,* more than 80 miles away.[15] The horrific effects on the crew were reported around the world and fed into the creation of the 1954 Japanese science fiction/horror film *Gojira*, better known in the Anglophone world as *Godzilla*. In the United States, concerns arose about the importation of radioactive fish and radioactive tea. But the dangers were rather closer at hand, with radioactive rain falling on Chicago in 1955 and deadly strontium-90 appearing in milk in 1959.[16] By the 1960s, studies of children's teeth showed significantly higher levels of strontium-90 in children born in the 1950s compared to older cadres.

While building up an enormous nuclear arsenal in the name of 'deterrence', the US government also began to try to assuage the public's fears of nuclear war, in part by fostering the impression that through 'Civil Defense' such a war might not be so deadly after all. (Likewise, Britain had its own Civil Defence Corps from 1949.) Lieutenant Commander Richard Gerstell's 'How You Can Survive an A-Bomb Blast', which appeared in the *Saturday Evening Post* in 1950, is an early instance of this propaganda programme.[17] The new Federal Civil Defense Administration launched its 'Alert America' campaign in June of 1951: in 1952 they sent convoys with informational exhibits throughout the United States, organizing pageants and recruiting photogenic young women for publicity shots, including a 'Miss Alert America'.[18] As for the exhibits themselves: 'The viewer sees the destruction of a city, of crops, of life. Then he sees how we might save himself, his neighbor, and sections of his city from fire. Or how he can save another city from the ravages of atomic bombing by joining Civil Defense.'[19] One might think of this as the 'edutainment' of terror. People were warned to be afraid of nuclear war and to expect massive casualties, but they were also encouraged to think of survival and the restoration of order. Less publicly, the government began to pour money into research on the long-term effects of radiation poisoning, including a thirty-year study conducted on some 1,200 beagles at UCD Davis and other research centres.[20]

Civil Defense literature on both sides of the Atlantic stressed that the blast could be survived and that fallout could be managed.[21] In the event of an attack, the family was to work as microcosm of the military: each member would have his or her own role, and a place in the hierarchical post-nuclear family; the paterfamilias would be the commanding officer. In the USA, improvised fallout shelters mushroomed around the nation, and such enterprising businessmen as the Swayze brothers tried to market luxury shelters to the well-to-do, securing the backing of Avon Products director Girard 'Jerry' B. Henderson for a model underground luxury home at the New York's World Fair in 1964.[22] Images promoting more ordinary DIY models shelters typically show relaxed nuclear families, camped out comfortably in their underground shelters: Father reads a book, Mother prepares a meal, the children play—the family pet, one assumes, is doomed.[23] The nuclear apocalypse would really be quite cosy.

One of the more seemingly far-fetched aspects of Leonard Wibberley's novel is that an expedition from Grand Fenwick arrives in New York to find the streets completely deserted because of a drill of some kind. But this episode is based on Cold War fact. In 1954, the year in which *The Mouse that Roared* began serialization in the *Saturday Evening Post*, America's 'Operation Alert', was first held on 14 and 15 June.[24] This elaborate Civil Defense simulated atomic attacks in forty-one 'target' cities across the country, including New York, Los Angeles, and Washington, and in ten provinces in Canada. In some areas these were largely paper exercises, but in others the public was required to evacuate the streets or their workplaces for 10 to 15 minutes, fake casualties were 'treated', and the Civil Defense patrolled the deserted streets. Those who refused to cooperate with drills could be and were arrested.[25] Part of such drills was the forecasting of horrendous casualties, with imagined death tolls—7 million in 1954—published in newspapers. As with 'Alert America', total annihilation was always ruled out.[26] Whether or not one agrees with Tracy C. Davis that such performances effectively trained people into certain forms of behaviour, it is difficult not so see that this literal theatre of war must have had an effect on how people experienced everyday life.[27] An imminent Soviet attack became taken for granted, and the fallout shelter became normal—by 1963 the USA is thought to have had a million underground shelters.

In the later years of Operation Alert Washington, President Eisenhower was whisked off to a new underground headquarters, Mount Raven, in Maryland. (The 1964 political thriller, *Seven Days in May*, imagines a military coup planned to take place during such a drill, while the president is isolated from his usual staff at Mount Raven.) And although by 1962 'Operation Alert' had ended, partly because of growing resistance from protesters, who refused to take cover for the requisite 15 minutes, plans for a post-cataclysm administration became ever more elaborate, not least because it was thought that the Soviet Union was spending vast sums on underground facilities. Sprawling subterranean complexes were developed at Mount Raven, Mount Weather in Virginia, Cheyenne Mountain in Colorado, and other sites around the country to ensure Continuity of Government. Britain too, increasingly integrated into the US nuclear defence system through its air bases, began to pour money into the expansion of bombproof infrastructure left over from the war, including bunkers for national and regional government and for radar facilities.[28] In the absence of hard information, speculation abounded about the exact nature of these buried secret worlds, and they became the stuff of popular legend, especially in the United States: according the *Washington Post* of 20 January 1977, Mount Weather contained an 'underground city, with streets, three-story buildings and a lake large enough for water-skiing'.[29]

Ruritania Gets the Bomb

Quite apart from state attempts to harness it for propaganda purposes, the realm of culture was inevitably marked internally by the climate of paranoia, suspicion, and anxiety.[30] For example, as Alan Nadel shows, the literary fiction of the United States in this era often eschews direct engagement with politics but is nonetheless concerned with the pressures of a conformist post-war society, and its anxious, 'other-directed', corporate-employee self.[31] 'Conformity' and 'anxiety' became keywords of the era, as psychosocial analysis entered its heyday.[32] Writers who directly tackled the political climate sometimes sought historical or metaphorical cover, most famously Arthur Miller with *The Crucible* (1953), in which the Salem witch trials of the seventeenth century evoke the feverish paranoia of McCarthyism. When we turn to the cinema of the period, we see some of the same allegorical tendencies at work: *High Noon* (1952), for example, is also a parable of the McCarthy years, as is *Bad Day at Black Rock* (1955). However, the most obvious mark that the Cold War and the Bomb left on the popular culture of this period is in the imagination of disaster and alien invasion, with science fiction and horror coming to offer powerful political modes. Classic post-apocalyptic novels include George R. Stewart's *Earth Abides* (1949), Richard Matheson's *I Am Legend* (1954), Pat Frank's *Alas, Babylon* (1959), and Walter M. Miller's *A Canticle for Leibowitz* (1960). Across the Atlantic, similar scenarios were conjured up in John Wyndham's *The Day of the Triffids* (1951), John Christopher's *The Death of Grass* (1956), and J. G. Ballard's *The Wind from Nowhere* (1961). On screen, fears of military and ideological invasion underpinned films as diverse as *The War of the Worlds* (1953), *Invasion of the Body Snatchers* (1956), and *Plan 9 From Outer Space* (1959).

But there was also a place for Cold War Ruritania. The chivalrous romantic adventure was now long past its heyday, and even the Buchanesque Ruritanian thriller no longer made much sense in a Europe dominated by the Iron Curtain. Instead fictional European lands begin to be deployed in comic approaches to the anxieties of the era. This fresh Ruritanian strand shows up first on stage and screen and includes the Bob Hope comedy *Where There's Life* (1947); the Ethel Merman Broadway musical *Call Me Madam* (1950; filmed 1953); Peter Ustinov's play, *Romanoff and Juliet* (1956; filmed in 1961) and *Carlton Browne of the F.O.* (1959). These deal with, respectively, Barovia, Lichtenburg, Concordia, and Gaillardia. When it comes to fiction, there are, perhaps, fewer candidates. Vladimir Nabokov's *Pale Fire* (1962), which features the deposed King of Zembla, can arguably be read as a Cold War Ruritanian story.[33] But it is Wibberley's *Mouse* series that stands out; beginning under the Eisenhower administration with *The Mouse that Roared* (1954–5), it lasted into the Reagan years with *The Mouse that Saved the West* (1981).

The 1947 romantic comedy hit *Where There's Life* (dir. Sidney Lanfield) is really a transitional work: there are a few wry references to splitting the atom and the Soviet Union, but the film does not possess the fully developed sense of menace that marks later Cold War comedy, and America's superpower status is downplayed. The title refers to a wartime tagline used

Figure 5.1. Publicity photo for the 1947 film Where There's Life (dir. Sidney Lanfield), showing William Bendix, Signe Hasso, and Bob Hope. ZUMAPRESS. com/Moviestills/age fotostock

to promote Bob Hope ('Where there's life there's Hope'), who plays Michael Valentine, an American radio announcer sponsored by Sparko Dog Food and the unwitting heir to the throne of Barovia, apparently somewhere in Eastern Europe (see Figure 5.1). In the opening scenes, set in Barovia, King Hubertus announces that he will hold democratic elections now that the war is over, but he is shot as he speaks by a member of a secret society, the Mordia. A trio of Barovians, including war hero General Katrina Grimovitch (Swedish actress Signe Hasso), fly to America to bring back the secret heir, but the Mordians are on his trail too. Michael, in the meantime, is finally about to marry Hazel, his fiancée of many years (Vera Marshe), but she drops him when he misses their wedding because of a Mordian attempt on his life and is subsequently found with another woman in his apartment— General Grimovitch. Michael finds himself drawn to the lovely General, a character largely borrowed from Greta Garbo's all-business Soviet official in *Ninotchka* (1939). Much of the film consists of their attempts to evade the murderous Mordia, and the clever set pieces include a long comic sequence in a department store. In the end, after he escapes another assassination attempt on the plane to Barovia, it is discovered that Michael is not the heir to the throne after all, leaving him free to pursue Katrina, who has realized that she loves him too.

It is a film of broad strokes: with William Bendix as the hot-headed brother, Hazel's Irish-American cop family are comic stereotypes, and the villains are straight from central European casting. The plot largely serves as an armature for a series of well-flagged farcical situations and visual and verbal gags. 'There is just so much beating with a slapstick that the normal intelligence can take,' Bosley Crowther cautioned potential audiences in the *New York Times*.[34] Barovia is likewise painted in bold colours, a land of political skulduggery and assassination, where love is less important than duty, but also a place where women take on 'masculine' roles. In this respect the statelet appears to be a hybrid of older Ruritanias, the pleasure-free land of Marsovia in *The Merry Widow* and John Buchan's volatile Evallonia, though it is also clearly meant to evoke the Soviet Union. America by contrast appears as the land of law, order, consumer plenty, and romance. Grimovitch becomes more 'womanly' as she falls not just for Hope but also more feminine American clothing in place of her Barovian military uniform, as we see in the department store sequence: 'I've never owned anything like this,' the General murmurs appreciatively about her new dress. In this light the film can be read as less about geopolitics and more of a post-war fantasy about the empowered, employed American women of the war years returning to their earlier roles as wives and consumers. However, that Hope is the voice of a dog-food company suggests a wry perspective on the media and consumer culture; and his hapless version of screen masculinity indicates a pretty rickety patriarchy.

Coming three years later, the Broadway musical comedy *Call Me Madam*, set in Lichtenburg, was inspired by the career of the 'hostess with the mostes' (sic), Perle Mesta, the Oklahoma-born American socialite and ambassador to Luxembourg.[35] Where the United States is a land of post-war consumer plenty in *Where There's Life*, here it is an actual economic superpower, capable of funding tiny and underdeveloped European states like Lichtenburg out of its spare change. Starring Ethel Merman, and with songs by Irving Berlin, the story is a modernized version of Graustarkian romance with a touch of *The Merry Widow*. There are also a few echoes of the Will Rogers screen comedy *Ambassador Bill* (1931), in which another plainspoken Oklahoman brings his American can-do spirit to Sylvania, and of *Rosalie* (1937). A long-running hit on Broadway, *Call Me Madam* also drew the crowds in London's West End before inspiring the 1953 Technicolor film directed by Walter Lang. In the film as on stage, the wealthy but plain-spoken American socialite from Oklahoma, Sally Adams (Ethel Merman), becomes ambassador to a picturesque but poor European country, the tiny Grand Duchy of Lichtenburg. She is in some doubt as to its location and visits Italy and Switzerland before finding the tiny Alpine country, which in the film looks very much like a lakeside Swiss village, complete with colourful peasants in lederhosen and dirndls. The new ambassador is a subject of great interest, as the Grand Duke and Duchess want to marry off their niece, the Princess Maria (Vera-Ellen), to Prince Hugo of Middledorf and hope to extract Marshall Plan money from Sally for the dowry. Sally, played by Merman with Mae West-like vigour, turns out to be rather less than pliable until she falls for General Cosmo Constantine (George Sanders), the Lichtenburgian foreign minister; however, he for his part thinks that the country should not depend on foreign aid. Meanwhile, Kenneth, Sally's press officer (Donald O'Connor), has fallen for the Princess, whom he meets in the music section of a department store, and though she knows their love is hopeless she seems just as taken with the young American. After various misunderstandings, Sally and Kenneth have to return to Washington, but they are followed by Constantine and Princess Maria. Constantine is now the Lichtenburgian ambassador to the United States, and the Princess is plain Miss Hammenschlaffen, having given up her title; all ends happily ever after as the ensemble reprise one of the earlier songs, 'You're Just in Love'.

More than anything else, *Call Me Madam* is a string of elaborate song and dance numbers, using such settings as a *Zenda*-style state ball, no fewer than three parties, and the Lichtenburg fête. For the most part, Lichtenburg itself is the descendant of all those backwards-looking, hidebound Graustarks that need a good dose of American spirit and romantic freedom more than money on easy terms, and Sally and Kenneth are there to provide it, with a whole series of upbeat songs and dance routines. Princess Maria's interest in American music is a sure sign that she is ready to be converted to the American way, and, like the Romanzan princess in *Rosalie*, she shows her natural longing for greater freedom by singing and dancing in the Lichtenburg fête. Constantine too is converted, admiringly informing Sally that she has 'brought a new vitality to Lichtenburg'. The Bomb is not mentioned, and while the plot centres on Marshall Plan funding, the Soviet alternative to US patronage is largely kept in the background. However, in one of her songs Sally Adams claims that a party-loving millionaire like herself is 'what they really need behind the Iron Wall': capitalism is fun. And the 'International Rag', originally written by Berlin in 1913, is updated here with a verse to the effect that 'someday even Commies' will be dancing to the International Rag. If the Rag stands for market values, the film can claim some prescience.

Peter Ustinov's *Romanoff and Juliet*, on the other hand, tackles head on the rivalry between the United States and the USSR. In the stage version, the unnamed 'smallest country in Europe' is besieged by the superpowers for its vote at the United Nations but manages to fend them off. Despite the chilly Cold War winds blowing through his country, the General (Ustinov) helps love to blossom between Juliet, the American ambassador's daughter, and Igor Romanoff, son of the Soviet ambassador, their love match anticipating a thaw in superpower relations. First produced on 2 April 1956 at the Manchester Opera House, the play became a critical and commercial success, the *Evening Standard* naming it best new play in January 1957. With David Hurst replacing Ustinov, it moved to London's Piccadilly Theatre in London; an excerpt of this production was televised by the BBC on 28 January 1957.[36] That October *Romanoff and Juliet* went on to Broadway's Plymouth Theatre (now the Gerald Schoenfeld), where it ran for 389 performances. Meant as a 'tilt at nationalism of all kinds', its only real villain, as the theatre programme proclaims, is the Cold War itself, which had created an atmosphere of 'prejudice, fear and hostility'.[37] Among those who saw it in London was Harry Truman, who sent the author what he remembered as a 'most perspicacious letter' about the play's political message.[38]

When Ustinov adapted *Romanoff and Juliet* for the screen in 1961, the unnamed country became Concordia, and the compressed action of the play—all three acts take place in the town square, and in the Soviet and US Embassies—was opened out somewhat. Location footage of the UN is used in the opening scenes, some picturesque Italian hilltop towns provide the Ruritanian backdrop, and there are cuts to Soviet and American back offices in Moscow and Washington, where paranoid cold warriors try to make sense of the information coming in from their embassies. Peter Ustinov directs, and plays the lead again, this time as the President of the Republic of Concordia (see Figure 5.2). Concordia is so small that it is often forgotten at the UN, and, as with many of its Ruritanian forebears, few know where it is on the map; the President's view, though, is that 'in an atomic age it's wiser to remain a small target'. And, small or not, its UN vote is important, so when the President flies home to his tiny country, the Americans set

Figure 5.2. Publicity photograph (1961) of Peter Ustinov in Romanoff and Juliet. Everett Collection Inc./Alamy Stock Photo

about courting him with offers of 'oil, uranium…last year's missiles'; the Russians for their part promise 'tractors, grain from the Ukraine, a power plant', and even a cultural bribe in the form of a visit by the Bolshoi Ballet. But despite his country's poverty—their principal income comes from selling deliberately defective postage stamps to collectors—the President wants Concordia to be left alone, knowing that any such aid will be the thin end of the Cold War wedge. He fights back by tricking both sides into believing that the tiny state has its own atomic arsenal and by engineering a clandestine romance and hidden-in-plain-sight marriage between Juliet (Sandra Dee, then at the height of her fame) and Igor Romanoff (John Gavin). Ustinov turns in a charming performance as the resourceful President, though Dee and Gavin as the romantic leads are somewhat less engaging. Reviews were mixed. *Variety*, for example, declared that while the film version lacked some of the 'satiric toxin' of the play, enough of the 'comic chemistry' remained; but others sided with the *Tatler*'s Elspeth Grant, who felt that the extended joke was just 'too fragile to sustain a film that runs for 103 minutes'.[39]

The 1959 Boulting Brothers comedy, *Carlton Browne of the F.O.*, also known as *The Man in a Cocked Hat*, in some ways resembles the Latin American variants of the Ruritanian narrative, since its setting is apparently a tropical island, Gaillardia. However, as usual nobody knows where Gaillardia is, and the island's struggle for power is between a King (Ian Bannen) and the Grand Duke (John Le Mesurier), who wants the Princess Ilyena (Luciana Paluzzi) to reign: such figures are more usually found in Europe than in Latin America. Gaillardia is a former British possession which becomes the subject of considerable international interest when it is found to be rich in cobalt, at the time seen to be a fresh source of weapons of mass destruction.[40] The Russians are the first to realize Gaillardia's strategic importance, sending in a team of geologists disguised as Cossack dancers, but Britain soon deploys its own men, masquerading as a team of Morris dancers. They also dispatch the eponymous hero, played by Terry-Thomas, a thoroughly incompetent Foreign Office official. He finds the young King reluctant to commit himself to any foreign power, but the corrupt Prime Minister (the ubiquitous Peter Sellers) is a good deal more tractable. The British persuade the United Nations to agree to partition the island, only to find that the cobalt is in the wrong half. In the end, following a revolution, the King prevails against his local foes and foreign meddling, and he and the Princess Ilyena fall in love, uniting the island's factions. *Carlton Browne*'s main appeal is Terry-Thomas as the foolish but likeable anti-hero, a role which he plays to comic perfection. That he is the dim-witted son of a highly successful diplomat adds point to the film's vision of Britain as a fading power, living on former glory. In the years after the Suez Crisis, the film's depiction of a

Britain keen to play its part in Cold War international politics but no longer really up to it had a certain bite. So much so that the Foreign Office thought it was not suitable for screening at the Moscow International Film Festival.[41]

The most successful of these Cold War Ruritanias takes a bolder approach to international affairs. Anthony Hope's Ruritania could never invade Britain, and Graustark is no scientific rival to the United States; that is simply not how those fictional lands work as fantasies. But in the 1950s a string of comic tales appears that imagines just those scenarios. In the novels of Leonard Wibberley, beginning with *The Mouse that Roared* (1954, 1955), Grand Fenwick, a tiny, semi-feudal country nestled somewhere between France and Switzerland, invades the United States, beats America and Russia to the moon, and comes generally to punch above its geopolitical weight.

Wibberley, as he occasionally pointed out, was himself from a very small, if not imaginary, country—Ireland—though he spent most of his life in Britain and the United States. Born in Dublin in 1915, he spent his early years in Cork, where his Lancashire-born father, Thomas, was the first Harrington Professor of Agricultural Research; Leonard's mother, Shinaid, or Sinaid, was Irish.[42] As his older sister Anna's semi-autobiographical novel *Time and Chance* describes, the household was deeply shaken by the political conflicts of the period, and in 1922 they moved to England.[43] His father's early death ended Leonard's schooling at the age of 15, and he worked in a publisher's stockroom and as a copy boy for the *London Dispatch*, before getting a job as a reporter for the *Daily Mirror*, perhaps helped by Anna, who was already a journalist. In 1936 he sailed for Port of Spain, Trinidad, where he was, inter alia, editor of the weekly edition of the *Trinidad and Tobago Guardian* and worked for a company building army bases and for Shell Oil. After a spell in New York he headed west to Los Angeles, where he wrote for the *Los Angeles Times*, among other papers, before becoming a full-time fiction writer. Living in Hermosa Beach, California, he knocked out three or four books a year and wrote a syndicated column, and there he died in 1983, having written more than 100 books, including juvenile fiction, mystery stories, screenplays, and more than a dozen non-fiction works.[44] (His son, Cormac Wibberley, is also a writer, best known for his screenplays for the *National Treasure* films.)

Between 1954 and 1981, Wibberley wrote the highly successful series of five 'Mouse' novels which introduced the world to the Duchy of Grand Fenwick. Originally published as 'The Day New York Was Invaded' in the *Saturday Evening Post* (December 1954–January 1955), *The Mouse that Roared* begins in Grand Fenwick, which we learn, was established in 1370 by one Roger Fenwick, head of a free company of bowmen in the service of Charles the Wise, somewhere 'in the southern reaches of France, bordering the Alps' (6). This tiny landlocked duchy has survived for centuries, its principal export a fine wine, Pinot Grand Fenwick. But after the Second World War, its rising population—now 6,000—creates a demand for imported goods that their wine exports struggle to match. The young Duchess Gloriana XII notices that the United States is giving large sums to Europe to keep communism in check, and she and her senior advisor, the Count of Mountjoy, first imagine that Grand Fenwick might cash in by forming a local communist party, recruiting a local contrarian, Tully Bascomb, to run it. They then decide to declare war on the United States, hoping that when they lose they will be given Marshall Plan aid, like Germany and Italy. Tully leads a shipload of archers to New York, unaware that the principal objective of his mission is to fail.

In the meantime, the United States has hatched the ultimate Cold War weapon, the Q-Bomb, using a new element, Quadium, developed by a Dr Kokintz, by coincidence also born in Grand Fenwick. Tully and company arrive during a version of 'Operation Alert', and they find the streets deserted, except for a Civil Defense team that takes them for men from Mars. Having read about Kokintz in a discarded newspaper, Tully and his men carry off the scientist and his prototype Q-Bomb from Columbia University, where he has been blithely unaware of the alarm. They sail off in their brig without the Americans ever knowing they have been invaded. When the rest of the world realizes what has happened, the geopolitical games begin: Russia offers to help Grand Fenwick by removing the Q-Bomb to Moscow for safekeeping; the Americans for their part mobilize troops in Europe and plan to offer their 'protection'. But the Grand Fenwickians will not give up their new leverage: threatening to detonate the bomb if the superpowers intervene, they assemble a League of Little Nations (the Tiny Twenty), and this body will henceforth have the power to subject the other nuclear powers to inspections. The 'Big Four Powers' (named as the United States, the Soviet Union, Britain, and Canada) agree to dismantle their atomic arsenals, and Gloriana and the heroic Tully marry. In the end Kokintz discovers that the Q-Bomb is, in fact, a dud, but he keeps this knowledge to himself.

The Mouse that Roared offers a compendium of the period's preoccupations and fears, but, like the Cold War plays and films we have considered, it combines whimsy and a light comic touch. In some ways it is a reductio ad absurdum of the Ruritanian formula, insofar as Grand Fenwick is not just small but absolutely tiny, some 15 square miles, with a minuscule court, army, and exchequer, and its attack on the United States is not so much David versus Goliath as a gnat versus Goliath. At one level this pokes fun at nationalism, as the Marx Brothers did with Freedonia in *Duck Soup*; and yet here the housefly wins. In fact, the size of Grand Fenwick makes a valid geopolitical point: any small country with a nuclear weapon could wield enormous power. This was not entirely an abstract issue in the early 1950s, as the two superpowers did not enjoy their monopoly on atomic weapons for very long. On 3 October 1952, in 'Operation Hurricane', Britain successfully tested its first atomic bomb in the uninhabited Monte Bello islands off the Australian coast; by 1954 they had plans for a hydrogen bomb. If there were going to be a special relationship between Britain and the United States, Britain did not want to be the hopelessly junior partner and desired its own nuclear arsenal. (France also had a nuclear programme, though it was 1960 before it tested its 'Gerboise Bleue' [blue jerboa] bomb in the Algerian Sahara.) In this light it is not so very difficult to recognize in Grand Fenwick a parodically small and backward version of Britain: Grand Fenwick was founded by an Englishman, and its population is Anglophone; it is a hereditary monarchy; they use the pound sterling as their currency; and its leaders read the London *Times*. But unlike Britain, the duchy is able to set the agenda of world affairs.

The novel is also quite insightful, though, about life in Wibberley's adopted home country. As it appears here, America is a paranoid place, with a population that has had fear drilled into it by the mass media, with commercial forces assisting the state in this. Here is Wibberley's skewering of 'Operation Alert':

> The warning of the coming alert was broadcast, courtesy of numerous automobile dealers, soap, soup, canned meat, furniture and other manufacturers every fifteen minutes twenty-four hours a day for a week. The same warning was given, at the same intervals and courtesy of much the same sponsors, over television... As the days passed, and the warnings continued through every medium of communication—the press, the radio, television, the cinema, from the pulpit and in a host of pronouncements from everyone with the slightest claim to public attention—a mild hysteria began to develop. (78–9)

The result, unsurprisingly, is a country where people are ready to latch onto any story that might give their inchoate anxieties a more definite shape.

When Tully's chainmail-clad group are seen by a Civil Defense decontamination unit, they are taken for Martian invaders, and the civilian population, driven into the subway stations by Operation Alert, almost welcome the rumours of aliens that trickle down to them:

> The word of an invasion from Mars... with frightful details of giant beings in metal suits, men equipped with strange and awesome weapons, spread from mouth to mouth among the teeming, scared, credulous multitude in the subway station. Their nerves had been keyed up for a full week. They had been warned of weapons which defeated all attempts of the imagination to describe. They had read innumerable stories of flying saucers; they had devoured a host of books on adventures in space; they had seen movies depicting every kind of invader from every kind of other world. They had been huddled underground and kept there, and they swallowed the story of an invasion from Mars, readily, avidly, and almost with relief. *At last they knew who the enemy was* whose onslaught they had been prepared to meet for seven days.   (105, my emphasis)

Grand Fenwick, by contrast, may be a quirky anachronism in the modern world, but its tiny population remains sane and level-headed, unfazed by the forces arrayed against them. Wibberley's ending, which sees the superpowers reined in by a league of nations, is far-fetched, perhaps, but no more so than the idea of Mutually Assured Destruction, whereby it was thought that no nuclear war would take place as long as the United States and the Soviet Union both possessed large enough nuclear arsenals to destroy each other.

The next novel in the series, *Beware of the Mouse* (1958), is a sort of prequel set in the Middle Ages, though it takes a few indirect swipes at the arms race. It was not until 1962 that Wibberley returned to modern times with *The Mouse on the Moon*, which sees the tiny country enter the space race. Again the Cold War provides the immediate context, the space programmes of the United States and the USSR being driven not just by international one-upmanship but by the wish to control space and potentially weaponize it.[45] It is the near future (1968), and the happy ending of *The Mouse That Roared* is unraveling:

> Possessed of the Bomb, Grand Fenwick had formed a League of Little Nations... and had been able to enforce an atomic inspection of the other nations. An uneasy peace between East and West ensued. But the inspection, the result of coercion rather than sincere agreement, was not working. Atomic rearmament was going on in spite of it. The bigger nations grew bigger and more menacing. The smaller nations dwindled to insignificance. The rivalry for control of the earth was even being taken into space, so that mastery of the moon and the planets was now part of the ambitions of East and West.   (4)[46]

Meanwhile in Grand Fenwick the Count of Mountjoy also feels that things are going badly: he cannot afford modern plumbing for the castle, nor a new fur coat for the Duchess, so he decides once again to use East–West rivalries to Grand Fenwick's advantage. The US president having made a number of speeches about the internationalization of space exploration, Mountjoy decides to take him at his word, requesting a loan from the United States of $550,000 to finance a manned Grand Fenwickian rocket to the moon and the purchase of an imperial sable coat for the Duchess (the $50,000). The United States decides that this is too small an amount and that a loan of $50 million will look like they genuinely wish for the internationalization of space, 'so that the moon does not become a second Berlin, divided between East and West' (24). (Berlin had become an icon of the divisions of the Cold War, thanks to the Berlin Blockade of 1948–9 and the construction of the Berlin Wall in 1961.) But to the astonishment of all concerned, Grand Fenwick does go to the moon. Dr Kokintz comes up with a new fuel derived from a rare element, Pinotium, found in Pinot Grand Fenwick, and, with the help of an old Saturn rocket donated by the United States, he constructs a space-worthy vessel of their own. The world is electrified by the news:

> Radio and television programs were interrupted to put it immediately on the air. Newspapers replated, flinging extra editions out on the streets in every city of the globe, and suddenly it was as if the whole distracted world had been silenced and all eyes and ears were directed towards the tiny Duchy tucked away in the Northern Alps between France and Switzerland.   (90)

US newspapers are a little more sceptical of this blow to their nation's prestige, with headlines such as 'Lilliput Heads For Moon In Junked U.S. Rocket' (92). Nonetheless, the Grand Fenwick team, made up of Kokintz and Vincent, Mountjoy's engineer son, reach the moon. They land and plant the Grand Fenwick flag just ahead of Russian and US teams, who have set off to 'help' them.

Despite its farcical elements and cynical view of politics, the novel reminds us that the world is a fragile place, threatened by the build up of nuclear arsenals. As Kokintz and Vincent survey the bleak lunar landscape, their own planet comes into view:

> Earth raised herself over the lunar desolation—a lovely huge blue liquid jewel, hung in a sky of sable. The sight was so entrancing that neither of them could speak... 'I never knew it was so beautiful' said Vincent at last. 'It is lovely beyond everything else in the heavens.'
>
> 'It is our home,' said Dr Kokintz simply and sadly.   (118)

In 1962 it seemed quite possible that it was a home that could be destroyed overnight.

The Mouse on the Screen

Given the essential Britishness of Grand Fenwick it is, perhaps, predictable that the film version of *The Mouse That Roared* (1959) was a Shepperton rather than a Hollywood affair, though it was directed by one American, Jack Arnold, and co-produced by two others, Walter Shenson and Carl Foreman. Shenson had optioned the *Saturday Evening Post* serial, and he enrolled Foreman, who was himself something of a Cold War victim: he had moved to Britain after his appearance before the House Un-American Activities Committee had made him unemployable in Hollywood; his *High Noon* is seen as a veiled attack on HUAC.[47] With a script by Roger MacDougall and Stanley Mann, *The Mouse That Roared* is essentially a Peter Sellers vehicle, with Sellers playing the roles of the Duchess Gloriana, the Count of Mountjoy, and Tully Bascombe.[48] Arnold was better known for such Cold War science-fiction features as *The Creature from the Black Lagoon* (1954), but he brought a lighter touch to *The Mouse that Roared*. With its cartoon titles and tongue-in-cheek voiceover, it captures the puckish spirit of Wibberley's novels, while also injecting a little more nuclear menace. The film follows the novel, with a few changes to the romance plot and to characterization. Gloriana is now the eccentric elderly widow of Leopold of Bosnia-Herzegovina and Tully a rather dreamy incompetent who cannot shoot an arrow. He is also, though, the hereditary Grand Constable of the Grand Fenwick army, aided by his more effective Sergeant, Will (William Hartnell, later the first Doctor Who.) Love interest, and some American star power, appears in the form of Jean Seberg as Helen, beautiful daughter of Professor Kokintz (David Kossoff), and in the end she and the hapless but curiously resourceful Tully are united.

Among the film's most striking scenes are those set in New York (see Plate 5.1). Following the novel, Tully and his men arrive in their dilapidated French tugboat just as a massive Air Raid Drill comes into effect, and they have Manhattan all to themselves. While the scenes of Tully's chain-mail troops clanking around were clearly done on a sound stage, the shots that show Manhattan's mid-town canyons completely empty are eerily post-apocalyptic. To make this a little less chilling, we see New Yorkers making the best of the Air Raid Drill by dancing to the radio in the underground shelters, but the net effect makes for uneasy comedy. Some of the film's other most successful touches are its inclusion of non-diegetic visual elements, including footage of an actual atomic test to give us a sense of what would happen if Kokintz's Q-Bomb should accidently fall, as it almost does on several occasions. The deadpan voiceover assures us that 'Ladies and gentlemen, this is not the end of our film. But we thought we should prepare you, and put you in the mood.' Again, in 1959 this must have been rather black comedy. The most biting satirical scenes occur late in the film when the Quadium bomb has reached Grand Fenwick, and the representatives of the various powers (Russia, the United States, Great Britain) have gathered at the border to offer their 'help' to the new nuclear power. To pass the time the bored ambassadors play a game of Diplomacy: to these high-level players the fate of the people affected by their gleeful dice-throwing is of little interest.[49] The aleatory nature of nuclear politics also underlies an extended visual gag sequence near the film's end, a sort of football game using the Q-Bomb: this is a game in which nobody wants to be left holding the ball.

Appropriately enough, one of the film's first screenings was at Ireland's Cork Film Festival. The *Irish Times* identified it as part of the long Ruritanian tradition that made hay of the 'pocket-sized principality'—'I suppose we all enjoy the idea of the world's smallest power humbling the world's greatest'— and it suggested readers go to see it 'if the world situation is getting you down'.[50] The *Mouse* was also well received in the USA, where Bosley Crowther of the *New York Times* thought the extended joke wore a little thin at times but nonetheless felt that the assembled talents 'whip up a lot of cheerful nonsense that makes wild fun of the awesome instruments of modern war and does so in terms of social burlesque and sheer Mack Sennett farce'.[51] The UK premiere was at the Odeon in Marble Arch: as a publicity stunt, invitations were sent to the representatives of smaller countries only, including Liberia, Yemen, and Nepal.[52]

This comic film has a sombre Cold War afternote. In August 1979, the 40-year-old Seberg was found dead in her car in Paris; she had taken an overdose of barbiturates, after a decade-long struggle with depression. Her mental illness, however, seems to have been exacerbated by her persecution by the FBI, who saw her as a dangerous figure of the left; a supporter of the Black Panthers, as well of more mainstream Civil Rights groups, she had been targeted in a campaign of surveillance and misinformation that had aimed to 'cheapen her image with the general public'.[53]

The Mouse on the Moon (UK, 1963) follows the visual style of the earlier film, including its use of cartoon credits. Directed by Richard Lester, who had worked on the *Goons* television series, it is less of a star vehicle and more of an ensemble piece than the earlier film, though Terry-Thomas steals the film as the comically incompetent spy, Maurice Spender, now a British rather than a Russian agent as in the novel. David Kossoff returns as Kokintz, but the other main parts go to a new cast: Margaret Rutherford plays the eccentric and bibulous Duchess Gloriana; Ron Moody is Mountjoy; the hapless Vincent is played by Bernard Cribbins; and June Ritchie plays the part of Cynthia. Britain features a good deal more prominently than it does in the novel, with John Le Mesurier in the role of the British UN delegate who decides to find out what the United States is up to with its Grand Fenwick loan. Indeed, like the earlier film *The Mouse that Roared, The Mouse on the Moon* emphasizes that Grand Fenwick is a refracted Britain. As the voiceover introduces Grand Fenwick as the 'smallest, least progressive country in the world... [a place that] clings loyally to her British traditions'; on screen we see a military parade that looks very familiar: 'One could almost imagine oneself back in London's Horseguards' Parade.' There are several gags along the same lines. Grand Fenwick's youthful protesters look like they have just wandered in from the Carnaby Street of the swinging sixties; their placards proclaim 'Keep off the Moon' 'And out of the Common Market'. The British television broadcast of the launch makes much of the fact that one of the astronauts will be wearing a British-made watch—the only British technology being used: 'Let no one say Great Britain is lagging behind.' Once America and Russia see a demonstration of the Grand Fenwick rocket, they scramble to send off their own. John Phillips, whom we met earlier as the US Ambassador to Concordia, appears here as the senior US diplomat, Bracewell, who leads their programme, and one of his team is a German rocket scientist who unconsciously gives a Nazi salute— anticipating *Dr Strangelove*, which was released the following year. There are a few nice comic details in the moon-landing sequence, including the sight of the Russian cosmonauts trying to construct a wall from moon rock— shades of the Berlin Wall. While the novel ends with Grand Fenwick's claim to the moon safely assured, the film shows the returned astronauts of all three nations squabbling over who got there first, and the closing shot is of a hideous astronaut statue, and its logo: *Per Harmoniam Ad Lunum*, glossed as 'Togetherness—Moonwise'. *The Mouse on the Moon* was well received on both sides of the Atlantic. The *New York Times* saw it as a 'delightful confounding of the great powers', while the London *Times* felt that it was more successful than its predecessor: with 'little message to speak of…[and] goonish gags', the film was a 'strangely likeable bundle of British rubbish'.[54] The reviewer seems to have missed the film's sideswipes at Britain as a Ruritanian territory trying to compete on the world stage as a third super-power, but without the money or technology to do so.

The Mouse's Long Tail

Grand Fenwick's later outings are often entertaining, but they did not enjoy the Zeitgeist-based success of the earlier novels, and neither of them was filmed. *The Mouse on Wall Street* (1969) looks at the more fantastic aspects of the financial markets and is less concerned with the Cold War. However, the last in the series, *The Mouse That Saved The West* (1981), returns to Wibberley's original focus. The young Duchess is now in her forties, a widow, and Mountjoy is truly an elder statesman. But as with the previous novels in the series, the focus is less on the characters and more on the issues of the day, this time the energy crisis that was triggered by revolution in Iran in 1979. The crisis, though, is clearly framed as a Cold War problem, and in the background is the Soviet invasion of Afghanistan as well as anti-American sentiment in Iran. When spiralling oil prices threaten the world economy— and deprive Mountjoy of his regular supply of hot water—he feels that it is time for Grand Fenwick to intervene once again in world affairs. He and a global oil mogul, Alfonso Birelli, conceive a scheme to pretend that oil has been discovered in the tiny duchy, relieving fears of a shrinking world sup-ply. Matters become more complicated when the incompetent geologists recruited by Mountjoy to bolster the story of a Grand Fenwickian oil field really do strike oil. But more dramatically, Mountjoy also plans to shift the balance of global power by giving the Arab states the Quadium bomb: with such a weapon, he explains to a Saudi Sheik, they can face the United States as an equal and stand up to Soviet pressure:

> Mountjoy reviewed the situation. The world supremacy of the OPEC nations, particularly those situated around the Persian Gulf, had made them a prime target for annexation by the Soviet Union. The anti-American moves in oil-rich Iran, and the Soviet adventure into Afghanistan, against which no countermove had been made by the United States, undoubtedly encouraged the Soviet planners to believe that if they move militarily into the Arab nations, the American response might be equally ineffective.   (146)

To protect the Arab nations, Grand Fenwick eventually gives them the Q-bomb—still a dud, of course. The novel ends with Kokintz's discovery of a source of free energy, which Mountjoy strictly forbids him from revealing, in the interests of global stability. It is, perhaps, a less successful comic fantasy than its predecessors, not least because, as the quoted passage indicates, Wibberley seems a little too eager to drive home his points about global affairs. *Kirkus Reviews* felt that it was 'pleasant, though a bit too talky when the oil economics is being explained: a just-passable sequel, with a handful of good chuckles, for *Mouse* enthusiasts'.[55]

When Wibberley died two years later it was only the first two novels in the Mouse series that were mentioned in his *New York Times* obituary. *The Mouse that Roared* and *The Mouse on the Moon* had captured the mood of their era in a way that the later novels failed to do. The independent Duchy of Grand Fenwick was at its most appealing when it seemed like the whole world was being carved up into East and West; the tiny feudal territory satirized Britain's lingering delusions of global power, but it also provided an imaginary space outside the binary logic of the Cold War. More than anything, perhaps, Wibberley's updated Ruritania had allowed people to laugh at their fears at a time when Armageddon really did seem to be just around the corner.

Ten years after the *Mouse* series ended the Cold War was effectively over. Its icy grip had lasted almost 50 years, and the political, physical, social, and mental vestiges lingered long after—indeed they linger still. Nonetheless, the formal end of the conflict was a major watershed, and if in the West the fearful spectre of the Soviet Union was soon replaced by the more amorphous phantasms of the 'War on Terror', the immediate danger of nuclear war receded. A whole vocabulary of fear—MAD, H-bombs, the missile gap, nuclear winter—gradually drifted from everyday use, and such places as Concordia and Grand Fenwick were no longer needed as glasses held up to the world's nuclear folly. But as the final chapter shows, Ruritania, that most adaptable and durable of tinsel territories, lives on. A staple of children's fiction in the first half of the twentieth century, in the 2000s Ruritania invaded the realm of young adult fiction, just as 'princess culture', and the relentless marketing of princess-themed films, clothes, and accessories to little girls, were taking hold.

6

The Ruritanian Makeover

The Princess Diaries and Princess Culture

Churchill's Iron Curtain was a powerful political metaphor for a partitioned world, but from August 1961 it also took on physical form as the Berlin Wall, built to stop mass emigration from the German Democratic Republic to the West. When in November 1989 free movement was restored between East and West Germany, and the crowds began to tear down the wall itself, it heralded the end of a political winter that had lasted more than 40 years. By the end of 1991 the Soviet Union had formally disappeared as a political entity, and the Warsaw Pact was dissolved. Geopolitical tensions between Russia and its neighbours, and indeed between it and the United States, continued, but the Cold War was over. This was a genuine historical watershed, dramatically transforming the lives of millions.

In the realm of culture, the drawing back of the Iron Curtain also had momentous effects. Genre and literary fiction alike were retooled to match the contours of a world in which the great binary oppositions organized around East and West were no longer relevant and in which Francis Fukuyama's much-cited 'End of History' actually seemed to be in prospect. The writers of popular thrillers had to work up a new set of plausible villains; and at the more literary end of the market, as Samuel Cohen has shown, there was a mushrooming of historical novels that sought to interrogate that 'end of history'.[1] A decade later, in the wake of the attacks of 11 September 2001, the map of a new *paysage moralisé* superimposed itself on the older model, with Middle-Eastern terrorists replacing Communists as the new bogeyman of the West, and Islamic fundamentalism emerging as the great ideological threat to its putative freedoms. In the small corner of cultural history that we have been exploring here, the end of the Cold

War removed Ruritania's role as a space outside the 'spheres of influence' of the superpowers. There was no longer an imaginative need for a Concordia or a Grand Fenwick. Indeed the original of the species seemed to be losing its role too, with no film version of *Zenda* after the Peter Sellers parody of 1979 and no television adaptation after the 1984 BBC production. Occasional homages have continued to appear in fiction, including John Spurling's *After Zenda* (1995), which imagines the twentieth-century history of Ruritania through the adventures of Flavia and Rassendyll's love child, and K. J. Charles's *The Henchmen of Zenda* (2018), which spices up Hope's world with homo-erotic interest. But there have been few signs that Hope's original is about to be revived in any more direct form.

However, one significant variant of Ruritanian fiction has entered some-thing of a boom period: the female-centred strain pioneered in McCutcheon's 1904 *Beverly of Graustark*. In 2000 the American writer Meg Cabot pub-lished a young adult novel, *The Princess Diaries*, the first in what has become at the time of writing a series of fourteen young adult novels, three middle school novels, and one book aimed at adult readers. Cabot had previously written historical romances under the pseudonym Patricia Cabot, but this was her first foray into YA fiction.[2] The books follow the comic tribulations of Mia Thermopolis, an American teenager who discovers one day that she is really the Princess of Genovia, a small principality not unlike Monaco. Acquired for an advance of $8,000 by a young assistant editor at Harper Collins, the novel sold slowly but steadily from a small first print run before becoming a bestseller.[3] It was given a massive boost in profile by the highly successful Disney film adaptation that followed in 2001, featuring the rela-tively unknown Anne Hathaway as Mia and Julie Andrews as her formidable royal *grand-mère*. In 2004 a second film appeared, *The Princess Diaries 2: Royal Engagement*; more loosely based on Cabot's work, it picks up Mia's story after college and is set in Genovia itself. As we shall see, the runaway success of the *Princess Diaries* is not entirely sui generis, Ruritanian settings having long been favourites among the authors of children's fiction. But there is more than literary history at work here: the *Diaries* also owe something to the real-life American princess story of Grace Kelly, who became Princess Grace of Monaco in 1956, and the story has been further shaped by the phenomenon of contemporary 'princess culture', in which Disney has played no small part. As we shall see in this chapter, *The Princess Diaries* represents a significant break with older fantasies of overnight royal status, a break that I will suggest resonates with America's changing sense of its place in the world.

The Princess Diaries

Cabot's novel takes its epigraph from Frances Hodgson Burnett's *A Little Princess* (1905). The heroine of that book, Sara Crewe, goes from riches to rags and back, and she observes that it is easy to be a princess when dressed for the part but 'a great deal more of a triumph to be one all the time when no one else knows it'.[4] It is a somewhat oblique clue to Cabot's novel in which our heroine does not want people to know that she really is a princess, but they find out anyway, forcing her to come to terms with her new role. When we first meet her, Mia Thermopolis is a 14-year-old American high school student who lives with her artist mother and their cat, Fat Louie, in a loft apartment in Greenwich Village; her father, long separated from her mother, lives overseas, in Genovia. A small territory situated somewhere between France and Italy, Genovia seems to bear more than a passing resemblance to Monaco, and Mia's Monegasque cousins are mentioned in passing. But on one of his visits her father reveals to her that he is not just a Genovian politician, as she has always believed, but the Prince of Genovia. She herself is thus no mere Mia Thermopolis but Amelia Mignonette Grimaldi Thermopolis Renaldi, Crown Princess of Genovia, and her domineering, sidecar-sipping grandmother is really the Dowager Princess. The novel follows Mia's attempts to assimilate this strange knowledge, while also nurturing a crush on the school heart-throb, Josh Richter, maintaining her friendship with the rather fierce Lilly Moscovitz, and absorbing her mother's romantic involvement with one of her teachers.

The diary of the novel's title is kept by Mia at her mother's urging: she wants her daughter to express her feelings about the blossoming relationship between her mother and Mia's algebra teacher, Mr Gianini. It records Mia's complex anxieties and desires but also becomes the receptacle for occasional stabs at algebra, and her many 'Things to do' lists, which comically combine the practical ('Buy cat litter') and the aspirational ('Achieve self-actualization'). This latter-day Beverly of Graustark has all of the usual teenage insecurities about her looks, regarding herself as a lanky 'flat-chested' 'freak' in size 8 shoes, sporting 'triangular' hair, and the age-appropriate roller-coaster of emotions she endures is often conveyed typographically in the text ('I CAN'T BELIEVE SHE'S DOING THIS TO ME!').[5] But, of course, unlike most teenagers Mia also has a whole set of other concerns: the clandestine romance between her mother and Mr Gianini is nothing compared to her own royal secret; and neither can be kept quiet forever.

Mia's situation is one that many people would regard as more of a delight than a trial. As she herself notes, her high school nemesis, the golden-haired teen beauty Lara Weinberger, would probably love to be a princess. That Mia herself does not feel this way is partly determined by her feelings about being the centre of attention; after her father's revelations she goes to see her favourite animal, the polar bear, at Central Park Zoo, noting that 'it must suck to have people looking at you all day' (38). The story, then, has fairy-tale qualities, but it is a fairy tale in which the business of being a princess is shown to be quite problematic for a modern girl who would rather wear Doc Martens and overalls than Chanel and heels.

Although the novel is relentlessly light in tone, like other young adult fiction it shows the young heroine confronting some serious issues: e.g., tensions between her unmarried parents; her father's testicular cancer; and bullying at the hands of Lara. And though she is no gun-toting Beverly, Mia overcomes her all-caps emotional turmoil to deal with these issues. She is still uncomfortable in her new role at the end of the novel, but she does begin to count her blessings, and she realizes that Lilly's older brother, computer genius Michael, who makes her laugh, is a far more suitable object for her affections than jock Josh Richter. The scales finally fall from her eyes when the narcissistic Josh invites her to the School's Cultural Diversity dance only with a view to attracting media attention to himself, engineering a kiss for the cameras on the school steps.

Broad comedy is the dominant mode, as when Mia gets the hiccups when her father tells her he is the Prince of Genovia, though there are more subtle literary touches too, as when Mr Gianini suggests to Mia that she would make a good Eliza Doolittle in the school production of *My Fair Lady*, anticipating her later 'Princess lessons' at the hands of her grandmother and her dramatic change in social status. It is also a very knowing novel when it comes to the mediated gender 'scripts' in which Mia is immersed, and the text is peppered with references to books, films, television, and Broadway shows that offer contrasting visions of the feminine, from Catherine Marshall's inspirational historical novel *Christy* (1967) to the 1990s stage musical *Beauty and the Beast* to the television series *Buffy the Vampire Slayer* (1997–2003).[6]

Disney spin-off *Beauty and the Beast* is Mia's favorite show, whereas Buffy is Michael's ideal woman, which hardly encourages Mia to believe that he might be interested in a girl like her. Gentle fun is also poked at the improbable scenarios of the romance novels read by Mia's new friend, Tina Hakim Baba. Disney looms large in Mia's world, in keeping with its dominance in children's popular culture, though it almost seems at times as if the novel foresees its own elevation into the ranks of Disney films, e.g., 'I don't care what Lilly says about Walt Disney and his misogynist overtones' (28); 'Princess Amelia Renaldo...it sounds like the name of some stupid line of make-up, or of somebody from a Disney movie' (39); though we also have 'Lilly started in about the Disneyfication of America, and how Walt Disney was really a fascist, and then everybody started wondering if it was really true about his body being frozen under the castle in Anaheim' (172–3).

Ruritania and Children's Fiction

Mia's up-to-the-minute diary entries descend from such foundational epistolary novels as Samuel Richardson's *Pamela* (1740) and Henry Fielding's parody, *Shamela* (1741). The novel's more direct antecedents include a number of late twentieth-century works, including Sue Townsend's 1982 bestseller, *The Secret Diary of Adrian Mole, Aged 13¾*, which amusingly reveals the inner life of the young Mole.[7] There are also echoes of the comic body-image and relationship anxieties of Helen Fielding's Bridget Jones, a latter-day Elizabeth Bennet, whose *Diary* began as a column in the *Independent* newspaper in 1995 before appearing in novel form (1996, 1999) and providing material for three enormously successful films (2001, 2004, 2016). In some respects Mia is a teen Bridget who just happens to be a princess.

But the novel also descends from a long line of Ruritanian children's fiction. The Frances Hodgson Burnett epigraph is in part a playful piece of indirection, since it is not so much *A Little Princess* that Cabot's Cinderella story directly recalls but Hodgson Burnett's later novel, *The Lost Prince* (1915), a variant for children of the Ruritanian line that we have been following. In that novel the boy-hero, Marco, helps to restore the rightful ruler of Samavia, a beautiful but unhappy principality found 'north of Beltrazo and east of Jiardasia'; the rightful ruler, it turns out, is his own father, and he himself is not plain Marco Loristan but Prince Ivor of Samavia. Hodgson Burnett was one of the first writers to realize that what worked for adult adventure romances would also appeal to children, and Ruritania went on to a long career in twentieth-century children's literature. One of the best-known instances is Violet Needham's 'Stormy Petrel' series, from *The Black Riders* (1939) to *The Red Rose of Ruvina* (1957). In the first in the series, the 11-year-old Dick Fauconbois (later the 'Stormy Petrel') becomes involved in political intrigue in a Ruritanian world; in *The Emerald Crown* (1940), young Etonian Basil Alexander discovers he is heir to the throne of Flavonia, though he must find the lost Emerald Crown to establish his claim. Like *The Lost Prince*, this a form of modernized fairy tale, recalling the pattern of behaviour that Sigmund Freud describes in his 1909 essay 'Family Romances', in which children imagine that they are really the offspring of much grander parents.

Other children's writers dipped into the Ruritanian well for less exotic stories. Biggles helps out the state of Maltovia in Captain W. E. Johns' *Biggles Goes to War* (1938). In both Noel Streatfeild's *The House in Cornwall* (1940) and Enid Blyton's *The Secret of Spiggy Holes* (1940), a Ruritanian ruler sequestered in contemporary Britain is rescued with the help of young protagonists. Such tales are in effect Buchan's *Castle Gay* turned into a school-holidays adventure, and, like their original, they owe more than a little to the presence of the boy-King Michael on the Romanian throne in the 1920s and the British press reports of May 1928 that Prince Carol had chartered two aircraft at Croydon with a view to secretly returning to Romania.[8] (British writers weren't the only ones who ventured over the border into Ruritania in these turbulent years for European politics: the eighth volume in the Belgian cartoonist Hergé's Tintin 1939 series, *Le Sceptre d'Ottokar*, sees the eponymous hero foil a plot against the King of Syldavia; the name of the novel's villain, Müsstler, is a none-too-oblique reference to both Mussolini and Hitler.) Even in later novels in which Ruritania is not centre-stage, it continued to enjoy a certain usefulness, as in Lorna Hill's ballet-school novel *Rosanna Joins the Wells* (1956), in which the young dancer is helped by Leopold, the former King of Slavonia.

Cabot's plot most closely resembles the *Lost Prince/Emerald Crown* strand among these stories, in which a young protagonist discovers that he or she has royal blood. But Cabot updates the earlier formula in significant ways: not only is adventure replaced by comic misadventure, but Mia's discovery of her royal status is a source of neither happiness nor awe. Casting considerable doubt on the desirability of being a modern princess, she even seems to question the value of monarchy itself. Mia is horrified at the attention her status will draw to her, for one thing, but her dislike of her 'Princess lessons' is also driven by her strong reluctance to embrace the version of adult femininity that the role—as prescribed by her grandmother—comprises. She has no wish to be like the Lara Weinbergers of her acquaintance, who wear nylon stockings, use make-up, and dress in chic but uncomfortable clothes. In this the novel is quite different to the film, which follows much more closely the long-established 'makeover' formula whereby the supposedly ugly duckling heroine comes to embrace her own physical transformation and finds her ideal mate.[9] Mia is made over in the novel—new hairstyle, new nails, new clothes—but that transformation remains rather secondary, and the story does not end with the heroine and Michael united at last, even if that does seem like a future possibility. At the same time Cabot does not wholly reject the older formula: Mia does remain a princess, and she finds that it is not all bad.

Monaco and Genovia

Cabot's modern American princess is more than the product of literary history, of course. As the series' occasional references to Princess Grace, Monaco, and the Grimaldis indicate, Cabot is also drawing on the royal mystique and glamour that came to surround the 26-year-old actress Grace Kelly when, in April of 1956, she became Her Serene Highness Princess Grace by marrying Prince Rainier III of Monaco.[10] Kelly was becoming, in effect, a real-life Beverly of Graustark, and occasional references to *Graustark* in newspaper accounts of the match suggest that memories of McCutcheon's work had not entirely dimmed, even if the *New York Times* seemed to think that Graustark appeared somewhere in *The Prisoner of Zenda*.[11] The Irish-American Kelly was already famous in her own right, having starred in a string of successful films, including *High Noon* (1952), *Rear Window* (1954), and *High Society* (1956), but this royal marriage took her to a new level of international celebrity. If the 'dollar princesses' of the turn of the century had married into the English aristocracy, becoming Ladies and occasionally Duchesses, Kelly went one better in the 'Wedding of the Century': she became an actual American princess, as well as acquiring some 142 other royal titles, since her husband was also the Duke of Valentinois, Duc d'Estouteville, Duc de Mazarin, Duc de Mayenne, and Prince de Château-Porcien, inter alia. While European and Hollywood royalty largely stayed away, the world's press—estimates of their numbers range from 1,600 to 1,800—gathered in force in Monte Carlo to relay the twin civil and religious ceremonies on 18 and 19 April.[12] American readers had been cheated of their American queen in 1936, when Edward abdicated before marrying Wallis Simpson in a private ceremony, but this time they would have their fairy tale and have it in elaborate detail. Columns reported at length on what Kelly had packed and what the couple would wear, and the cameras captured every moment from her departure from New York aboard the USS *Constitution* to her marriage to Prince Rainier at Saint Nicholas Cathedral to her departure aboard the Monegasque royal yacht for a month-long honeymoon in the Mediterranean.[13] The minutiae of the trip, and of her $30,000 trousseau and her $7,000 wedding dress by MGM designer Helen Rose, were all relayed to an avid public; they could marvel at the 450 yards of fine Brussels lace used in Rose's design or at Aristole Onassis's hiring of a seaplane to drop carnations on Kelly as she arrived.[14]

The pièce de resistance was the live television coverage of the cathedral wedding ceremony. As we saw in chapter 3, Ivor Novello's *Glamorous Night* was oddly prescient in imagining the effect that television would have on royalty, as was made clear by the televised coronation of Queen Elizabeth in 1953, watched by some 20 million.[15] But the Wedding of the Century added another element, and this cocktail of Hollywood celebrity, the older glamour of royalty, and blanket media coverage turned out to be heady indeed. There was even some drama as well as spectacle, of course, insofar as Prince Rainier had been under considerable pressure to marry and provide an heir, since without one the tiny principality reverted to France under a 1918 treaty. (With the birth of Princess Caroline the following year, the future of Monaco was secured; and it was made even more certain with the birth of Prince Albert the following year.) With all these elements in play, some 30 million viewers turned on their sets to see MGM's Wedding of the Century, and millions more saw the newsreel coverage by Pathé and others in cinemas. Whether or not the wedding was a deliberate effort by Rainier and Monaco investor Onassis to boost Monaco's flagging fortunes, as has been suggested, it certainly had that effect.[16] Its consequences in the United States were more evident in the cultural sphere: as Maya Cantu notes, the Broadway stage was thronged for some time with tales of latter-day Cinderellas and European royalty, from *My Fair Lady* (March 1956) to *Happy Hunting* (December 1956); arguably even *The Sound of Music* (1959) belongs to this moment.[17]

Cabot draws on this American princess story in a number of ways to fill out her pocket principality. Genovia is, like Monaco, somewhere on the coast between Italy and France. Like Monaco, it was invaded by the Italians during the Second World War and has a strong interest in promoting its tourist industry, though it does not depend on revenue from gambling. Its ruler, Prince Phillipe, a prematurely bald, American-educated playboy with a string of international girlfriends, bears more than a passing resemblance not to Prince Rainier but to his son, Prince Albert, who, like his sisters, was the subject of endless press coverage in the 1980s and 1990s. Indeed, it is tempting to speculate that Cabot may have come across a newspaper account of a paternity suit taken by a Californian woman, Tamara Rotolo, against Albert in 1992, naming Albert as the father of her daughter, Jazmin—she was later acknowledged as his daughter by Albert, in what one newspaper described as a '*Princess Diaries* moment'.[18]

Princess Culture

The novel may also have taken its cue, though, from the recognizable and distinct 'princess culture' that was coalescing in the 1990s, offering young girls a very particular model of gendered identity. At the time of writing this international trend is still very much with us: 'Princesses are everywhere there are girls. Donning pink tulle dresses and sporting glittering tiaras, little princesses appear in preschools and playgrounds, backyards and bedrooms.'[19] Students of this phenomenon argue that while young girls have been fascinated by princesses for a very long time, the current pink tide is something quite distinct.[20] Its commercial roots are in fact very recent and are linked to one of the world's largest media companies, Disney. Disney had already created a whole series of princess icons in its films, but the Disney Princesses brand itself emerges at almost exactly the same moment as the *Diaries*. In 2000, the year that *The Princess Diaries* was published, Disney marketing employee Andy Mooney noticed that many of the girls attending a *Disney on Ice* show were wearing princess costumes, though Disney did not sell any such outfits, and he realized that they should 'get as much product out there as we possibly can that allows these girls to do what they're doing anyway: projecting themselves into the characters from the classic movies'.[21] The result was the careful repackaging of Disney's existing princess icons (Cinderella, Snow White, Pocahontas, Belle, and others) as the Disney Princesses and the creation of a whole new range of merchandise, including Princess costumes, shoes, tiaras, accessories, DVDs, televisions, dolls, toys, figurines, and tea sets. Would-be princesses (or their parents) could spend less than 10 euros on a fork and knife set or, in the case of the young princess who has everything, purchase the 'Arribas Jewelled Collection, Cinderella Castle Large Figurine' for around 6,000 euros. Ultimately the success of the line led to the creation of new Princess movies like *Frozen* (2013), a sort of cross between *The Snow Queen* and Christina Rossetti's *Goblin Market*. But even before that extraordinarily lucrative property, the Princess line had become a $4 billion industry.[22] Other manufacturers, of course, also saw the possibilities of the princess market, and everything from a princess mobile-phone cover to a princess tent is now available to the parents of any aspiring young royal.

I do not want to suggest that *The Princess Diaries* is simply another variety of this tiara-mania. Indeed, aimed at a slightly older teenage audience, the novel appears to be as much a critique as a part of the princess phenomenon. Mia, as we have noted, does not want to be a princess, and, even when she reconciles herself to the role, she sees it as more constrictive than enabling. Although her favourite Broadway show is the musical version of the Disney film *Beauty and the Beast*, which she has seen seven times, there is very little evidence that Mia aspires to being Belle or wants to live in a fairy-tale world of magical transformation. The list of women she most admires includes one princess—the late Diana, Princess of Wales—but also some very different figures, e.g., Hillary Rodham Clinton, Madonna, and Joan of Arc. (Her grandmother, for her part, thinks that Princess Grace and Coco Chanel should be her models.)

Being a princess for Mia ultimately means attempting to hold onto her sense of self while treading the tricky path to adult femininity. As she learns to at least sometimes change her overalls for couture, she comes to realize that this initially uncomfortable shift does bring with it its own form of power. Her new-found popularity at school may derive for the most part from her royal status, but her grandmother's grooming regime is also a factor. When the young Princess stands up to the nice but rather overpowering Lilly, she records in her diary: 'Maybe it was the fingernails. I never had fingernails before. They sort of made me feel strong.' And although she is slow to admit this, her new look plays some part in steering her and Michael towards each other. He sees her with fresh eyes, and she sees that he finds her attractive: '"Whoa," he said, backing up. I wasn't sure if he said whoa and backed up because of what I'd said, or how I looked' (110). As readers, we tend to favour the latter explanation. Nonetheless, the narrative of Mia's transformation and romantic fulfilment is not a simple one, and although she and Michael come together briefly at the school dance towards the end of the first volume, it takes several more books in the series for Mia to realize that he likes her at least as much as she likes him. While the novel is at one level, then, a modern fairy tale of noble birth, sudden wealth, and social status, it remains somewhat sceptical about the benefits that go with those. There are no magical solutions to Mia's problems. At the novel's close she remains insecure, and socially awkward, though she realizes that her life is not really that bad, especially when 'princess lessons' are cancelled.

Disney Does Ruritania

With Disney's vested interest in princesses, Walt Disney Pictures were quick to option Cabot's novel and issue it in their summer schedule for 2001, as a co-production with Whitney Houston's BrownHouse Productions. Garry Marshall, the director, was an industry veteran who had created such TV sitcoms as *Happy Days, Laverne and Shirley*, and *Mork and Mindy* and had also directed that rather different modern fairy tale, *Pretty Woman*.[23] The screen-play by Gina Wendkos tracks the plot of the novel, but there are some significant differences. Played by 20-year-old newcomer Anne Hathaway, Mia is 15, a year older than in the novel, and she and her mother (Caroline Goodall) live not in a Manhattan loft but in a former San Francisco firehouse.[24] Her father is dead rather than merely resident in Europe, a story change that enlarges the role of Julie Andrews, who plays Mia's grandmother, Queen Clarisse. She is a formidable presence, though far more likeable than in the novel, and is provided with her own romantic subplot. The school's alpha couple, Lana (singer Mandy Moore) and Josh (Erik von Detten), remain prominent, but Tina Hakim Baba has disappeared from the story entirely, as has Mr Gianini. Instead we see more of Mia's stoic but sympathetic bodyguard, Joe (Hector Elizondo, a frequent Marshall collaborator), who is also Queen Clarisse's long-term partner, sub rosa.

With some additional suspense, as in the novel, the story focuses on Mia's uncertainty about her new royal role and her gradual realization that Michael (Robert Schwartzman), not Josh, is the one for her. Hathaway's Mia is more of a standard romantic comedy heroine, though, stumbling from one comic mishap to another. For instance, her humiliation at the hands of Josh and the media is played up: Josh's media kiss takes place at a beach party, at which the press also photograph her changing clothes, and an image of her clad only in a towel appears in the newspapers. (As Roger Ebert drily noted, it is hard to see any contemporary royal family being greatly taken aback by such images.)[25] Nonetheless, her ambivalence about her new identity ends at last when she finds a letter from her dead father, which sets her off on a last-minute drive in the rain to the Genovian Independence Day Ball, where she announces that she has decided that she wants to be Princess Mia after all; she and Michael come together, and there is even a heel-raising kiss in the garden of the Genovian consulate.

Genovia itself is largely an absent presence, though we do get a glimpse of it from Mia's private jet at the end of the film. The real heart of the film is in fact its makeover narrative, which is naturally far more prominent in the visual medium than it is in the novel. Her grandmother teaches her how to walk, eat, and dance in a suitably regal way, to considerable comic effect. And however predictable it is, the film's most memorable scene comes when the frizzy-haired, bespectacled Mia is transformed by stylist Paulo (Larry Miller) and his team into a doe-eyed beauty with a perfect smile and good hair (see Figure 6.1).[26]

Figure 6.1. Anne Hathaway as the madeover Mia in the 2001 film version of *The Princess Diaries* (dir. Garry Marshall). TCD/Prod.DB/Alamy Stock Photo

Of course, as critics pointed out, it did not really take a great deal of work to turn 20-year-old duckling Hathaway into a photogenic swan. Subsequent scenes emphasize her new visual power. Thus the state dinner and in particular the Genovian Independence Day Ball are in the best Ruritanian tradition, but they also create opportunities to spotlight and linger on the madeover Mia in suitably Princess-like dresses. The veteran Julie Andrews was an ideal choice to preside over these transformation and exhibition scenes. Not only had she starred in the Cinderella-like *Sound of Music*, but at Hathaway's age she had played the role of Eliza Doolittle, the Cockney flower-girl transformed into a lady by Professor Henry Higgins (Rex Harrison), in the first Broadway production of *My Fair Lady* in 1956.

Reviews of the film were mixed, with *Variety* suggesting that the film had a 'pre-fab quality' and others seeing a waste of the leads' comic gifts.[27] British magazine *Sight and Sound* growled, 'As a study in America's on-going sense of isolationism, its odd view of democracy, and its blind belief in the superiority of its casual, laid-back way of doing things, this awful film is almost interesting.'[28] Others saw the film as an attempt to reroute the novel towards a more Disney-friendly narrative. Elvis Mitchell of the *New York Times* noted: 'Its happy ending could simply be product placement. The royal castle in Genovia looks like an attraction at the happiest place on Earth. In other words, Mia's going to Disney World!'[29] At least one critic believed that the target audience was not so much girls of Mia's age as '10-year-old girls who think they're 14', which also suggests that the film was aimed at preserving the Disney Princess idea and extending its reach.[30] At any rate, the cinema-going public liked it: the film grossed $108 million in the domestic market, and as of 2018 it had earned over $165 million globally, having cost $26 million to make.[31]

For the 2004 sequel, *The Princess Diaries 2: Royal Engagement*, the producers decided to bypass Cabot's series and to create an original narrative set almost entirely at the Genovian court. Directed again by Garry Marshall, it features most of the original cast, though former love interest Michael does not appear.[32] Shonda Rhimes' screenplay opens with Mia's graduation from the Woodrow Wilson School of Public and International Affairs at Princeton, before taking us to Genovia, which appears in the film to be a composite of Hollywood Europe, with some landscape shots recalling England and others Switzerland; the capital, likewise, is as much alpine *village perché* as Riviera town. As Queen Clarisse plans to step down, Mia is to become Queen of Genovia. But there is a complication: the Genovian Parliament, manipulated by Viscount Mabrey (John Rhys-Davies), rules that Mia can only ascend the throne if she is married; otherwise the crown will go to Mabrey's nephew, Nicholas, Lord Devereaux (Chris Pine, in his first major role). The Princess has just 30 days to find a suitable husband; and while an acceptable candidate is located in the form of Andrew Jacoby (Callum Blue), the English Duke of Kenilworth, there appears to be little magnetism between him and Mia. In the end the American Princess walks out of the wedding, and though she and Nicholas are drawn to each other, she persuades the Genovian Parliament that she can rule alone. The Queen and Joe get married, Mia becomes Queen of Genovia, and the film's final shots show women entering the Genovian Parliament as members for the first time. Like Graustark many years before, Genovia is a place that needs some American can-do spirit, and Mia not only reforms the rules of succession but also manages to brighten the lives of the nation's surprisingly numerous and ethnically diverse orphans, turning the Winter Palace into a new children's shelter.

A plot summary gives very little sense of the film, which, like its predecessor, is largely driven by Hathaway's performance as the likeably klutzy princess and Andrews' turn as the long-suffering Queen who is struggling to make her American granddaughter slightly more regal. Thus while Mia models one elaborate costume after another, the danger of the film becoming a purely static spectacle is allayed by a whole set of sight gags and slapstick episodes, and even the elaborate wedding, with its $50,000 in flowers, is essentially played for laughs. As reviews noted, while Mia has now turned 21, the film 'is still aimed at preteen girls', and the fun is, by and large, their kind of fun, including a giant slumber party at the palace.[33] Maintaining the upbeat mood, pop numbers alternate with wistful strings in the familiar soundtrack pattern of Hollywood romantic comedy, though there is also one awkward duet between Andrews and the pop singer Raven-Symoné, who plays Mia's friend, Princess Asana.[34] Lest we miss the point, the feminist ending, in which Mia is crowned to reign alone, is underscored by another Raven-Symoné song, *This Is My Time*.

And what of Genovia? The film was entirely filmed in Los Angeles, except for some aerial shots of Longford Castle in Wiltshire. Marshall had apparently considered 'going to Czechoslovakia' (sic) to film in Prague 'because it has a lot of castles', but he 'took one look at the world and said, "Genovia's in Burbank"'.[35] And so it is: the capital of Genovia is in the fact the 'Little Europe' set on the backlot of Universal Studios, and all of the palace interiors were

Figure 6.2. Mia inspects her Genovian troops in *The Princess Diaries 2: Royal Engagement* (dir. Garry Marshall, 2004). Entertainment Pictures/Alamy Stock Photo

put together especially for the film, a relatively unusual decision in an era of location shooting (see Figure 6.2).[36] It is a reminder, should it be needed, that Genovia is more a heterotopia for contemporary America than a fantasy about Europe itself. In this respect, of course, it is not so very different from *Beverly of Graustark* and other earlier royal fantasies, for most of which Europe itself was of limited importance.

Some reviewers felt that it was not a very successful flight of fancy, more EuroDisney than Genovia, with the royal palace resembling 'a lesser Marriott'. If Ruritanian fantasy had always conjured with 'cardboard kingdoms', this was very thin cardboard indeed. It was largely dismissed as a run-of-the-mill sequel lacking the original's charm, an 'unfunny, cheap looking romp aimed at the 'tween girl audience' and 'too blandly insubstantial to expand its appeal beyond its target demographic'.[37] One reviewer noted with approval the film's overt feminism message, 'promot[ing] a positive image of female empowerment for its young audience'. Yet as Scott Brown of *Entertainment Weekly* put it, 'the film's generic feminism pales beside its bloated sense of privilege'.[38] The film does indeed seem to suggest that women should be recognized as the equal of men, but only in a deeply hierarchical world in which the lucky few are born to royal position and others are naturally subjects: the rules of gender may bend and even break, but the rules of class seem immutable. Despite, or perhaps because of, these contradictions, the film was a commercial success, if not quite at the level of its predecessor. The *Princess Diaries* franchise appears to be still thriving. By 2014 the novels in the series had sold some 5 million copies.[39] The possibility of a third film became less likely after the death of director Garry Marshall in July 2016, but stories about it continue to appear in the press, and a number of the principals have said they would like to make a third film.[40]

What does the multi-platform success of the *Diaries* tell us about what Ruritania or Graustark means now? The most striking aspect is that older daydreams of a match between new American power and wealth and old European prestige seem to have been superseded. Now you can be an American Princess without marrying and without ever having to step outside the United States: Mia just *is* a princess. She is uncomfortable with her new prestige, and indeed Mia's discomfort is very much the point of the first novel, if not the whole series. But perhaps the Princess doth protest too much, and we might see this reluctance as a sort of screen fantasy that dissimulates a deeper narcissistic fantasy that links Mia Thermopolis the American Princess and America's more general sense of its place in the world. Fiction does not simply reflect national politics, but as we have seen there are structures of feeling, to use Raymond Williams's phrase, that link the two: just as the spirit of adventure in Hope's *Zenda* drew from as it contributed to the self-assurance of the British empire, Graustarkian reveries of American royalty were always bound up with the contemporary sense of America's national vigour and manifest destiny. This confidence in America's uniqueness has not gone away, of course. After the First World War, as the United States displaced Britain as a global power, the manifest destiny of McCutcheon's era was replaced with a more strident sense of America's international preeminence. During the Cold War the idea that America was the 'leader of the free world' became an unironic part of national political discourse; and the collapse of the Soviet Union, which left the United States as the last superpower standing, seemed to confirm that view of the country's special status as a shining city on a hill.[41] Does this understandable, but potentially malignant, sense of grandiosity trickle down? In his 1979 jeremiad *The Culture of Narcissism: American Life in an Age of Diminishing Expectations*, Christopher

Lasch saw evidence everywhere of clinical narcissism, the unintended consequence of unfettered capitalist individualism, inter alia. More recently, Jean M. Twenge and W. Keith Campbell have written about what they see as an 'epidemic of narcissism' in the United States, which they attribute to such diverse factors as parenting, the Internet, and the credit boom.[42] But at some level, we might speculate, individual narcissism could simply be a symptom of the political variety. Against this backdrop, the blue-blood fantasies of *The Princess Diaries* seem not merely predictable but inevitable.

Afterword

'You're the Prince of Castlebury, and I'm just a poor girl from Buffalo'
(A Princess for Christmas)

Ruritania and its offspring have provided looking-glass versions of Britain and the United States for more than 120 years now. In the late nineteenth century, pocket kingdoms offered pageantry, adventure, and romance; on the musical stage of the early twentieth century, they represented the pull of tradition and the past; during the Cold War they provided an image of a small world outside the madness of Mutually Assured Destruction; and in the 2000s they appeared in Young Adult fiction as both critique and embrace of Princess Culture. But what does the future hold for Ruritania?

In the United States, following the success of *The Princess Diaries*, there has been something of a revival of Graustarkian films of plucky American women finding love and tiaras in picturesque European kingdoms. With more than a whiff of Mills and Boon about them, these narratives cleave to 'traditional' romance plots far more than the *Diaries* itself, which even in its Disney version pushes against the Cinderella story of commoners and royalty, though they share its fascination with Old World prestige, courtly trappings, and pocket-sized principalities. An early instance is *The Prince and Me* (dir. Martha Coolidge, 2004), a successful feature film that was followed by three straight-to-video sequels (2006, 2008, 2010). In the original, Julia Stiles plays an academically focused Midwesterner, Paige Morgan, at the University of Wisconsin who falls in love with a visiting student from Denmark, Eddie (Luke Mably), only to find that he is really Crown Prince Edvard. Since his father (James Fox) is about to abdicate because of ill health, the formerly wayward Eddie will soon be King, and our heroine is torn between her original dream of working with Medécins Sans Frontières and the prospect of becoming Queen of Denmark.[1] This is not, strictly speaking, a Ruritanian plot, as Edvard is set to rule a real country, rather than some gossamer imaginary statelet, even if the film's vision of feudal Denmark must have startled most Danish viewers. Nonetheless, *The Prince and Me* and its sequels do contain many of the usual tropes of disguise, pageantry, and the constrictions of court protocol.

The successful series paved the way for a host of small-screen royal love stories that are more squarely set in tinsel Ruritanian territory. These family-friendly romantic comedies have been aimed specifically at the Christmas market, though it is not clear whether this seasonal mutation came about because Christmas is a time of the year associated with Old World tradition, because of the linkage between Christmas and fairy tales, or simply because reliably formulaic content was needed for the Christmas television market.[2] In *A Princess for Christmas* (2011), for instance, our heroine, Jules Daly (Katie McGrath), lives in Buffalo and is guardian to her nephew and niece, her sister and her husband having died suddenly, in an accident we assume. Jules loses her job just before Christmas, but her luck turns when she is invited by the children's paternal grandfather (Roger Moore), a duke, to spend the holidays at his castle in the aptly named Castlebury, somewhere in Europe. After surprisingly few complications she and her brother-in-law's brother (Sam Heughan), who happens to be a prince, fall in love, and all ends happily ever after; she even manages to find time along the way to teach the gruff Duke the real meaning of Christmas.[3]

The film originally aired on the Hallmark Channel (Crown Media Family Networks), which has perfected the art of producing cheap and quick feel-good 'family' TV films, aimed primarily at women.[4] Each costs around $2 million and is made in just a few weeks.[5] In the last few years the channel has returned to the same castles-in-the-snow formula with such features as *A Royal Christmas* (2014, Cordinia), *Crown for Christmas* (2015, Winshire), and *Christmas at the Palace* (2018, San Senova), while *Royal Matchmaker* (2018, Voldavia) makes use of the same basic recipe, though without the snow, for their 'Spring Movies Series'. Other channels have attempted to trump Hallmark's court cards, with Starz producing *A Prince for Christmas* (2015, Balemont) and Lifetime offering *My Christmas Prince* (2017, Madelvia). Recognizing the potential of such holiday features, the dominant streaming media provider Netflix has recently joined the war for, or on, Christmas viewers with *A Christmas Prince* (2017, Aldovia), *A Christmas Prince: The Royal*

Wedding (2018, Aldovia), and *The Princess Switch* (2018, Belgravia). This is not a comprehensive list, but it gives some sense of the recent pervasiveness of snowflake Ruritania. Nearly all of these films contain motifs from both the page and musical stage versions of Ruritania—mistaken identities, court pageantry (a coronation, or at least a court ball), romance with a prince, and overcoming the constraints of protocol—but there are also seasonal sleigh rides and open fires, and sleigh bells tinkle mercilessly through the perky orchestral scores. Sometimes we get a few touches that are clearly borrowed from the *Diaries* films, such as comedy archery scenes or the remarkable royal interest in orphans. The chocolate-box kingdoms themselves are always conveniently Anglophone, and the European princes are played by actors from the UK: Luke Mably, Chris Geere, Will Kemp, Ben Lamb, Callum Alexander, Sam Heughan, and Sam Palladio. More curiously, perhaps, the American heroines have often been played by non-American actors, including Viva Bianca (Australian), Rose McIvor (a New Zealander), and Katie McGrath (Irish). If there is a certain sameness to the picturesque snowy settings, this is because of the shared use of location shots of Romania to conjure up Old World Mitteleurope—Peleş Castle in Sinaia in particular has been worked hard in at least four films.[6] But whatever their fascination with the quaint trappings of feudal Europe, love is always a more powerful force than tradition and protocol in these resolutely upbeat films, in which free rein is given to the fairy-tale elements that Anthony Hope, George Barr McCutcheon, and Meg Cabot tended to keep somewhat in check.

Why have there been so many of these films in the last few years? Is the renewed power of these Princess stories underwritten by the waning of democracy in an age of oligarchs and strong-men leaders? Do they appeal by wrapping up in romance, braid, and tinsel the structural inequalities of late capitalism? Or do they simply testify to the enduring power of the fantasy of transformative romantic love, a kind that will not simply unite us with an ideal partner but utterly change our humdrum lives? We can, I think, identify at least one less abstract reason for their current vogue—and for their use of British actors. These films trade on the American republic's long fascination with royalty and Old World tradition, but in the last few years they have had a more immediate source of inspiration in the form of the American princess story of Meghan Markle. In 2016 the Los Angeles–born actress began seeing Prince Harry, younger son of the Prince of Wales and of the late Diana, Princess of Wales, creating a surge of princess-mania that peaked in May 2018 when the couple were married at Windsor Castle.

As the entertainment website *Enews* pointed out about these Christmas movies: 'Royalty, so hot right now.'[7] Markle's African-American ancestry added further media interest to this match between New World and Old. To date this element of the story has not found its way into the Christmas movies. Even if African-American friends to the heroine have begun to appear—in *A Christmas Prince, My Christmas Prince,* and *Princess Switch,* for instance—these remain very much stories of a white Christmas.

As for the country that gave birth to Ruritania, at the time of writing no such revival is under way. With the prospect of Britain's exit from the European Union after the 2016 referendum, what Tom Nairn describes in *The Enchanted Glass* as the 'Ukanian' side of Britain seems to have come into sharper focus. According to the *Financial Times,* people were wondering in 2017 'how Britain had so quickly descended from a self-confident, economically successful world power into a country more closely resembling Ruritania.'[8] Simon Jenkins in the *Guardian* worried that Britain's departure from the European Union could transform the country into 'a Ruritania of border guards, tariff clerks and temporary work permits.'[9] Likewise, Drew Allan claimed in the Glasgow *Herald* that Britain was 'relapsing into a state of nostalgic, flag-waving, post-imperial reminiscences, becoming a latter-day Ruritania.'[10] It is not the Ruritania of adventure and romance that these writers are contemplating, clearly, but that other image of the country as a somewhat backwards if picturesque place, a petty principality, overfond of tradition and uniforms—as we have seen, this is the version that derives from the musical stage rather than from the adventure novel. It is, perhaps, unwise to speculate about what popular culture will or will not produce next, but, in light of such commentary, it seems unlikely that there is going to be a revival of *Zenda*-style romance any time soon in Britain. It is one thing to conjure up escapist adventures set in picturesque pocket kingdoms when you are writing from the capital of a global empire, but quite another to do so when you fear that your own country is turning into a Ruritanian backwater.

Notes

INTRODUCTION

1. Romance is a term with a long critical history. As a term for prose fiction in which the imagination is given free rein, it has often been used to define the edges of the more serious realm of the novel. See, for instance, Laurie Langbauer, 'Romance', in Stephen Arata, Madigan Haley, J. Paul Hunter, and Jennifer Wicke, eds., *A Companion to the English Novel* (Oxford: Wiley Blackwell, 2015), 103–16.

2. The term 'Ruritanian romance' appears in, for instance, 'Amusements', *The Sphere*, Saturday, 4 May 1901, 28; and 'Literature and Art', *Sheffield Daily Telegraph*, 8 April 1903, 3.

3. 'Novels', *Saturday Review*, 13 January 1900, reviewing H. B. Marriott Watson's *The Princess Xenia*.

4. 'The Uses and Abuses of Fictional Geography', *Academy*, 13 October 1906.

5. Clive Bloom suggests that Hope's novels 'create the style for the escapist adventure set within an international political crisis'. See his *Bestsellers: Popular Fiction Since 1900*, 2nd edition (Houndmills: Palgrave Macmillan, 2008), 170.

6. Madox Ford wrote *The New Humpty Dumpty* (set in the fictional Galizia) under the pseudonym Daniel Chaucer.

7. Mark J. P. Wolf, *Building Imaginary Worlds: The Theory and History of Subcreation* (New York: Routledge, 2012), 4.

8. See M. M. Bakhtin, *The Dialogic Imagination: Four Essays*, trans. Caryl Emerson and Michael Holquist (Austin: University of Texas Press, 1981). Critics of science fiction sometimes deploy the term 'polder' for such isolated time-space worlds. See the *Encyclopedia of Science Fiction*, edited by John Clute, David Langford, Peter Nicholls, and Graham Sleight, online.

9. Wallace, 'Cardboard Kingdoms', *San José Studies* 13.2 (Spring 1987): 23–34 (25). Wallace locates George Meredith's sprawling Bildungsroman *The Adventures of Harry Richmond* (1870–1) as the first of the breed and describes its descendants as 'Graustarkian' rather than 'Ruritanian', though he somewhat inconsistently allows that Anthony Hope 'found the formula'.

10. Vesna Goldsworthy, *Inventing Ruritania: The Imperialism of the Imagination* (1998; London: C. Hurst and Co., 2013), xxvi.

11. Michel Foucault describes a heterotopia as a space set apart from the everyday world in which the usual rules do not apply. See his 'Of Other Spaces, Heterotopias', *Architecture, Mouvement, Continuité* 5 (1984): 46–9.

12. 'London Theatres: The Palace, King's Rhapsody', *The Stage*, 22 September 1949, 7.

13. 'Ruritanian Romance', *The Globe*, 16 March 1918.

14. Adam Tooze, *The Deluge: The Great War and the Remaking of Global Order 1916–1931* (London: Allen Lane, 2014).

15. Joseph Adamson and Jean Wilson, eds., *Northrop Frye, The Secular Scripture and Other Writings on Critical Theory*, vol. 18, 1976–1991 (Toronto: University of Toronto Press, 2005), 5.

16. Jeffrey Richards, *Swordsmen of the Screen: From Douglas Fairbanks to Michael York* (London: Routledge and Kegan Paul, 1977), 5.

17. Nairn, *The Enchanted Glass: Britain and its Monarch*, new edition (1989; London: Verso, 2011), 35. On the shifting attitudes to titled elites in Britain itself in the early twentieth century, see Billy Melman, *The Culture of History: English Uses of the Past 1800–1953* (Oxford: Oxford University Press, 2006).

18. Frank Prochaska, *The Eagle and the Crown: Americans and the British Monarchy* (New Haven: Yale University Press, 2008).

19. For the former event, see chapter 6; on the latter, see Frank Reuven, 'The Great Coronation War', *American Heritage* 44.8 (1993), online.

CHAPTER I

1. For biographical details I have drawn for the most part on Anthony Hope's own memoir, *Memories and Notes* (London, 1927), and on Sir Charles Mallet, *Anthony Hope and His Books, Being the Authorized Life of Sir Anthony Hope Hawkins* (London, 1935). On the Casey and Comerford families, see Patrick Comerford's 'Comerford Profiles 20: the Revd. Edwards Comerford Hawkins (1827–1906) and The Prisoner of Zenda' on his blog on the Comerford, Comberford, and Quemerford families. Web, accessed 8 November 2013.

2. Sir Henry Hawkins had acted in two trials for the side of the Tichborne family that rejected the claimant, whose real name was Arthur Orton. See Hawkins' entry in the ODNB, and the two-volume *Reminiscences of Sir Henry Hawkins, Lord Brampton* (London: Edward Arnold, 1904).

3. Mallet, *Anthony Hope*, 59.

4. 'The Triumph of the Weak Brother', *Glasgow Herald*, 12 January 1895. The previous year Grant Allen had published an article in the *Fortnightly Review* on the need for a 'New Hedonism' that put pleasure before duty and that recognized the importance of the sex instinct.

5. 'Sport Royal', in *Sport Royal and Other Stories* (1893; New York: Henry Holt, 1895), 98.

6. 'The Love of the Prince of Glottenberg: A Zenda Story by Anthony Hope' also appeared in *McClure's Magazine* for December, 1895.

7. Mallet, *Anthony Hope*, 73; *Memories and Notes* 111–12.

8. Rassendlyll refers to his sister-in-law as a countess, so Lord Burlesdon is presumably an earl.

9. Anthony Hope, *The Prisoner of Zenda: Being the History of Three Months in the Life of an English Gentleman* (London: J. W. Arrowsmith, 1894), 14. Subsequent references are given in parentheses in the text.

10. Hawkins would have preferred a one-shilling edition (Mallet, *Anthony Hope*, 74). Most sources give its publication date as April 1894, without specifying a date. In the *Evening Standard* for Saturday, April 7, it appears in the summary of 'Yesterday's New Books', suggesting that it had either been published on the previous day or received that day for review.

11. 'New Publications: A Bright and Stirring Romance', *New York Times*, 27 May 1894; see also 'Recent Publications', *New Haven Morning Herald*, 11 October 1894. Sarah Barnwell Elliott, 'Some Recent Fiction', part 2, *Sewanee Review* 3.1 (November 1894): 90–104 (97).

12. Richard D. Altick, 'Nineteenth-Century English Bestsellers: A Third List', *Studies in Bibliography* 39 (1986): 235–41 (238).

13. Based on the 'Monthly Report of the Wholesale Book Trade' (England). See Troy J. Bassett and Christina M. Walter, 'Booksellers and Bestsellers: British Book Sales as Documented by The Bookman, 1891–1906', Appendix 2, *Book History* 4 (2001) 205–36 (230).

14. On bestsellers and steady sellers, see Clive Bloom, *Bestsellers: Popular Fiction Since 1900*, 2nd edition (Houndmills: Palgrave Macmillan, 2008), 1–5.

15. According to Mallet, Henry Holt sold 260,000 copies (79). In 1905, for instance, the novel was serialized in *The National Tribune* (DC) and other papers. Hope's later books did not go to Holt, something the publisher resented. See 'The Publishing Reminiscences of Mr Henry Holt', *The Publisher's Weekly*, 12 February 1910: 929–33 (931).

16. The French edition was translated by Robert de Cerisy, under the pseudonym Mme Gaston-Bruno-Paulin Paris. The Spanish edition combines *Zenda* with *The Dolly Dialogues* (*El prisionero de Zenda; Charlas con Dolly: versión española*).

17. This game was rereleased with a different cover to exploit the publicity around the 1937 film version of the novel. Parker Brothers are better known for *Monopoly* (1935).

18. 'Sensational Magical Illusions', *The Strand*, January 1903, 63–6. For a list of US Zendas, see the US Geographic Names Information System (GNIS), though it is possible that not all were named for Hope's novel.

19. *Rupert of Hentzau* (Bristol: Arrowsmith, 1898), 384.

20. Mallet, *Anthony Hope*, 134.

21. Mrs Hope's red hair is described in ' "Anthony Hope's" Debutante Daughter', *The Sketch*, 2 August 1922, 31.

22. *Condensed Novels: New Burlesques* (London: Chatto and Windus, 1902), 10.

23. Grier was the pseudonym of Hilda Caroline Gregg.

24. The term 'Ruritanian romance' appears early on in, for instance, 'Amusements', *The Sphere*, Saturday, 4 May 1901, 28; and 'Literature and Art', *Sheffield Daily Telegraph*, Wednesday, 8 April 1903, 3.

25. See, for instance, Laurie Langbauer, 'Romance', in Stephen Arata, Madigan Haley, J. Paul Hunter, and Jennifer Wicke, eds., *A Companion to the English Novel* (Oxford: Wiley Blackwell, 2015), 103–16.

26. 'The Uses and Abuses of Fictional Geography', *Academy*, 13 October 1906.

27. As discussed in the Introduction, in his analysis of what he terms 'Cardboard Kingdom' fiction, Raymond P. Wallace identifies seven recurring features: a fictitious country, usually a small monarchy; a threat to the state; a 'Wicked Uncle' or similar villain; an 'intervening stranger', our hero or heroine; a 'remarkable coincidence', here physical resemblance; a chase; and a duel. See his 'Cardboard Kingdoms', *San José Studies* 13.2 (Spring 1987): 23–34 (23–24). He suggests that Hope established the formula for this kind of fiction.

28. John G. Cawelti, *Adventure, Mystery, and Romance: Formula Stories as Art and Popular Culture* (Chicago: University of Chicago Press, 1976), 39–40.

29. Joseph Adamson and Jean Wilson, eds., *Northrop Frye, The Secular Scripture and Other Writings on Critical Theory, vol. 18, 1976–1991* (Toronto: University of Toronto Press, 2005), 5. As Tony Watkins notes, Hope saw himself as writing within the Romance tradition and gave a public lecture on Romance in 1897. See Watkins, ed., *The Prisoner of Zenda* (Oxford: Oxford World's Classics, 1994), ix.

30. A 'swashbuckler' was originally a particularly boisterous type of historical or fictional warrior: to swash means to make noise; a buckler is a small shield. The OED's first example of the term 'swashbuckling' is from the *Boston Transcript* of 4 July 1888. On the spread of the bretteur/swashbuckler novel through Europe, see Jacques Migozzi and Farid Boumédiène, Circulation transnationale des romans et séries de la culture populaire en Europe (1840–1930)', *Géographie poétique et cartographie littéraire*, PULIM, 2012. Andrew Lang and A. E. W. Mason's *Parson Kelly: A Story of a Jacobite Plot* (1900), for instance, was described as 'swashbuckling romance at its very best' in 'Publishers' Announcements', *Daily News*, 5 March 1900.

31. On the novel's use of the chivalric code, see, for instance, Watkins, 'Introduction' to the 1994 OUP *Zenda*, and Joseph A. Kestner, *Masculinities in British Adventure Fiction, 1880–1915* (Farnham: Ashgate, 2010), 154–6.

32. Jeffrey Richards, *Swordsmen of the Screen: From Douglas Fairbanks to Michael York* (London, Henley and Boston: Routledge and Kegan Paul, 1977), 4.

33. Wallace names George Meredith's *The Adventures of Harry Richmond* (1871) as early example of his 'Cardboard Kingdoms' subgenre, but it is difficult to see that novel's sprawling bildungsroman-cum-romance as a model for Hope's adventure, even if its Princess Ottilia of Eppenwelzen may be a model for Princess Flavia. Stevenson's 1882 collection *New Arabian Nights* also makes uses of pocket kingdoms: Prince Florizel of Bohemia is the hero of two of the stories; ultimately deposed, he becomes a tobacconist in Rupert Street in Soho.

34. Dornford Yates, *Fire Below* (1930; London: Ward, Lock, 1949), 34.

35. More theoretical consideration of miniatures include Gaston Bachelard's *The Poetics of Space* (1964; New York: Penguin, 2014) and Susan Stewart's *On Longing: Narratives of the Miniature, the Gigantic, the Souvenir, the Collection* (Baltimore: Johns Hopkins University Press, 1984). Bachelard links literary miniatures to dream

states and suggests that there is something restful about them, as they allow us 'to be world conscious at slight risk' (161). For Stewart they are connected to nostalgia, interiority, and the imaginary transcendence of time and labour.

36. 'Literary Notes', *Freeman's Journal*, 3 May 1895.

37. See, for instance, Richard Menke, 'The End of the Three-Volume Novel System, 27 June 1894', *BRANCH: Britain, Representation and Nineteenth-Century History*, edited by Dino Franco Felluga, an extension of Romanticism and Victorianism on the Net; and Troy Bassett's 'At the Circulating Library: A Database of Victorian Fiction, 1837–1901' on Victorianresearch.org.

38. In a less focused form, mystery had also been a part of the domestic novel, of course, including Charles Dickens' *Bleak House* (1852–3) and the 'Sensation' novels of Wilkie Collins, Mrs Braddon, and others.

39. Robert Louis Stevenson, 'A Gossip on Romance', *Longman's Magazine* 1 (November 1882): 69–79 (73, 77). Stevenson later crossed swords with Henry James over the nature of the novel, responding to James's 'Art of Fiction' essay of 1884 with his own 'A Humble Remonstrance' (also 1884). The two subsequently became good friends and regular correspondents.

40. Lang, 'Realism and Romance', *Contemporary Review* 52 (1887): 683–93.

41. Andrew Lang, 'Tendencies in Fiction', *North American Review* 161.465 (August 1895), 153–60.

42. In his memoir, Hope remembered Lang as an intellectual who 'championed the sort of thing the ordinary man likes to read—novels of rapid narrative, stirring incident, and normal emotions' (173).

43. John Fearnley and Sarah Barnwell Elliott, 'Some Recent Fiction', *Sewanee Review* 3.1 (November 1894), 81–104 (98). Part 2 (90–104) is by Elliott, the first section by John Fearnley.

44. On scepticism towards Nordau's work in Britain, see Nicholas Freeman, *1895: Drama, Disaster and Disgrace in Late Victorian Britain* (Edinburgh: Edinburgh University Press, 2014), 79–81.

45. Max Nordau, *Degeneration* (1892; London: William Heinemann, 1895), 39.

46. 'Novels and Stories', *Saturday Review*, 26 May 1894.

47. Paul J. Niemeyer, 'The Royal Red-Headed Variant: The Prisoner of Zenda and the 1893 Heredity Debates', *College Literature* 42.1 (Winter 2015): 112–38.

48. For a different reading of such Anglo-German interchangeability, see Michael Denning, *Cover Stories: Narrative and Ideology in the British Spy Thriller* (London: Routledge, 1987), 48.

49. 'Theatrical Gossip', *The Era*, 16 June 1894; Mallet, *Anthony Hope*, 94.

50. A typescript of Rose's adaptation exists in the Houghton Library, Harvard, and is available online through Harvard's Digital Collections. The British Library does not have a copy of Rose's text but interestingly does have a number of other adaptations for the stage, indicating that the play has been performed several times by amateur groups over the last thirty years or so.

51. 'Theatrical Gossip', *The Era*, 13 July 1895. Edward Askew Sothern had entertained several generations as Lord Dundreary in Tom Taylor's *Our American Cousin*, one of the most successful comic plays of the century. The younger Sothern was

educated in England but was in fact born in America and spent much of his career there; he is often referred to as an American actor.

52. 'The King of Ruritania', *New York Times*, 5 September 1895.

53. 'The King of Ruritania'; see also 'The Drama in America', *The Era*, 21 September 1895. Sam Sothern, Edward's brother, played Bertram Bertrand, and another English actor, Rowland Buckstone, son of playwright and actor Henry Buckstone, played the part of Colonel Sapt, an indication of how closely inter-linked the British and American theatre worlds were in this period.

54. 'The Prisoner of Zenda', *The Evening World*, 5 September 1895. See also 'Original Performances of Plays at the Lyceum Theatre and The American', *The Sun* (New York), 5 September 1895.

55. See Daniel Frohman, *Memories of a Manager: Reminiscences of the Old Lyceum and Some Players of the Last Quarter Century* (New York: Doubleday, Page, 1911), 71–2 (72).

56. 'Matinée Idols, Past and Present', *Munsey's Magazine*, January 1904, 576–85 (582–3).

57. Frohman, *Memories of a Manager*, 72.

58. 'The theatrical welkin has been ringing for a week with praise of Hackett's remarkable versatility and his physical charms. With that length of limb, dash of manner and tenderness in love-making, his doom as a matinee girl's idol is already sealed.' 'The Stage', *San Francisco Call*, 11 October 1896. He is listed in 'Matinée Idols, Past and Present' along with Sothern, William Faversham, and Edward J. Morgan as one of the quartet of younger idols.

59. 'The Theatres', 16 February 1896.

60. David Carroll, *The Matinée Idols* (New York: Arbor House, 1972), 78–9.

61. 'Amusements', *The Record-Union* (Sacramento), 22 October 1896.

62. See, for example, 'Hackett Revives His Biggest Hits', *San Francisco Call*, 14 August 1910.

63. Sidle [sic] Lawrence, 'Saccharine Drama: Whose the Blame', *Los Angeles Herald*, 31 May 1908.

64. 'Extravagant Heroics of New Stage Duels', *San Francisco Call*, 2 February 1902. The article mentions Alexander Salvini in Dumas's *The Three Guardsmen* as a predecessor and Kyrle Bellew as a contemporary stage swordsman.

65. 'Music and Drama', *Milwaukee Journal*, 1 September 1896, 3.

66. 'Emphatic Success of James K. Hackett in Rupert of Hentzau at the Hollis', *Boston Daily Advertiser*, 3 January 1899, 5.

67. On the success of these stage swashbucklers, see Jeffrey Richards, *Swordsmen of the Screen: From Douglas Fairbanks to Michael York* (London: Routledge, 1977), 12–13.

68. It is an unstable term: sometimes taken to be an affluent woman with time on her hands, in effect an unescorted lady of leisure (and this version has more traction in Britain), she is also the shop assistant or telephone girl who spends much of her income on the theatre. See, for instance, 'The Matinee Girl', *Manchester Times*, 3 November 1899, citing William Archer's article, 'The American Stage' in the *Pall Mall Magazine*, November 1899. These were not the

only views abroad: in 'A Chat With Leonard Boyne', *The Era*, 7 July 1894, the popular Irish actor suggested that the matinee girl had 'keen eyes' and was 'on the whole…a good influence on thoughtful work'. On London's matinee audiences for avant-garde fare, see Susan Torrey Barstow, ' "Hedda Is All of Us": Late-Victorian Women at the Matinee', *Victorian Studies* 43.3 (Spring 2001): 387–412.

69. As Richard Butsch notes, this evocation of a female audience marks a shift from the discussion of theatre audiences in terms of the 'Bowery b'hoys' at mid-century. Richard Butsch, *The Making of American Audiences: From Stage to Television* (New York: Cambridge University Press, 2000).

70. 'The Matinee Girl', *Munsey's Magazine*, October 1897, 34–9 (35). The term 'matinée idol' was subsequently given currency by, among other things, the comic short American film *The Matinée Idol* (July, 1907), in which matinee girls hunt down an unfortunate young actor; an English film with the same title and theme (September 1907); *The Saleslady's Matinée Idol* (1909); another short film called *The Matinee Idol*, starring Pearl White (1910); and *The Girl and the Matinee Idol* (1915); as well as the successful stage musical *A Matinee Idol* (28 April 1910, Daly's Theatre).

71. Butsch, *The Making of American Audiences*, 123–4.

72. Joel H. Kaplan and Sheila Stowell, *Theatre and Fashion: Oscar Wilde to the Suffragettes* (Cambridge: Cambridge University Press, 1995), 11. For a detailed account of the St James's and Alexander's management, see W. Macqueen Pope, *The St. James's: Theatre of Distinction*; Barry Duncan, *The St. James's Theatre: Its Strange and Complete History* (London: Barrie and Rockliff, 1964), 215–96; A. E. W. Mason, *Sir George Alexander and the St. James's Theatre*; and Joseph Donohue and Ruth Berggren, eds., *Oscar Wilde's The Importance of Being Earnest: A Reconstructive Critical Edition* (Gerrards Cross: Colin Smythe, 1995), 23–33, 44–51.

73. Shaw Desmond, *London Nights in the Gay Nineties* (New York: Robert M. McBride, 1928).

74. The play centres on the protagonist's dilemma: whether he should enter the priesthood or marry to prolong the family line. For a description of the play's failure, see Leon Edel, ed., *Guy Domville: A Play in Three Acts* (Philadelphia: Lippincott, 1960), 96, and Barry, *The St. James's Theatre*, 238–42. Alexander remained proud of his attempt to bring such intellectual works to the St James's and included a photograph of himself as Guy Domville in *Parts I Have Played: Photographic and Descriptive Biography of Mr George Alexander* (London: Abbey Press, *c.* 1910) (V&A biographical file). No photograph of *The Importance of Being Earnest* appears there.

75. At Alexander's request, Wilde persuaded Wyndham to give up the play in exchange for the promise of a future play. See Donohue and Berggren, *Oscar Wilde's The Importance of Being Earnest*, 40.

76. Richard Ellmann, *Oscar Wilde* (New York: Vintage, 1988), 430–1; Duncan, *The St. James's*, 243.

77. A. E. W. Mason argues that while Frank Harris criticized Alexander for taking Wilde's name from the bills, this course was deliberately taken to earn more money for Wilde at a time when he desperately needed it. Mason, *Sir George Alexander*, 80–1.

78. Henry Arthur Jones, *The Triumph of the Philistines* (New York: Samuel French, 1899).

79. Macqueen Pope, *St James's*, 141; Duncan, *The St. James's*, 244–5; Jones, *The Triumph of the Philistines*, xi; Freeman, *1895: Drama Disaster and Disgrace in Late Victorian Britain*, 126–7.

80. 'St James's Theatre', 25 November 1895.

81. Among those who appeared as character witnesses was Arthur Wing Pinero, who described Alexander as a 'very high-minded man' ('Police', *Times*, 5 November 1895). See 'The Charge Against Mr George Alexander', 6 November 1895; Duncan, *The St. James's*, 246–8; and 'Mr George Alexander and the Police', *The Sketch*, 13 November 1895, 120. The *Sketch* remained pro-Alexander and regularly featured articles and photographs about the theatre and its stars, including a special feature on *The Prisoner of Zenda*.

82. For a full cast list and subsequent changes of personnel, see Duncan, *The St James's*, 248–9.

83. 'Picturesque Ruritania: Production of the Prisoner of Zenda', *Pall Mall Gazette*, 7 January 1896.

84. The Saxe-Meiningen company were an experimental German theatre company led by the Duke of Saxe-Meiningen, known for their emphasis on rehearsal and naturalistic settings.

85. Harvard typescript of Edward Rose's *The Prisoner of Zenda*, Act 1, 25.

86. 'The London Theatres: The St James', *The Era*, Saturday, 11 January 1896.

87. See also untitled review from *The Referee*, 12 January 1896 (Production file, V&A).

88. Ellmann, *Oscar Wilde*, 422–3; Christopher Craft, 'Kiss Me With Those Red Lips: Gender and Inversion in Bram Stoker's *Dracula*', *Representations* 8 (Autumn, 1984): 107–33.

89. According to Frank Harris, Alexander snubbed Wilde at Cannes in December, 1898, but A. E. W. Mason suggests that this story was fabricated by Harris, and he reprints a letter from Wilde to Alexander that suggests that in 1900 they were on excellent terms. Alexander approached Wilde in Paris in 1900 with a voluntary offer of royalties on the performance of the plays that he had bought in Wilde's bankruptcy sale (*The Importance of Being Earnest* and *Lady Windermere's Fan*), and he promised to bequeath the rights of these to Wilde's sons. Ellmann, *Oscar Wilde*, 571, 579; Mason, *Sir George Alexander*, 82–6.

90. 'The Prisoner of Zenda', *Pall Mall Gazette*, 8 April 1895.

91. A. A. B., 'St James's Theatre: The Prisoner of Zenda Revived', *Daily Mail*, 21 October 1896.

92. Dramatic Opinions and Essays, volume 2 (New York: Brentano's, 1922), 66. Elsewhere he suggests that Alexander could have used the 'exchequer of the kingdom of Ruritania' to finance matinees of a more intellectual kind (130).

93. *Lady Windermere's Fan* ran for 156 performances in London and had a short tour. R. C. Carton's *Liberty Hall*, which had been a 'smashing success', ran for 183 performances. When *Earnest* was revived by Alexander in 1909, it ran for 324 performances. The St James's greatest hit in all of Alexander's period (1891–1917) was, in fact, Pinero's largely forgotten *His House in Order*, which achieved 427 performances in 1906–7. See W. Macqueen Pope, *St. James's, Theatre of Distinction* (London: W. H. Allen, 1958), 122–3, 175, 180, and Mason *Sir George Alexander*, 109–10.

94. Mason, *Sir George Alexander*, 108–9.

95. Mallet, *Anthony Hope*, 98.

96. 'London Correspondence', *Freeman's Journal*, 26 October 1896; 'Public Amusements', *Lloyds Weekly Newspaper*, 12 January 1896.

97. Howland appeared in quite a few comic films, her career lasting into the sound era.

98. 'Dramatic and Musical: Rudolf and Flavia Again', *New York Times*, 11 April 1899. See also 'The Week at the Theatres', *New York Times*, 16 April 1899, where Hackett's range as an actor is contrasted with his impression of 'breeding' and the exhibition of 'plastic grace and youthful agility'.

99. 'St. James's Theatre', *The Era*, 13 January 1900. 'Mr George Alexander and His New Playhouse, Drama and Dog', *The Sketch*, 31 January 1900, 21.

100. It was 'at the present moment a needlessly painful spectacle'. 'Reviews', *Times*, 6 February 1900; 'Occasional Notes', *Pall Mall Gazette*, 6 February 1900, 2. See also Barry, *The St. James's*, 256. Hope himself noted that 'we have flung the lying in state scene to the wolves, but things don't look well' (Mallet 145).

101. Duncan, *The St. James's*, 256, and see programmes from the revival.

102. *The Garden of Lies* was an adaptation of a 1902 novel by the American writer Justus Miles Forman.

103. 'Ruritanians All', *The Stage Year Book* (1909), 26.

104. 'Death of Sir George Alexander: A Quarter of a Century at the St James's', *Times*, 16 March 1918.

105. 'Miss Evelyn Millard', *Times*, 14 March 1941.

106. He wrote a number of pamphlets himself but was also chief literary advisor at Wellington House, assessing the usefulness for propaganda purposes of huge volumes of material. See Peter Buitenhuis, *The Great War of Words: British, American and Canadian Propaganda and Fiction, 1914–1933* (Vancouver: UBC Press, 1987), 31–2.

107. 'Sir Anthony Hope Hawkins: The Creator of Ruritania', *Times*, 10 July 1933.

CHAPTER 2

1. Jeffrey Richards, *Swordsmen of the Screen: From Douglas Fairbanks to Michael York* (London: Routledge, 1977), 4.

2. The classic account of this transition is offered by the History of the American Cinema series. See Charles Musser, *The Emergence of Cinema: The American Screen*

to 1907, History of the American Cinema, vol. 1 (New York: Charles Scribner, 1990); Eileen Bowser, *The Transformation of Cinema, 1907–1915*, History of the American Cinema, vol. 2 (New York: Charles Scribner, 1990); and Richard Koszarski, *An Evening's Entertainment: The Age of the Silent Feature Picture, 1915–1928*, History of the American Cinema, vol. 3 (New York: Charles Scribner, 1990). See also studies such as Charlie Keil's *Early American Cinema in Transition: Story, Style, and Filmmaking, 1907–1913* (Madison: University of Wisconsin Press, 2001).

3. 'The Cinema of Attraction: Early Film, Its Spectator and the Avant-Garde', *Wide Angle* 8.3 & 4 (Fall 1986): 63–70.

4. See, for instance, Bowser, *The Transformation of Cinema*; Kelly Brown, *Florence Lawrence, the Biograph Girl* (Jefferson, NC: McFarland & Company, 1999), and the entries for Lawrence and Turner in the *Women Film Pioneers Project* database by Kelly Brown and Charlie Keil respectively.

5. Paramount Pictures Corporation Christmas ad, cited in Bowser, *The Transformation of Cinema*, 135.

6. Adolph Zukor, *The Public is Never Wrong* (New York: G. P. Putnam's, 1953), 61, 64–72. On Bernhardt and early cinema, see Victoria Duckett, 'The Actress-Manager and the Movies: Resolving the Double Life of Sarah Bernhardt', *Nineteenth Century Theatre and Film* 45.1 (September 2018): 27–55.

7. Ramsaye, *A Million and One Nights: A History of the Motion Picture* (London: Frank Cass, 1964), 598.

8. 'Prisoner of Zenda Again: Hackett's Revival of Hope's Play Warmly Applauded', *New York Times*, 22 September 1908.

9. 'Stage Scenery at Auction', *New York Times*, 27 July 1909.

10. See the entry for Hackett in Dumas Malone, ed., *Dictionary of American Biography* (New York: Charles Scribner's, 1943), volume 8; and Walter Browne and E. De Roy Koch, eds., *Who's Who on the Stage 1908* (New York: B. W. Dodge, 1908). See also 'Hackett's Career Has Been Active', *San Francisco Call*, 10 July 1910, for a career summary to that point.

11. 'Zenda Licensed', *Weekly Variety*, 14 March 1913. 'The Patents co. has licensed another 'outlaw' film.'

12. For a meandering account of the set but some useful photographs, see Louis Reeves Harrison, 'Studio Saunterings: Stealing a March on the Famous Players Company', *Moving Picture World*, vol. 15, (Jan–March 1913), 26–8.

13. A slight exaggeration, since Helen Gardner's six-reel *Cleopatra* had appeared the year before. Other companies were also beginning to realize that longer features could compete with one- and two-reel films.

14. 'Daniel Frohman Gets Big Stars to Act for Movies', *New York Times*, 22 December 1912.

15. Charles Musser, *Before the Nickelodeon: Edwin S. Porter and the Edison Manufacturing Company* (Berkeley: University of California Press, 1991), 466.

16. See George Blaisdell, 'At the Sign of the Flaming Arcs', *Moving Picture World*, vol. 15, (Jan–March 1913), 455.

17. For a rather fulsome review of the gala screening at the Lyceum, see W. Stephen Bush, 'The Prisoner of Zenda', and George Blaisdell, 'Observed in the Audience', in *Moving Picture World*, vol. 15 (Jan–March 1913), 871–2. The mostly theatrical audience applauded the outdoor scenes in particular. A print of the film survives in the collection of the Eastman Museum in Rochester, New York.

18. Full-page ad, *Moving Picture World*, vol. 15 (Jan–March 1913), 431.

19. Reviews excerpted in page ads for the film in the *Moving Picture World*, vol. 15 (Jan–March 1913), 961.

20. See W. V. Knoblauch, 'Aus dem Englischen Buchhandel', *Börsenblatt für den Deutschen Buchhandel*, 6 April 1914 (Jg. 81) Nr. 79, S.497–9. I am grateful to Annemone Ligensa for bringing this to my attention.

21. Lee Grieveson and Peter Kraemer, 'Introduction: Feature Films and Cinema Programmes', in Grieveson and Kraemer, eds., *The Silent Cinema Reader* (London: Routledge, 2004) 187–95 (190).

22. Hayakawa's extraordinary popularity was largely overlooked in film histories until recently, but see Daisuke Miyao, *Sessue Hayakawa: Silent Cinema and Transnational Stardom* (Durham: Duke University Press, 2007).

23. They had also filmed works by other late Victorians, including Hall Caine, R. C. Carton, and Henry Arthur Jones. See Rachael Low, *The History of the British Film, 1914–1918, vol. 3 of the History of British Film* (1950; London: Routledge, 1997), 76.

24. 'The Prisoner of Zenda on the Film', *Times*, 10 March 1915; Mallet, *Anthony Hope*, 224.

25. It was the Mexican-born Novarro's first major role; he appears in the cast list under the name Ramon Samaniegos, closer to his birth-name, José Ramón Gil Samaniego.

26. On Ingram, see Liam O'Leary, *Rex Ingram: Master of the Silent Cinema* (1980; London: BFI, 1993); and the recent biography by Ruth Barton, *Rex Ingram: Visionary Director of the Silent Screen* (Lexington: University Press of Kentucky, 2014).

27. W. H., 'Notable Film: Success of the "Prisoner of Zenda"', *Pall Mall Gazette*, 30 January 1923, 4.

28. 'The Prisoner of Zenda at the Palace Theatre', *The Sketch*, 14 February 1923, 318.

29. Quoted in an ad in *Motion Picture News*, 26 September 1922.

30. 'The Screen', *New York Times*, 1 August 1922. For additional reviews see Barton, *Rex Ingram*, 109–10.

31. He later published an account of his experiences, *Stand To: A Diary of the Trenches, 1915–1918* (1937). Rex himself joined the Royal Canadian Flying Corps during the war but did not see action.

32. W. H., 'Notable Film'. See also, for instance, 'A Social Diary', in the 'Women of Today' section of the *Pall Mall Gazette*, 30 January 1923, 6.

33. 'The Prisoner of Zenda: New Film at Palace Theatre', *Times*, 30 January 1923, 8.

34. Richards, *Swordsmen of the Screen: From Douglas Fairbanks to Michael York* (London: Routledge, 1977), 160.

35. On the producer's colourful life, see David Thomson, *Showman: The Life of David O. Selznick* (London: André Deutch, 1993), and Ronald Haver, *David O. Selznick's Hollywood* (Los Angeles: Bonanza Books, 1980).

36. Walpole's career overlapped with Hope's during World War I, when they both served under John Buchan in the new Ministry of Information.

37. Thomson, *Showman*, 169, 222. Silvia Schulman married Ring Lardner Jr in 1937, and they were divorced in 1945. Since Thomson attributes this story to an interview with Lardner in 1988 it should, perhaps, be treated with some caution.

38. Haver, *David O. Selznick's Hollywood*, 21.

39. There were rumours of a more direct treatment. See 'Hollywood May Pick Up Wally-Windsor Yarn', *Boxoffice*, 15 May 1937, 43.

40. See Prochaska, *The Eagle and the Crown: Americans and the British Monarchy* (New Haven: Yale University Press, 2008), 138–45.

41. Thomson, *Showman*, 233.

42. Brenda Davies, *John Cromwell* (London: BFI Publications, 1974), 11.

43. See the captioned picture of Sigvard and Madeleine Carroll in *Boxoffice*, 15 May 1937, 43. Sigvard Bernadotte had himself lost his royal title after marrying a commoner in 1934.

44. 'Courtesy of the Public Library', *New York Times*, 9 May 1937, 3.

45. The *Oxford Dictionary of National Biography* and her *New York Times* obituary give her real name as Marie-Madeleine Bernadette O'Carroll, but she was christened Edith Madeleine Carroll. The only biography at the time of writing is Derek Chamberlain, *39 Steps to Stardom: The Life and Times of Madeleine Carroll* (Leicester: Matador, 2010).

46. Sarah Booth Conroy, 'Star Memories', *Washington Post*, 12 May 1983. Lassie, however, was not released until 1940. In another version of the story Fairbanks more plausibly mentions Rin Tin Tin, an earlier canine star.

47. One exception in Michael's camp is the English actor Montagu Love, who plays Detchard.

48. On the various sides of his career, see David Rayvern Allen, *Sir Aubrey: A Biography of C. Aubrey Smith* (1982; Ewell, Surrey: J.W. Mckenzie, 2005).

49. 'Newsreels Cover Coronation With Color, Television', *Motion Picture Herald*, 15 May 1937, 42; and 'NBC, Selznick Plan Coronation Air Show', *Motion Picture Daily*, 24 April 1937, 4.

50. Sheridan Morley, *The Brits in Hollywood: Tales from the Hollywood Raj* (1983; London: Robson, 2006), 161.

51. See Nick Evangelista, *The Encyclopedia of the Sword* (Westport, CT: Greenwood, 1985), 117–19.

52. Display ad for Lucky Strikes, *New York Times*, 29 July 1937, 11.

53. 'The New Pictures', *Time* 30.11, 13 September 1937, 36.

54. 'Hollywood Hatchet', *Time* 30.16, 18 October 1937, 30.

55. 'The Screen: The Prisoner of Zenda Opens at the Music Hall', *New York Times*, 3 September 3 1937.

56. 'The Screen', *Brooklyn Daily Eagle*, 3 September 1937, 10.

57. Tino Balio, *Grand Design: Hollywood as a Modern Business Enterprise*, History of the American Cinema, vol. 5 (New York: Scribner's, 1993), 405.

58. The Mountbattens, like the Windsors, had come to play down their Germanic links during the First World War.

59. See, for instance, 'Film First Night', the *Times*, 3 November 1937, 17; 'The Odeon's Gala Opening Performace: The Prisoner of Zenda', the *Sketch*, 10 November 1937, 252; and 'This is a Landmark Cinema', *Daily Herald*, 3 November 1937, 11. On the deaths of Prince Ioann, Grand Duchess Elizabeth, and other members of the royal family at Arapayevsk, see, for instance, Antony Lambton, *Elizabeth and Alexandra* (New York: E. P. Dutton, 1985), 402–5.

60. Michael Orme, 'The World of the Kinema', *Illustrated London News*, 13 November 13, 1937, 858; 'The Prisoner of Zenda', *Times*, 3 November 1937, 12.

61. James Agate, 'The Prisoner of Zenda', *Tatler*, 24 November 1937, 332. He noted that 'Sapt is essentially German, and our one and only Aubrey is more English than the playing-fields of England'.

62. 'Punch and Judy at the Vaudeville', *Illustrated London News*, 30 October 1937, 772.

63. 'MGM's New Box-Office Giant!', a full-page ad in *Film Bulletin*, 17 November 1952, 2.

64. Prochaska, *The Eagle and the Crown*, 165.

65. 'Managers Get The Results', Motion Picture Herald, November 22, 1952, 48; 'Chatter: Broadway', Variety, October 22, 1952, 62.

66. 'The Prisoner of Zenda, *Focus: A Film Review* 6.2 (February 1953): 36–7 (37). The review was by 'V', one of Focus's 'Panel of Priests'.

67. 'The New Pictures', *Time* 60.18 November 3, 1952, 102.

68. Its direct source was a novel of the same name by Bengali writer Sharadindu Bandyopadhyay.

69. Richards, *Swordsmen of the Screen*, 160–1.

70. Alexander Walker, *Peter Sellers* (London: Macmillan, 1982), 305.

71. For Mirisch's account of the film, see his *I Thought We Were Making Movies, Not History* (Madison: University of Wisconsin Press, 1988), 348–56.

72. On Sellers' erratic behaviour on the set, see Roger Lewis, *The Life and Death of Peter Sellers* (London: Arrow, 1994), 659–60, 792.

73. Mirisch, *I Thought We Were Making Movies, Not History*, 353–55, and Ed Sikov, *Mr Strangelove: A Biography of Peter Sellers* (New York: Hachette, 2003), 355–6.

74. Gary Arnold, 'Hollywood Breaks Out Laughing', *Washington Post*, 22 April 1979. The article notes that some hundred major comedy projects were under way in Hollywood.

75. Janet Maslin, 'Screen: Sellers in New "Zenda": A Comic Version', *New York Times*, 25 May 1979.

76. '"Zenda" Out In the Fifth', *Washington Post*, 25 May 1979.

77. Ray Conlogue, 'Ruritania Done For Good', *The Globe and Mail* (Canada), 28 May 1979.

78. Arthur Thirkell, 'Not Two of the Best Sellers', *Daily Mirror* 7 December 1979, 21.

79. See the online BBC guide to classic episodes of the series: http://www.bbc. co.uk/doctorwho/classic/episodeguide/androidsoftara/detail.shtml.

80. John Corry, 'Prisoner of Zenda is Presented on A&E', *New York Times*, 12 August 1986.

CHAPTER 3

1. A comparison of the frequency of use of the words 'Ruritania' and 'Graustark' using the Google Ngram Viewer gives very different results, with the former showing its greatest peak after the Second World War, while the latter has its major peak around 1903–4, a later spike in the 1920s, and then a decline to very low levels after the 1940s.

2. There are, however, a Graustark Street in Houston, Texas, and a Graustark Path in Wooster, Ohio; in 1963 the novel also lent its name to a famous racehorse.

3. 'Geo. B. M'Cutcheon Dies at a Luncheon', *New York Times*, 24 October 1928, 1; Frank Mott, *Golden Multitudes* (New York: 1947); for additional figures see the *20th-Century American Bestsellers* website hosted by the University of Virginia.

4. Ad for *Beverly of Graustark*, the *New York Clipper*, 14 February 1914, 13.

5. It was published by a small press, Lightyear Press of Laurel, New York. In 1971 the Scholarly Press, St Clair Shores, Michigan, had also published an edition. More recently, print-on-demand, OCR editions have appeared from such presses as Wildside and Norilana. More surprisingly, there is an Australian audiobook version of *Graustark* from 1992.

6. For the biographical details that follow I have largely relied on the only major study of McCutcheon, A. L. Lazarus and Victor H. Jones's *Beyond Graustark: George Barr McCutcheon, Playwright Discovered* (Port Washington, New York: Kennicat Press, 1981). Lazarus and Jones present McCutcheon as a neglected playwright and are less interested in his bestselling career. Other useful biographical sources include *Drawn from Memory: The Autobiography of John T. McCutcheon* (Indianapolis: Bobbs-Merrill, 1950); the novelist's own literary ledger in the collection of the Beinecke Library, Yale; his entry in volume 12 of Dumas Malone, ed., *Dictionary of American Biography*, 20 volumes (New York: ACLS/Charles Scribner's, 1934), 12–13; articles in the *Bookman* and other contemporary periodicals; and his obituaries.

7. Lazarus and Jones, *Beyond Graustark*, 12–13.

8. McCutcheon, *Drawn from Memory*, 30.

9. According to *Drawn from Memory* (182), he was offered a $15,000 advance by Dodd, Mead for *The Sherrods* (1903).

10. James L. W. West III, 'George Barr McCutcheon's Literary Ledger', *Yale University Library Gazette* 59.3–4 (April 1985): 155–61 (161).

11. *Graustark* (1901; New York: Grosset and Dunlap, *c.*1911), 2. Subsequent references in parentheses in the text.

12. Theodore Roosevelt, *The Strenuous Life* (New York: Review of Reviews, 1910), 7–8. For the nation more generally, the strenuous life was to mean involvement

outside its own borders, specifically intervention in the Philippines. See also Grant Cohran Knight, *The Strenuous Age in American Literature* (Chapel Hill: University of North Carolina Press, 1954), and Amy Kaplan, 'Romancing the Empire: The Embodiment of American Masculinity in the Popular Historical Novel of the 1890s', *American Literary History* 2.4 (Winter 1990): 659–90. On fiction and the Gilded Age, see James D. Hart, *The Popular Book: A History of America's Literary Taste* (Berkeley: University of California Press, 1950), 180–200.

13. Marion Davies, star of *Beverly of Graustark* (1925), played Mary Tudor in the 1922 film version of Major's novel.

14. In *Arms and the Woman*, for instance, an American falls for Hildegarde, the Princess of Hohenphalia, who renounces her title to marry him; his first love, Phyllis, raised as an American, turns out to be her lost twin and thus a princess. McGrath was highly successful himself, and many of his novels were filmed.

15. West, 'George Barr McCutcheon's Literary Ledger', 159.

16. 'Books in Demand', *New York Times*, 22 June 1901, 14. An American Civil War novel, Winston Churchill's *The Crisis*, was the most popular title in all the cities covered. The author was, of course, the popular Missouri-born novelist (1871–1947), not the British politician of the same name.

17. *Publisher's Weekly*, 21 September 1901. Reproduced on the *American Bestsellers* website, hosted by the University of Virginia.

18. 'Graustark', *Urbana Daily Courier*, 1 May 1903.

19. 'Tonight: At the Colonial, Graustark Beautifully Staged', *Athens Banner*, 15 October 1910, 1.

20. There was also a Canadian edition by McLeon and Allen in 1903. The 1913 Norwegian translation was published in Decorah, Iowa, by the B. Anundsen publishing company. Yale's Beinecke Library has an extensive collection of McCutcheon editions.

21. 'New Books of the Month', *Bookman*, May 1902, 71.

22. 'Graustark', *Athenaeum* review of the Grant Richards 6 shilling edition, 26 April 1902, 525.

23. Galbraith, 'Our American Letter', *The Bookman* 32.217 (October 1909), 8. He thought, though, that some might remember the stage version of *Brewster's Millions*, which had been a hit for Charles Frohman in 1907 at the Hicks Theatre, now the Gielgud Theatre.

24. West, 'George Barr McCutcheon's Literary Ledger', 157.

25. See Amy Kaplan, 'Romancing the Empire'. For a different view that sees the romance of the period as underwriting the exceptional yet normal violence of empire through its narrative combination of the everyday and the extraordinary, see Andrew Hebard, 'Romantic Sovereignty: Popular Romances and the American Imperial State in the Philippines, *American Quarterly* 57.3 (September 2005): 805–30. See also Nancy Glazener, *Reading for Realism* (Durham: Duke University Press, 1997), 147–88, on the 'Romantic Revival' of this period.

26. These were collected and published by the *Chicago Record-Herald* as *The Cartoons That Made Prince Henry Famous* (1902).

27. *Beverly of Graustark* (New York: Dodd, Mead, 1904), 1. Subsequent page references in the text.

28. Number 1 that year was a historical romance set against the backdrop of the colonization of Kentucky and Tennessee, *The Crossing*, by bestselling American author Winston Churchill.

29. 'Back to Graustark', *New York Times*, 1 October 1904, 661.

30. Montrose Moses, 'Geo. Barr McCutcheon: Believes in the Happy Endings not for its Commercial Value But Because of his Philosophy of Art', *New York Times*, 21 July 1912, 417.

31. 'Graustark: Revived in Sequel', *San Francisco Sunday Call*, 9 October 1904.

32. 'Beverly of Graustark', *Athenaeum*, No. 4044, 29 April 1905, 524.

33. The 'Dollar Princesses' are described in Gail MacColl and Carol McD. Wallace's *To Marry an English Lord or, How Anglomania Really Got Started* (New York: Workman, 2009).

34. For instance, William Randolph Hearst's St Bernard de Clairvaux was imported in 1926; in the same year Warwick Priory began to arrive in the United States to form the Weddell family's Virginia House. Brianna Nofil and Jake Purcell's *Medieval America* website maps the extraordinary transfer of medieval material to the US.

35. Prochaska, *The Eagle and the Crown*, 112.

36. In a 1916 cartoon John T. McCutcheon depicted the King of England recouping the expenses of the war by creating new noblemen, each of whom comes back from America newly wedded to an American heiress. The cartoon is described by Jennie Franklin Purvin in 'Politics', *Illinois Sentinel*, 15 December 1916, 8.

37. While appearing in novel form it was also published as a serial in *Ainslee's Magazine* and elsewhere. Dodd Mead advertised it as the 'best selling novel in America' in their pre-Christmas ads. See, for example, *Athens Banner*, 23 December 1909, 11.

38. Established in Britain by Thomas Cook (1808–92), by this period Thomas Cook and Son were major international travel agents.

39. The comment about 'yellow' arrivals is probably an oblique reference to the Chinese Exclusion Act of 1882, which had been made permanent in 1902.

40. 'New McCutcheon Book', *New York Times*, 23 May 1908, 296 (a review of *The Husbands of Edith*).

41. George Barr McCutcheon was himself not against union activity per se and supported the 1916 plan to affiliate the Authors League of America to the American Federation of Labor. See Richard Fine, *James M. Cain and the American Authors' Authority* (Austin: University of Texas Press, 1992), 83.

42. The US was not the only country to deport those perceived to represent a socialist threat. The Spanish government forcibly dispatched 800 aboard the *Manuel Calvo* earlier that year. See Robert Gerwarth, *The Vanquished: Why the First World War Failed to End, 1917–1923* (London: Allen Lane, 2016), 154.

43. Presumably McCutcheon found such material more palatable than the sexual frankness of the contemporary 'sex novel'. In a 1917 interview with Joyce Kilmer, he made it clear that he 'has no respect for the type of novel, increasingly popular of late, in which the author devotes page after page to glowing accounts

of immorality with the avowed intention of teaching a high moral lesson... "The so-called sex novel [sc. a reference to the work of such writers as Elinor Glyn]...is one of our gravest fatalities."' 'McCutcheon, "Magazines Cheapen Fiction"', in Alfred Joyce Kilmer, ed., *Literature in the Making, By Some of its Makers* (New York: Harper and Bros., 1917), 157–68 (159–60).

44. Alice Payne Hackett and James Henry Burke, *80 Years of Bestsellers, 1895–975* (New York: R. R. Bowker, 1977), 73. See also the *20th-Century American Bestsellers* Database.

45. *Literary Digest* review cited in Justina Leavitt Wilson and Clara Elizabeth Fanning, *Book Review Digest* (Minneapolis: H. W. Wilson, 1909), 285. 'One Hundred Christmas Books: *Truxton King*', *New York Times*, 5 December 1909, 34.

46. 'Book Reviews: Truxton King', *Evening Star* (North Dakota), 25 September 1909, 5; 'Truxton King', *San Francisco Call*, 10 October 1909, 7.

47. The novel was serialized in various Sunday newspapers in 1914, with illustrations by R. F. Schaebelitz, as well as appearing in volume form.

48. *Athens Banner*, 19 September 1914, 4.

49. *East of the Setting Sun* (New York: Dodd, Mead, 1924), 8.

50. Cited in Gerwarth, *The Vanquished*, 96.

51. Robert K. Murray, *Red Scare: A Study in National Hysteria, 1919–1920* (New York: McGraw Hill, 1955).

52. See Murray, *Red Scare*, 84–88, and Julian F. Jaffe, *Crusade against Radicalism: New York During the Red Scare, 1914–1924* (Port Washington, NY: Kennikat Press, 1972), 227–8.

53. *The Inn of the Hawk and the Raven: A Tale of Old Graustark* (New York: Dodd, Mead, 1927), 93, 94.

54. See 'Theatrical Gossip', *New York Times*, 13 June 1901, as well as McCutcheon's ledger. McKee's interests included a share in Florenz Ziegfeld's highly successful *Follies*.

55. 'Graustark at Harlem Opera House', *New York Times*, 21 January 1908; 'Harlem', *New York Clipper*, 25 January 1908. John Craig played Grenfall Lorry, and Beatrice Morgan was Yetive.

56. 'Grace Gatts sues Ferris', *New York Times*, 1 December 1911. A musical version of Hayward's *Graustark*, entitled *Lovetime / The Melody of the Mountains*, was written by the Australian composer Dudley Glass in 1943 but does not seem to have been produced. See 'New Musical Play', *The Age* (Melbourne), 27 November 1943, and the Dudley Glass papers in the National Library of Australia.

57. They followed up the success of *Graustark* with a drama set in the fictional Ehrenstein, *The Goose Girl*, which blended Ruritanian elements and a Cinderella story.

58. 'Graustark', *Spartanburg Herald-Journal*, 12 March 1910; 'Graustark: Greatest of All Leading Romantic Plays Now On', *Athens Banner*, 13 October 1910, 3.

59. Compare, for example, the Frontispiece to the photo-illustrated Grosset and Dunlap edition (no date given) and the publicity still for the Baker and Castle production reproduced in the Pittsburgh Press of 26 May 1911.

60. 'See American Men Win Two Graustark Beauties', *Pittsburgh Press*, 26 May 1911.

61. 'Graustark to Play Return Date', *Bryan Times*, 10 November 1911. Similarly worded puffs appear in other regional newspapers.

62. Ad for the United Play Company's production at the Elks' Theatre, Prescott, Arizona, from the *Prescott Journal Miner*, 18 January 1913.

63. See 'Graustark', *Weekly Variety*, 23 May 1913.

64. 'Present Road Shows', *Variety*, 27 March 1925.

65. A print survives in the Library of Congress Paper. See Kemp R. Niver, *Motion Pictures from the Library of Congress Paper Print Collection, 1894–1912* (Berkeley: University of California Press, 1967). A scene-by-scene synopsis that includes subtitles was published by Klaw and Erlanger in September 1914.

66. Mark Klaw had worked as the Frohmans' lawyer, and Klaw and Erlanger joined Charles Frohman and his partners in the Theatrical Syndicate in 1896, effectively forming a monopoly of theatre bookings in the US.

67. Now Hořice na Šumavě in the Czech Republic. See Charles Musser, *The Emergence of Cinema: The American Screen to 1907*, volume 1 (Berkeley: University of California Press), 209–12.

68. See John C. Tibbets, *The American Theatrical Film: Stages in Development* (Toledo: Popular Press, 1985), 71–6.

69. Linda Arvidson, *When the Movies Were Young* (New York: E. P. Dutton, 1925), 225.

70. This scene-by-scene summary, including subtitles, appears in the printed script, *Beverly of Graustark* (n.p.: Klaw and Erlanger, 1914). This synopsis was presumably published for copyright reasons.

71. 'Comments on the Films: Beverly of Graustark', *Moving Picture World*, 3 June 1916.

72. Synopsis in the online *American Film Institute Catalog of Feature Films*.

73. A copy of this poster was sold by Heritage Auctions on 13 August 2017 and can be seen in their online catalogue.

74. See the online *American Film Institute Catalog* entry.

75. 'Graustark Heralded as one of the World's Greatest Dramas', *Camas Prairie Chronicle*, 24 December 1915.

76. Neil G. Caward, 'Essanay's Graustark', *Motography* 13.19 (January–June 1915), 742. This review also features two stills from the film.

77. Hazel Simpson Naylor, 'As Others See You, or Gleanings from the Audience', *Motion Picture Magazine* (August 1915–January 1916), 132, 168. Francis X. Bushman, 'From the Inside of the Studio', *Picture Play Weekly*, 10 April 1915, 1–4 (3).

78. 'Photoplay Classics', *Motion Picture Magazine* (February–May 1916), 141–2, 181.

79. 'Russian Ballet in Prince of Graustark—at Strand', *Athens Banner*, 22 April 1917, 7.

80. 'The Prince of Graustark Filmed from Famous Novel', *Athens Daily Herald*, 25 April 1917, 7.

81. 'Prince of Graustark', *Weekly Variety*, 3 November 1916, 25.

82. 'American Film in London', *Weekly Variety*, 1 October 1915.

83. See, for instance, 'Truxton King: Class A', a review in the trade paper for exhibitors, *Screen Opinions* 11.15 (March 1923), 232. 'John Gilbert Has Good Vehicle in George Barr McCutcheon Story', *Film Daily*, 4 February 1923, 15.

84. 'When you book a 'Book Title' Picture, Remember the Bookseller in Your Town', *Exhibitors Herald*, 24 February 1923, 26.

85. Marc McDermott appeared as Prince Gabriel, Roy D'Arcy as Dangloss, and Wanda Hawley as Dagmar. A few reels survive at the Library of Congress.

86. 'Talmadge's Lot Move', *Weekly Variety*, 18 March 1925.

87. *Photoplay* review, late 1925, reproduced on the Norma Talmadge Website.

88. 'Graustark', *Weekly Variety*, 9 September 1925.

89. See James L. W. West, *American Authors and the Literary Marketplace Since 1900* (Philadelphia: University of Pennsylvania Press, 1988), 121.

90. By 1926 he had interests in production and distribution, in partnership with the Metro-Goldwyn-Mayer conglomerate, and he also owned several high-profile cinemas. On Hearst and the film industry, see Louis Pizzitola, *Hearst Over Hollywood: Power, Passion and Propaganda in the Movies* (New York: Columbia University Press, 2002).

91. According to one interview, Davies had, in fact, wanted to do a version of *Twelfth Night*, and the heavily adapted *Beverly* had been a compromise. See Jane Tilton, 'Beverly of Hollywood', *Motion Picture Magazine* (June 1926), 37. On the significance of cross-dressing in early cinema, see Laura Horak, *Girls Will Be Boys: Cross-Dressed Women, Lesbians, and American Cinema, 1908–1934* (New Brunswick: Rutgers University Press, 2016).

92. The costumes were by André-ani (Clément Henri Andreani), Kathleen Kay, and Maude Marsh.

93. 'Extraordinary Special Feature: Palace Theatre', *Athens Banner-Herald*, 16 June 1926, 5.

94. Cal York, 'Studio News and Gossip, East and West', *Photoplay*, 26 February 1926, 40.

95. 'Beverly of Graustark: Lovely Picture', *Athens Banner-Herald*, 18 June 1926, 3.

96. See, for instance, the reviews quoted in the page ad for *Beverly* in *Film Daily*, 21 April 1926, 3; George T. Pardy, 'Beverly of Graustark', *Motion Picture News*, 8 May 1926, 2266; 'Beverly of Graustark', *Variety*, 21 April 1926, 34.

97. 'The Biggest Money Makers of 1926', *Exhibitors Herald*, 25 December 1926, 38–9. Though released the previous year, *Graustark* also made the list.

98. 'New Talmadge Vehicle', *Moving Picture World*, 22 November 1924, 345; 'Stroheim Plays Villain for Constance Talmadge', *Exhibitors Herald*, 8 August 1925, 39; 'Presenting Mr Pidgeon', *Picture-Play Magazine*, September 1926, 47.

99. On Stroheim as a filmmaker, see Herman G. Weinberg, *Stroheim: A Pictorial Record of His Nine Films* (New York: Dover, 1975); and Richard Koszarski, *Von: The Life and Films of Erich Von Stroheim* (1983; New York: Limelight, 2001).

100. Koszarski, *Von*, 167.

101. Koszarski, *Von*, 202.

102. Koszarski, *Von* 202–3. See, for instance, the First National ad for *East of the Setting Sun*, *Exhibitors Herald*, 18 April 1925, between pages 10 and 11.

103. The draft script and related documents are part of the Howard Estabrook Papers at the Margaret Herrick Library in Beverly Hills.

104. See, for example, J. O. Engleman, 'Outside Reading', *The English Journal* 6.1 (January 1917), 20–7; Wilfred Eberhart 'Evaluating the Leisure Reading of High-School Pupils', *The School Review* 47.4 (April 1939), 257–69; David H. Russell,

'Reading Preferences of Younger Adolescents in Saskatchewan', *The English Journal* 30.2 (February 1941), 131–6.

105. Based on a newspaper comic strip created by Dashiell Hammett and Alex Raymond.

106. P. E. Schneider, 'Graustark Becomes A Boom Town', *New York Times*, 15 February 1959.

107. Souvanna Phouma, 'Pro-Western Neutral', *New York Times*, 17 August 1960; C. L. Sulzberger, 'The Man Who Would Not Be King', *New York Times*, 7 March 1955.

108. See, for instance, the short note in the 'Individual Writers' section of the *Annual Review of the Journal of Modern Literature* 9.3/4 (December 1982): 397–564.

109. Ashbery, 'Beverly of Graustark', *The American Poetry Review* 28.33 (May/June 1999): 7–8.

CHAPTER 4

1. 'London Theatres: The Palace, King's Rhapsody', *The Stage*, 22 September 1949, 7.

2. J. C. Trewin, 'The World of the Theatre: Off the Map', *Illustrated London News*, 8 October 1949, 552.

3. Gerald Bordman, *American Operetta: From H.M.S. Pinafore to Sweeney Todd* (New York: Oxford University Press, 1981), v.

4. For detailed accounts, see Richard Traubner, *Operetta: A Theatrical History* (London: Victor Gollancz, 1984), and James Harding, *Folies de Paris: The Rise and Fall of French Operetta* (London: Chapell/Elm Tree Books, 1979).

5. Traubner, *Operetta*, 20.

6. On early operetta in Paris, see James Harding, *Folies de Paris*.

7. Quoted in Graeme Gilloch, 'The Word on the Street: Charles Baudelaire, Jacques Offenbach, and the Paris of their Time', in Christian Hermansen Cordua, ed., *Manifestoes and Transformations in the Early Modernist City* (Farnham: Ashgate, 2010), 59–76 (64).

8. On the Emperor's and Czar's visits, see 'Occasional Notes', *Pall Mall Gazette*, 26 April 1867, and 4 June 1867.

9. There is an actual town called Gerolstein in Germany, but it has never been a duchy, let alone a grand duchy.

10. 'The London Theatres', *The Era*, 24 November 1867.

11. Robert Louis Stevenson, *Prince Otto* (London: Chatto and Windus, 1885), 4. Oddly enough, Gilbert and Sullivan, who delighted in the use of imaginary settings, did not pursue Offenbach's Ruritanian lead until their last opera, *The Grand Duke* (1896), set in the Duchy of Pfennig-Halbpfennig, and produced two years after *The Prisoner of Zenda* had appeared.

12. On Ruritanian operetta in America in these years, see William A. Everett, *Sigmund Romberg* (New Haven: Yale University Press, 2007), 78.

13. 'The Prince of Pilsen Comes', *New York Times*, 18 March 1903.
14. On this operetta, see Orly Leah Krasner, 'Birth Pangs, Growing Pains, and Sibling Rivalry: Musical Theatre in New York, 1900–1920', in William A. Everett and Paul R. Laird, eds., *The Cambridge Companion to the Musical* (Cambridge: Cambridge University Press, 2002), 29–46 (31–3).
15. Traubner, *Operetta*, 243.
16. In its source text, Henri Meilhac's *L'Attaché d'ambassade* [1861], the German principality of Birkenfeld is the off-stage space. For a discussion of the resonance of the names of people and places in the operetta, see Raymond Knapp, *The American Musical and the Performance of Personal Identity* (Princeton: Princeton University Press, 2009), 21–31.
17. The first adaptation was by Edward Morton, with lyrics by Adrian Ross, though Basil Hood was later brought in to make further changes. Meilhac, as we have seen, had also collaborated on libretti for Offenbach, including that of *La Grande-Duchesse de Gérolstein*.
18. On *The Merry Widow*'s shift from comedy to romance, and on centrality of dance, see Traubner, *Operetta*, 232–6; Rick Altman, *The American Film Musical* (Bloomington: Indiana University Press, 1987), 163.
19. *The Merry Widow, New Musical Play, Adapted from the German of Victor Léon and Leo Stein, Lyrics by Adrian Ross, Arranged for the Piano by H. M. Higgs, Vocal Score* (London: Chapell, 1907), 20–1.
20. On *Die lustige Witwe* as a Viennese fantasy about the Balkans, see Everett, *Sigmund Romberg*, 43–4.
21. Ronald Pearsall, *Edwardian Popular Music* (Newton Abbot: David and Charles, 1974), 191.
22. The lascivious dance was presumably the can-can. Sitwell and Bennett are cited in Ronald Pearsall, *Edwardian Popular Music* (Newton Abbot: David and Charles, 1974), 38–9.
23. Traubner, *Operetta*, 235; Pearsall, *Edwardian Popular Music*, 37.
24. David Parkinson, *The Rough Guide to Film Musicals* (London: Rough Guide, 2007), 11. See also Bordman, *American Operetta*, 74–87, on the *Widow*'s impact.
25. See Bordman, *American Operetta*, 80; Pearsall, *Edwardian Popular Music*, 38; 'P.I.P. Playgoer', *Penny Illustrated Paper*, 7 March 1908. The article comments on the parody of *The Merry Widow* and other popular plays in The Follies at the Apollo Theatre.
26. This extravagant hat, like other items of Lily Elsie's costume in the London production, was the creation of the couturier 'Lucile', sister of the popular novelist Elinor Glyn. See Joel H. Kaplan and Sheila Stowell, *Theatre and Fashion: Oscar Wilde to the Suffragettes* (Cambridge: Cambridge University Press, 1995), 116.
27. Marlis Schweitzer, *When Broadway Was The Runway: Theatre, Fashion, and American Culture* (Philadelphia: University of Pennsylvania Press, 2009), 1–4; see also Traubner, *Operetta*, 236, and Pearsall, *Edwardian Popular Music*, 37–8.
28. Traubner, *Operetta*, 206.

29. 'The Balkan Princess', *Playgoer and Society Illustrated* 1.6 (June 1910): 99.

30. For a detailed illustrated review, see *The Playgoer and Society Illustrated*, 6.33 (June 1912): 65–83.

31. See, for example, James Ross Moore, 'Girl Crazy: Musicals and Reviews Between the Wars', in Clive Barker and Maggie B. Gale, eds., *British Theatre Between the Wars* (Cambridge: Cambridge University Press, 2000), 88–112.

32. *Chu Chin Chow*, a 'Musical Tale of the East', loosely based on the Arabian Nights, ran for 2,238 performances, the longest British run until 1958's *The Mousetrap*. See E. D. Mackerness, *A Social History of English Music* (London: Routledge and Kegan Paul, 1964), 242–3, and Brian Singleton, *Oscar Asche, Orientalism, and British Musical Comedy* (Westport, CT: Praeger, 2004).

33. Everett, *Sigmund Romberg*, 78–9.

34. Traubner notes that this operetta was first produced in Marseille as *La Reine s'amuse* in 1913; its title was a play on Victor Hugo's *Le Roi s'amuse*, which had provided the plot of Verdi's *Rigoletto* (*Operetta*, 305).

35. B. W. Findon, 'The Naughty Princess: Opera Bouffe in Two Acts', *Play Pictorial* 37.225 (October 1920): 86–97.

36. Herbert Farjeon, 'The London Stage: The White Camellia', the *Graphic*, 9 March 1929, 12. See also Singleton, *Oscar Asche*, 186.

37. 'Old Heidelberg', *The Era*, 23 March 1903.

38. 'Old Heidelberg Again', *New York Times*, 13 October 1903; 'Topics of the Drama', *New York Times*, 18 October 1903.

39. The best-known silent version is Ernst Lubitsch 1927 film, starring Ramon Novarro and Norma Shearer. See Bruce Babington, 'Herr Lubitsch Joins the Corps Saxonia: History, Gesture and Homosociality in *The Student Prince of Old Heidelberg*', in Phil Powrie, Ann Davies, and Bruce Babington, eds., *The Trouble with Men: Masculinities in European and Hollywood Cinema* (London: Wallflower Press, 2004), 122–33.

40. Quoted in Everett, *Sigmund Romberg*, 130.

41. Everett, *Sigmund Romberg*, 127, 131.

42. Abel., 'The Student Prince', *Variety*, 10 December 1924; Traubner, *Operetta*, 385; Everett, *Sigmund Romberg*, 128.

43. On the uniforms, see 'His Majesty's: The Student Prince', *The Stage*, 11 February 1926, 18. It was positively reviewed in many papers. See, for instance, 'The Student Prince', *The Era*, 10 February 1926, 8. The *Times* singled out its Americanism and the paucity of humour ('His Majesty's Theatre', *Times*, 4 February 1936, 10). For a review more critical of the play's music and comedy, see, for instance, 'Heidelberg to Music', *Sporting Times*, 6 February 1926, 7. On 3 March 1926 the *Era*'s 'Theatrical Gossip' reported that the management of the His Majesty's production wanted to clear up various misapprehensions about the operetta; among other things, the article mentions that the male chorus were all British, and many of them ex-soldiers.

44. Everett, *Sigmund Romberg*, 129.

45. Everett, *Sigmund Romberg*, 151.

46. Sisk., 'Princess Flavia', *Variety*, 18 November 1925.

47. See, for example, the record of returns for Philadelphia and Baltimore in the weekly *Varietys* for the months of April and May 1926.

48. Howard Pollack, *George Gershwin: His Life and Work* (Berkeley: University of California Press, 2006), 418–23; Philip Furia, *Ira Gershwin: The Art of the Lyricist* (Oxford: Oxford University Press, 1996), 68.

49. On Novello's life and work, see W. Macqueen Pope, *Ivor: Story of an Achievement* (London: W. H. Allen, 1951); Peter Noble, *Ivor Novello, Man of the Theatre* (1951; London: White Lion, 1975); and James Harding, *Ivor Novello: A Biography* (1987; Cardiff: Welsh Academic Press, 1997). For production photographs from *Glamorous Night*, see David Slattery-Christy, *In Search of Ruritania* (Milton Keynes: Author House, 2008). For a recent reappraisal, see Stewart Nicholls, 'West End Royalty: Ivor Novello and English Operetta, 1917–1951', in Robert Gordon and Olaf Jubin, eds., *The Oxford Handbook of the British Musical* (Oxford: Oxford University Press, 2017), 199–223.

50. Anon, 'Noel Coward and Ivor Who?', *The Economist*, 27 November 1993, 96.

51. Harding, *Ivor Novello*, 61.

52. Harding, *Ivor Novello*, 37.

53. 'Glamorous Night', *Play Pictorial* 66.398 (June 1935): 3–9. The article provides a lavishly illustrated summary of the play.

54. 'James P. Cunningham, '400 Do Coronation Job', *Motion Picture Herald*, 15 May 1937, 40.

55. Maurice Willson Disher's review in the *Daily Mail* describes Lord Radio's office as 'a futurist setting'. Cited in Noble, *Ivor Novello*, 203. The superheterodyne, or 'superhet', was a type of radio receiver, an improvement on the heterodyne.

56. Additional photographs of the original sets are included in *Glamorous Night: A Romantic Play With Music by Ivor Novello, Lyrics by Christopher Hassall, Amateur Version Prepared by Sydney Box and Conrad C. Carter, Under the Supervision of the Author* (London: Samuel French, 1939).

57. The story of the operetta, as summarized in the Drury Lane programme, is that of a Prince and Princess of neighbouring territories who are betrothed without ever having seen each other; incognito, they pass a 'glamorous night' together and fall in love before discovering their real relationship. It is the basic plot of several Edwardian musical comedies, including *The King of Cadonia*, and looks forward to Novello's own *King's Rhapsody*.

58. Traubner, *Operetta*, 349.

59. A. L. Easterman claims that the name Magda was coined by the Italian press, who assumed that Elena was short for Magdalena. See his *King Carol, Hitler, and Lupescu* (London: Victor Gollancz, 1942), 75. For contemporary views, see Hector Bolitho, *Roumania Under King Carol* (London: Eyre and Spottiswoode, 1939), and, for a more recent account, see Maria Bucur, 'King Carol II of Romania', in Bernd Fischer, ed., *Balkan Strongmen: Dictators and Authoritarian Rulers of Southeast Europe* (London: Hurst and Company, 2007), 87–117.

60. Easterman suggests that the British press in this period uncritically reprinted tales circulated by Carol's Romanian enemies about his 'promiscuous philanderings, champagne bibbings [and] gambling orgies', (*King Carol*, 43).

61. 'Carol's Crown', *Time*, 16 June 1930. In May 1928 the British press was full of reports that Carol was sequestered in Godstone, Surrey, planning a secret flight to Romania to recapture the throne; eventually he was forced to leave Britain under police escort.

62. 'Playboy into Statesman', *Time*, 13 November 1939. For a fictional—and enthusiastic—representation of Carol's Straja Tarii, a sort of scouting movement, see Buchan's *House of the Four Winds*. Carol's political tendencies became clearer in the years after *Glamorous Night*: by 1938 Carol was in effect a royal dictator, presiding over anti-Semitic policies while also violently suppressing the Iron Guard, the main fascist opposition. But the Guard, backed by Hitler, were not so easily suppressed. By 1940, orchestrated mobs were besieging the Royal Palace, shouting 'Death to Lupescu' and 'Death to the Jewess'. In September of that year Carol and Elena gathered their four dogs and fled the country. For a period, at least, Carol plotted another return to Romania, but he died in Estoril, Portugal, in 1953 and was buried in the Church of St Vincent in Lisbon; Elena lived on until 1977. See Richard Cavendish, 'Death of Carol II of Romania', *History Today* 53.4 (April 2003).

63. Cited in Frank Prochaska, *The Eagle and the Crown: Americans and the British Monarchy* (New Haven: Yale University Press, 2008), 138.

64. Coward had himself ventured into Ruritanian territory in his play The *Queen Was in the Parlour* (1926), which features the lovelorn Queen of Krayia; film versions followed in 1927 and 1932.

65. *King's Rhapsody: A Musical Romance*, Devised, Written and Composed by Ivor Novello, Lyrics by Christopher Hassall (London: Samuel French, 1955).

66. J. C. Trewin, 'The World of the Theatre: Off the Map', *Illustrated London News*, 8 October 1949.

67. 'King's Rhapsody', *Yorkshire Post and Leeds Intelligencer*, 16 September 1949; 'The London Theatres', *The Scotsman*, 17 September 1949. *Observer* and *Times* reviews cited in Noble, *Ivor Novello*, 259–60.

68. On *Gay's the Word*, see Dominic Symonds, 'The American Invasion', in Gordon and Jubin, *The Oxford Handbook of the British Musical*, 225–48 (239–42).

69. Adrian Wright, *A Tanner's Worth of Tune: Rediscovering the Post-War British Musical* (Woodbridge, Suffolk: Boydell Press, 2010), 38.

70. Its basic plot was already familiar to Broadway audiences, since it is based on Terence Rattigan's *The Sleeping Prince* (1953), which had been filmed as *The Prince and the Showgirl* (1957), with Marilyn Monroe and Laurence Olivier.

71. See Charles Morrow, 'It's Good to be the King: Hollywood's Mythical Monarchies, Troubled Republics, and Crazy Kingdoms', in Andrew Horton and Joanne E. Rapf, eds., *A Companion to Film Comedy* (Chichester: Wiley Blackwell, 2012), 251–72.

72. On Stroheim's *The Merry Widow* and his films more generally, see Herman G. Weinberg, *Stroheim: A Pictorial Record of His Nine Films* (New York: Dover, 1975); and especially Richard Koszarski, *The Man You Loved To Hate: Erich Von Stroheim and Hollywood* (Oxford: Oxford University Press, 1983).

73. According to the IMDB, both Clark Gable and Joan Crawford had uncredited dancing parts in the waltz scene.

74. 'The Screen: The Merry Widow', *New York Times*, 27 August 1925.

75. Andre Sennwald, 'The Merry Widow', *New York Times*, 12 October 1934.

76. See Brian Taves, P. G. *Wodehouse and Hollywood: Screenwriting, Satires and Adaptations* (Jefferson, NC: McFarland, 2006), 33–5; and 'McGuire's MG *Rosalie* Readied for Cameras', *Variety*, 16 December 1936, 3.

77. 'My Lips Betray', *Screenland*, February 1934, 9; 'My Lips Betray', *New Movie Magazine*, February 1934, 101.

78. I have excluded the 1931 Wheeler and Woolsey comedy vehicle *Cracked Nuts* from this survey, since it is set in the Latin American territory of El Dorania rather than ersatz Europe, but it is worth mentioning in passing here for its anticipation of the zaniness of *Duck Soup*.

79. John Mundy, *The British Musical Film* (Manchester: Manchester University Press, 2007), 33.

80. See Lawrence Napper, *British Cinema and Middlebrow Culture in the Interwar Years* (Exeter: University of Exeter Press, 2009); Stephen C. Shafer, *British Popular Films 1929–1939: The Cinema of Reassurance* (London: Routledge, 1997).

81. Stephen Guy, 'Calling all Stars: Musical Films in a Musical Decade', in Jeffrey Richards, ed., *The Unknown Thirties: An Alternative History of the British Cinema* (London: I. B. Tauris, 1998), 99–120. See also Mundy, *The British Musical Film*, 71–4. The 'quota' system had been introduced by the Cinematograph Films Act of 1927.

82. Quoted in Jeffrey Richards, *The Age of the Dream Palace: Cinema and Society in Britain 1930–1939* (London: Routledge and Kegan Paul, 1984), 247.

83. For a detailed and extensively illustrated account of a production of the operetta at the Palace Theatre on 21 October 1926, see *Play Pictorial* 49.297 (October 1926): 89–108.

84. 'Lucky Girl', *Motion Picture Herald*, 2 July 1932.

85. 'Film Reviews: *Glamorous Night*', *Variety*, 19 May 1937, 23. On its American prospects, see also the *Motion Picture Review Digest* entry for *Glamorous Night*, January–December 1938, 37.

86. John Mundy, 'Britain', in *The International Film Musical*, edited by Corey K. Creekmur and Linda Y. Mokdad (Edinburgh: Edinburgh University Press, 2012), 1–28 (18).

87. Neagle and Flynn had already been paired in another Wilcox film, *Lilacs in the Spring* (1954).

88. For a set of colour production stills from the film, see 'King's Rhapsody', *Australian Women's Weekly*, 20 July 1955, available online through the Trove database.

89. Thomas McNulty, *Errol Flynn: The Life and Career* (Jefferson, NC: McFarland, 2004), 261.

90. A Pan paperback edition of the novel appeared in 1968, to cater to the demand created by the film version.

91. One of the wealthiest men of his time, and related to the Astor family, Zborowski was killed in an accident in the Italian Grand Prix at Monza at the age of 29.

92. Authorship of this interpolated episode is somewhat uncertain. One might assume it to be the work of Dahl, but Ken Hughes claims that he himself wrote 'every fucking word in that bloody script' because Broccoli had dismissed Dahl's slow-to-arrive version as 'shit'. See Jeremy Treglown, *Roald Dahl: A Biography* (London: Faber and Faber, 1994), 169–70 (170). Treglown notes that Dahl later distanced himself from the project (170).

93. Joshua Hagen, 'The Most German of Towns: Creating an Ideal Nazi Community in Rothenburg ob der Tauber', *Annals of the Association of American Geographers* 94.1 (March 2004): 207–27 (213).

94. Dick Van Dyke in Chitty was one of the attractions of the Battersea Easter Parade that year, and The *Daily Express* ran a competition for readers to win the 'Truly Scrumptious', the car driven by Sally Ann Howes' character in the film. 'While the Marathon Goes On', *Daily Express*, 3 December 1968.

95. 'The Sweet Yell of Success', *Daily Mirror*, 28 November 1968.

96. Ronald Bergan, 'Obituary: Ken Hughes: Director who Yearned for Serious Films but Won Fame with *Chitty Chitty Bang Bang*', *Guardian*, 1 May 2001.

97. Aliza Weinberger, 'Author Meg Cabot returns to Genovia for more "Princess Diaries"', Mashable.com, 2 June 2015.

CHAPTER 5

1. Winston Churchill, 'March 5, 1946, Westminster College, Fulton, Missouri', text from the website of the International Churchill Society.

2. Odd Arne Westad, *The Cold War and World History* (London: Allen Lane, 2017), 106, 266.

3. The full text of Kennan's telegram is given in the Cold War Documents section of the National Security Archive at George Washington University, available online.

4. The standard history of the period is Melvyn Leffler and Odd Arne Westad, eds., *The Cambridge History of the Cold War*, 3 vols. (Cambridge: Cambridge University Press, 2010–12), and see also Odd Arne Westad, *The Global Cold War: Third World Interventions and the Making of Our Times* (Cambridge: Cambridge University Press, 2007), his *The Cold War: A World History* (London: Allen Lane, 2017), and William Blum, *The CIA, a Forgotten History: U.S. Global Interventions Since World War 2* (London: Zed Books, 1986).

5. William J. Broad, 'From the Start, the Space Race Was an Arms Race', *New York Times*, 25 September 2007.

6. William J. Broad, 'Star Wars Traced to Eisenhower Era', *New York Times*, 28 October 1986.

7. On Soviet cultural diplomacy see, for instance, Cadra Peterson McDaniel, *American–Soviet Cultural Diplomacy: The Bolshoi Ballet's American Premiere* (Lanham: Lexington Books, 2014), and Kiril Tomoff, *Virtuosi Abroad: Soviet Music and Imperial Competition during the Early Cold War, 1945–1958* (Ithaca, NY: Cornell University Press, 2015). On American efforts, see Frances Stonor Saunders, *Who*

Paid the Piper? The CIA and the Cultural Cold War (London: Granta, 1999), and Peter Finn and Petra Couvée, *The Zhivago Affair: The Kremlin, the CIA, and the Battle Over a Forbidden Book* (New York: Pantheon, 2014).

8. See, for instance, Hugh Wilford, 'The Information Research Department: Britain's Secret Cold War Weapon Revealed', *Review of International Studies* 24.3 (July 1998): 353–69; and Andrew N. Rubin, *Archives of Authority: Empire, Culture, and the Cold War* (Princeton: Princeton University Press, 2012), 37–8.

9. A comment made in the *New York Times* of 8 August 1945, cited in Boyer, *By the Bomb's Early Light* (1985; Chapel Hill: University of North Carolina, 1994), xxi.

10. David W. Dunlap, '1950: "Atomic Bomb Is Not The Weapon"', *New York Times*, 10 August 2017.

11. See Oliver Stone and Peter Kuznick, *The Untold History of the United States* (New York: Gallery Books, 2012), 241.

12. See, for example, 'Noah's Ark for Atom Bomb Test', *Aberdeen Press and Journal*, 25 February 1946, 1.

13. Jean Watin-Augouard, *Le dictionnaire des marques* (Paris: JV&DS–Sediac, 1997), 54; Hannah Betts, 'The Bikini Is 70 Years Old Today—So Why Is It Still One of the Hardest Items to Buy?', *Daily Telegraph*, 5 July 2016.

14. Such items regularly appear in auctions such as those of Hake's Americana and Collectibles. For a wry look at the bomb-flavoured culture of this period, see *The Atomic Café* (1982, dir. Jayne Loader, Kevin Rafferty, Pierce Rafferty).

15. See, for instance, 'New Efforts to Ban H-Bomb are Expected: Fisherman Dies', *Yorkshire Post and Leeds Intelligencer*, 24 September 1954, 7. Ralph E. Lapp's *The Voyage of the Lucky Dragon* (1957), serialized in *Harper's Magazine* in 1957–8, describes the events and the global outcry they created.

16. Boyer, *By the Bomb's Early Light*, 352.

17. Richard Gerstell, 'How You Can Survive an A-bomb Blast', *The Saturday Evening Post*, 7 January 1950, 23, 73–6, later revised as *How to Survive an Atomic Bomb* (New York: Bantam, 1950).

18. Guy Oakes, *The Imaginary War: Civil Defense and American Cold War Culture* (New York: Oxford University Press, 1995), 82–4. See also Gerard J. DeGroot, *The Bomb: A Life* (Cambridge: Harvard University Press, 2005).

19. Reproduced from an unnamed Los Angeles newspaper on the *Cold War: L.A.* website. For 'Alert America', see Bill Geerhart's *Conelrad* website.

20. Richard C. Paddock, 'Column One: Fallout From Toxic Beagle Experiments', *Los Angeles Times*, 8 February 1994.

21. See, for instance, the British Home Office–issued *Civil Defence Handbook No. 10: Advising the Householder on Protection Against Nuclear Attack* (1963), and the Irish Civil Defence pamphlet *Bás Beatha: Survival in a Nuclear War, Advice on Protection in the Home and on the Farm* (1965).

22. Michelle DeArmond, 'Avon Founder Buried His Doorbell Deep in Las Vegas', *Los Angeles Times*, 9 June 1996.

23. See, for instance, the cover image of Chuck West's 1962 publication for Fawcett Publications, *Fallout Shelter Handbook*.

24. Oakes, *The Imaginary War*, 84–104.

25. The Underground Home exhibit was sponsored by Jerry Henderson and his Underground World Home Corporation. Judith Miller, 'Civil Defense Notions Change But the Skepticism Remains', *New York Times*, 4 April 1982.

26. See, for example, 'A-Raid Test Stills Boro: Imaginary "Bomb" Dropped Downtown', *Brooklyn Daily Eagle*, 14 June 1954; 'Refugees Fill Torrance in Mock Atomic Attack', *Torrance Herald*, 17 June 1954; Jon Hunner, *Inventing Los Alamos: The Growth of an Atomic Community* (Norman: University of Oklahoma Press, 2004), 179.

27. Davis, 'Between History and Event: Rehearsing Nuclear War Survival,' *TDR: The Dramatic Review* 46.4 (2002): 11–45.

28. On Britain's extensive underground facilities, see, for instance, Nick McCamley, *Cold War Secret Nuclear Bunkers: The Passive Defence of the Western World During the Cold War* (Barnsley: Pen and Sword Military, 2002). The public was probably first alerted to this secret infrastructure by Peter Laurie's *Beneath the City Streets: A Private Inquiry into the Nuclear Preoccupations of Government* (London: Allen Lane, 1970).

29. Paul Hodge, 'Plans for City Evacuation in Case of Nuclear War Studied; Civil Defense Studies Plan for Evacuation of Washington Area', *Washington Post*, 20 January 1977. The lake is not, in fact, so far-fetched, since there is apparently one at NORAD headquarters in Colorado Springs. Mount Weather is now the headquarters of FEMA. For a recent account of these strange structures, see Garrett M. Graff, *Raven Rock: The Story of the U.S. Government's Secret Plan to Save Itself—While the Rest of Us Die* (New York: Simon and Schuster, 2017).

30. For reappraisals of the cultural significance of the Cold War, see, for instance, Ann Douglas, 'Periodizing the American Century: Modernism, Postmodernism, and Postcolonialism in the Cold War Context', *Modernism/Modernity* 5.3 (September 1998): 71–98; Adam Piette, *The Literary Cold War: 1945 to Vietnam* (Edinburgh: Edinburgh University Press, 2009); and Andrew Hammond, ed., *Global Cold War Literature: Western, Eastern and Postcolonial Perspectives* (New York: Routledge, 2011).

31. Alan Nadel, 'Fiction and the Cold War', in John N. Duvall, ed., *The Cambridge Companion to American Fiction After 1945* (Cambridge: Cambridge University Press, 2012), 167–80. The term 'other-directed' was popularized by David Riesman (with Nathan Glazer and Reuel Denney) in *The Lonely Crowd: A Study of the Changing American Character* (1950).

32. Thomas Hill Schwaub, *American Fiction in the Cold War* (Madison: University of Wisconsin Press, 1991), 17.

33. Nabokov's fictional Zembla recalls the real Nova Zembla (or Novaya Zemlya) archipelago, used by the Soviet Union as an atomic test-site from the 1950s. In 1961 it was used to test the AN602, or Tsar Bomba, the largest-ever hydrogen bomb. I am grateful to Scott Hamilton for pointing this out to me. On the AN602, see Westad, *The Cold War: A World History*, 303–4.

34. 'Three Films Have Premieres at Midtown Theatres—Hope at Paramount', *New York Times*, 25 December 1947.

35. Her life as a Washington socialite and ambassador in Luxemburg is described in her *Perle: My Story* (New York: McGraw Hill, 1960).

36. There were many provincial productions. For the critical response, see John Miller, *Peter Ustinov: The Gift of Laughter* (London: Orion, 2003), 102–3.

37. Programme note to the production at the Theatre Royal in Bristol in November, 1957. Peter O'Toole played the General in this Bristol Old Vic production.

38. Peter Ustinov, *Dear Me* (New York: Random House, 1977), 284.

39. 'Romanoff and Juliet', Variety, 31 December 1960; 'Elspeth Grant on Films', *Tatler*, 12 July 1961, 89.

40. In the end no cobalt bombs were ever built, though they were a source of speculation in the 1950s and drifted into the popular imagination, e.g., in Nevil Shute's *On the Beach* (1957).

41. Tony Shaw, *British Cinema and the Cold War* (New York: I. B. Tauris, 2006), 174.

42. 'Agricultural Education at University College Cork', *Cork Examiner*, 25 November 1919. In his diary for 7 April 1929, Plunkett describes him as 'a Lancashire [Roman Catholic]' who had survived 'the troubles' in Ireland, despite being 'equally objectionable to the Black & Tans and the extreme Sinn Feiners'. See 1929 'Diary of Sir Horace Curzon Plunkett (1854–1932)' in the online collections of the National Library of Ireland.

43. Anna Wibberley, *Time and Chance* (New York: Simon and Schuster, 1973); 'Professor T. Wibberley', *Times*, 24 December 1930; 'Professor Wibberley', *Irish Examiner*, 24 December 1930; 'Death of Professor Wibberley', *Irish Independent*, 24 December 1930.

44. Some of this extensive output was written under the aliases Christopher Webb, Leonard Holton (for the screenplays), and Patrick O'Connor. See Peter Kerr, 'Leonard Wibberley, 68, Dies; Wrote "Mouse that Roared"', *New York Times*, 25 November 1983; and "Author of "Mouse that Roared" Leonard Wibberley Dead at 68', *Daytona Beach Morning Journal*, 24 November 1983. See also the biographic note in the Finding Aid for the Leonard Wibberley Papers, in the collection of the University of Southern California, available online from the Online Archive of California. There is a brief description of his time in Trinidad in one of his syndicated articles, 'A Cheer is Offered for Wise Policemen', *Reading Eagle* (Pennyslvania), 2 July 1981. See also 'Author Wibberley: Roaring Philosopher', *The Nashua Telegraph* (New Hamphire), 6 October 1982.

45. This fresh instalment from the tiny Duchy received a warm critical reception: 'a hilarious trip to the moon', said *Life Magazine*; 'Fantastic, irreverent, cockeyed, funny and irresistible', said the *Library Journal*; 'Delightful, delicious and devastating', opined the Associated Press. Quoted in the paperback Bantam Pathfinder edition of 1965.

46. *The Mouse on the Moon* (New York: William Morrow, 1962).

47. Shaw, *British Cinema and the Cold War*, 123.

48. Arnold also directed a television pilot of *The Mouse that Roared*, starring Sid Caesar in multiple roles, but this failed to attract network interest.

49. This looks like an adapted version of Monopoly rather than the board game of the same name that appeared that same year.

50. 'Film Notes by Our Cinema Correspondent: Victory by Mistake', *Irish Times*, 5 October 1959. The *Irish Press* noted the resemblance to *Carlton-Browne of the F.O.* See Michael Mills, 'A Mouse With Reason to Roar', *Irish Press*, 5 October 1959. The *Cork Examiner* reported that the Irish-born 'Leonard Patrick O'Connor Wibberley' had now 'returned to Ireland, and [was] living at Roundstone, Co. Galway' ('Cork Film Festival', 1 September 1959).

51. Bosley Crowther, 'Movie Review: The Mouse That Roared', *New York Times*, 27 October 1959.

52. 'Snub', *Daily Herald*, 17 July 1959, 2.

53. 'FBI Admits Spreading Lies about Jean Seberg', *Los Angeles Times*, 14 September 1979. 'The Jean Seberg Affair Revisited', The Daily Mirror blog, *Los Angeles Times*, 22 March 2009.

54. Bosley Crowther, 'Screen: British Spoof of Space Race and Statecraft; 'Mouse on the Moon' Opens at Cinema I; Tiny Duchy Is Victor Over Great Powers', *New York Times*, 18 June 1963. Our Film Critic, 'Bette Davis and Joan Crawford as Sisters,' *Times*, 2 May 1963, 6.

55. '*The Mouse That Saved the West*, by Leonard Wibberley' *Kirkus Reviews*, 22 April 1981.

CHAPTER 6

1. Samuel Cohen, *After the End of History: American Fiction in the 1990s* (Iowa City: University of Iowa Press, 2009), which charts the explosion of 'historiographic metafiction' in the wake of the Cold War.

2. Though it was quickly followed by the first book in her supernatural Shadlowland series for young adults, *The Mediator* (2000).

3. Sue Corbett, 'The Accidental Bestseller', *Publishers Weekly*, originally published on 24 November 2014, available on publishersweekly.com.

4. Frances Hodgson Burnett, *A Little Princess* (1905; New York: Charles Scribner, 1917), 146. *A Little Princess* is an expanded version of Hodgson Burnett's earlier 'Sara Crewe or What Happened at Miss Minchin's', which had been published in *St Nicholas* magazine in 1888. The novel was adapted for the screen in 1939 as *The Little Princess* with Shirley Temple in the role of Sara.

5. Meg Cabot, *The Princess Diaries* (New York: HarperTeen, 2000), 1, 4, 139.

6. The idea of gender scripts has become commonplace in theories of childhood development. Theories of gender itself as a performance appear in the work of writers as different as Simone de Beauvoir and Judith Butler.

7. The novel and its sequels were successful enough to sustain radio and stage adaptations and three television series.

8. On the political turn in wartime children's fiction, see Owen Dudley Edwards, *British Children's Fiction in the Second World War* (Edinburgh: Edinburgh University Press, 2007).

9. See Elizabeth A. Ford and Deborah C. Mitchell, *The Makeover in Movies: Before and After in Hollywood Films, 1941–2002* (Jefferson, NC: McFarland, 2004), 20–8. Ford and Mitchell cite *Now, Voyager* (1941) as the first major example of the makeover genre.

10. For accounts of the courtship and wedding, see, for instance, Randy J. Taraborrelli, *Once Upon a Time: Behind the Fairy Tale of Princess Grace and Prince Rainier* (New York: Grand Central Publishing, 2003), and Wendy Leigh, *True Grace: The Life and Times of an American Princess* (New York: Thomas Dunne Books, 2007). Leigh notes that Grace Kelly was not, in fact, the first American-born Princess of Monaco, since Alice Heine, who later married Prince Albert I, was born in New Orleans.

11. 'Graustark-on-the-Mediterranean; Here are Some Scenes of the Improbable Land of Monaco', *New York Times*, 8 April 1956.

12. Taraborrelli gives the number of journalists as 1,500; Leigh reports 1,600.

13. See, for instance, 'Prince Rainier will wear Sky-Blue Trousers for Wedding to Grace Kelly', *Belfast Newsletter*, 7 April 1956; 'Monaco Welcome Princess-to be', *Hartlepool Northern Daily Mail*, 12 April 1956.

14. Onassis was a major investor in Monaco through ownership of shares in the *Société des Bains de Mer*, which controls the Casino.

15. Joe Moran, 'Why Elizabeth II's 1953 Coronation is the Day that Changed Television', *Radio Times*, 2 June 2013. As Moran notes, cameras had not been allowed at Elizabeth's wedding ceremony at Westminster Abbey in 1947. See also his *Armchair Nation: An Intimate History of Britain in Front of the TV* (London: Profile, 2013).

16. See Leigh, *True Grace*, 109, 140; Taraborrelli, *Once Upon a Time*, 203–9.

17. Maya Cantu, *American Cinderellas on the Broadway Musical Stage: Imagining the Working Girl from 'Irene' to 'Gypsy'* (New York: Palgrave, 2015), chapter 4.

18. See, for instance, Rone Tempest, 'Move Over, Charles and Di: The House of Windsor isn't the Only Royal Mess. Just look at the Grimaldis of Monaco', *Los Angeles Times*, 24 November 1992; Jeff Wilson, 'A 'Princess Diaries' Moment for Albert's Daughter', *Washington Post*, 5 June 2006; and Romy Otulski, 'Exclusive: Grace Kelly's Granddaughter Jazmin Grace Grimaldi Opens Up', *Harper's Bazaar*, August 2015.

19. Miriam Forman-Brunell and Rebecca C. Hains, 'Introduction' to Forman-Brunell and Hains, eds., *Princess Cultures: Mediating Girls Imaginations and Identities* (New York: Peter Lang, 2015). See also, for instance, Miriam Forman-Brunell and Julie Eaton, 'The Graceful and Gritty Princess: Managing Notions of Girlhood from the New Nation to the New Millennium', *American Journal of Play* 1.3 (Winter 2009): 338–64.

20. See, for example, Sherianne Shuler, 'Raising (Razing?) Princess: Autoethnographic Reflections On Motherhood and The Princess Culture', *The Popular Culture Studies Journal*, 3.1 and 3.2 (2015): 458–86 (461).

21. Megan Condis, 'Applying for the Position of Princess: Race, Labor, and the Privileging of Whiteness in the Disney Princess Line', in Forman-Brunell and

Hains, eds., *Princess Cultures*, 25–44 (27). Condis cites the anecdote from Peggy Orenstein's 2006 *New York Times* magazine article, 'What's Wrong with Cinderella'.

22. Shuler, 'Raising (Razing) Princess', 461.

23. *Newsweek* dubbed *The Princess Diaries* a 'genial, G-rated Pretty Woman'. Devin Gordon, 'She's Getting the Royal Treatment', *Newsweek*, 8 May 2001.

24. The relocation to the west coast was apparently to suit Marshall's schedule. Dina Rabinovitch, 'Author of the Month: Meg Cabot', *Guardian*, 27 October 2004.

25. Roger Ebert, '*The Princess Diaries*', 3 August 2001, on rogerebert.com.

26. For Susan Wloszczyna writing in *USA Today*, the film was in 'too great a rush to get to the magic moment' of the makeover. See her 'Girls Will Royally Enjoy "The Princess Diaries"', *USA Today*, 2 August 2001. For a detailed analysis of this scene, see Ford and Mitchell, *The Makeover in Movies*, 20–8.

27. Robert Koehler, 'The Princess Diaries', *Variety*, 27 July 2001.

28. Gilda Williams, 'The Princess Diaries', *Sight and Sound* 12.2 (February 2002): 57–8.

29. Elvis Mitchell, 'Film Review; Pygmalion for Another Fair Lady', *New York Times*, 3 August 2001.

30. Wloszczyna, 'Girls Will Royally Enjoy "The Princess Diaries"'.

31. Joe Leydon, 'Review: "The Princess Diaries 2: Royal Engagement"', *Variety*, 11 August 2004; Justin Kroll, 'Princess Diaries 3 Is Not Currently in Development', *Variety*, 17 June 2015.

32. According to the website of American Humane, the part of Fat Louie is played by two cats, Othello and Zorro.

33. Ali Jaafar, 'Princess Diaries 2: Royal Engagement', *Sight and Sound* 14.12 (December 2004): 59–60.

34. Andrews stopped singing on screen after a 1997 operation on her throat. See David Germain, 'Mary Poppins Sings Again, Sort of, in *Princess Diaries 2*', *Toronto Star*, 10 August 2004.

35. 'Summer Movie Preview', *Entertainment Weekly*, 30 April 2004.

36. Peter Haldeman, 'The Princess Diaries 2', *Architectural Digest* 61.7 (July 2004): 152–5. According to this article various paintings of the Genovian royal family are in fact portraits of production designer Albert Brenner and some of the film's producers and writers. African-Americans Whitney Houston, Debra Martin Chase, and Shonda Rhimes do not appear to be among them.

37. Tom Gliatto 'The Princess Diaries 2: Royal Engagement', *People*, 23 August 2004; Noh, 'The Princess Diaries 2'; Leydon, 'Royal Return Engagement'; Jaafar, 'Princess Diaries 2'.

38. Scott Brown, 'The Princess Diaries 2: Royal Engagement', *Entertainment Weekly*, 20 August 2004.

39. Corbett, 'The Accidental Bestseller', 7.

40. See, for example, Stefan Kyriazis, 'Princess Diaries 3 Confirmation: Julie Andrews and Anne Hathaway "Very Keen" to Start', *Daily Express*, 3 March 2017; and Noelle Devoe, 'Anne Hathaway and Julie Andrews Want to Make "Princess Diaries 3" Even Though Their Director Died', *Seventeen*, 2 March 2017.

41. On the long life of the term since its first use in 1948, see Dominic Tierney, 'What Does It Mean That Trump Is "Leader of the Free World"? The puzzling resilience of a Cold War concept', *The Atlantic*, 24 January 2017.

42. Lasch, *The Culture of Narcissism: American Life in an Age of Diminishing Expectations* (New York: W. W. Norton, 1979); Twenge and Campbell, *The Narcissism Epidemic: Living in the Age of Entitlement* (New York: Free Press, 2009).

AFTERWORD

1. Stiles is replaced by Kam Heskin in the sequels; Mably reappears in the second film, but he is replaced for the other two by Chris Geere. The third film, *The Prince and Me: A Royal Honeymoon*, takes us to Ruritania proper, in the form of Belavia.

2. On the more general issue of films that represent Christmas while also being part of its patterns of consumption, see, for example, Lauren Rosewarne, *Analyzing Christmas in Film: Santa to the Supernatural* (London: Lexington, 2018).

3. Prince Ashton, we are told, is a prince through his mother's side of the family, though this is never explored.

4. 'Our target audience is women', according to Michelle Vicary, executive vice president of programming and network publicity for Crown Media Family Networks. See Dinah Eng, 'Meet the Woman Behind Hallmark's Christmas Movie Juggernaut', *Fortune* (online), 27 November 2015.

5. Nicole Kobie, 'Inside the Christmas Movie Mega-complex Churning out Festive Films', *Wired* (UK), 21 December 2018.

6. This striking building appears as a royal setting in *A Princess for Christmas*, *A Prince for Christmas*, *A Christmas Prince*, and *Royal Matchmaker*. Built in neo-Renaissance style, the former summer palace is a late-nineteenth-century structure, completed in the early twentieth century.

7. Tierney Bricker, 'Netflix's *A Christmas Prince* vs. Lifetime's *My Christmas Prince*: A Royal Showdown', *Enews*, 13 December 2017. On the royal Christmas vogue, see also Liz Shannon Miller, " 'A Christmas Prince: The Royal Wedding': Holiday Rom-Coms Are Harder Than They Look", *Indiewire*, 2 December 2018. As Miller notes, these Christmas TV movies had already attracted the invidious attention of *Saturday Night Live*'s comedy team, whose fake trailer of Hallmark's Christmas offerings include a film called *Prince Santa*. This 'Hallmark Channel Christmas Promo' featuring James Franco appears in *Saturday Night Live*, Season 43, Episode 10, which aired in the United States on 9 December 2018; it is available on YouTube's *SNL* channel.

8. George Parker and Alex Barker, 'Intrigue and Betrayal Stalk UK's Corridors of Power', *The Financial Times*, 1 July 2016.

9. Simon Jenkins 'After Ivan Rogers, Britain Will Still Need Friends in Europe – and Diplomats', *Guardian*, 4 January 2017. See also, for instance, Vince Cable's attack on the 'Ruritanian' honours system in ' "Dave's Cronyism Stinks . . . I Thank the Lord I Said No to my Peerage": Former Business Secretary Vince Cable Says 2016 Britain Is Just Like *The Goon Show*', *Mail Online*, 7 August 2016; Tom Dyckhoff's

'Let's Move to Windsor & Eton, Berkshire: "A Metaphor for the Nation"',
Guardian, 3 November 2017, in which he advises potential housebuyers to
'think of Ruritania, and you're halfway there'; and Simon Jenkins' 'It's Delusional
to Think Britain Should Be a Global Military Power', *Guardian*, 28 June 2018,
in which he argues that 'Britain's defence structure is Ruritanian, drenched in
ceremonial, institutional history and abstract nouns.' The royal wedding in
May 2018 made others think of Anthony Hope: see, for instance, Kevin Maguire,
'Austerity for the Many ut Not for This Pair Reveals that We Really Are Not
All in This Together; Royal Wedding: Anger as Taxpayers Handed £2m Bill;
Storm Is Brewing for Freeloaders', *Daily Mirror*, 13 October 2018; and John
Edwards and Lynda Lee Potter, 'The End of the Prince's Playboy Years: *Daily
Mail* Relives the Day Andrew Married Flame-Haired Fergie with Original
Newspaper Reports from 1986—from the £35,000 Wedding Dress to Pageboy
William Who Stole the Show', *Mail Online*, 14 May 2018.

10. Drew Allan, 'UK on the Way to Becoming a Minor Entity', Glasgow *Herald*,
19 December 2017.

Bibliography

Most British newspapers have been cited from the British Library's online *British Newspaper Archive*. For historical US newspapers, I have used the Library of Congress's *Chronicling America: Historic American Newspapers* as well as the online archives of individual publications. For early film trade papers and periodicals, I found the *Media History Digital Library* an invaluable resource.

SELECT RURITANIAS

Buchan, John, *Castle Gay* (London: Hodder and Stoughton, 1930).

Buchan, *The House of the Four Winds* (London: Hodder and Stoughton, 1935).

Beverly of Graustark (dir. Sidney Franklin), Cosmopolitan, MGM, 1926.

Beverly of Graustark (n.p.: Klaw and Erlanger, 1914).

Cabot, Meg, *The Princess Diaries* (New York: HarperTeen, 2000), 26.

Carlton Browne of the F. O. (dir. Roy Boulting, Jeffrey Dell), Charterhouse, 1959.

Chitty Chitty Bang Bang (dir. Ken Hughes), Dramatic Features, Warfield, 1968.

Ford, Ford Madox, *The New Humpty Dumpty* (New York: John Lane, 1912).

Graustark (dir. Dimitri Buchowetzki), Joseph M. Schenck Productions, 1925.

Harte, Bret, *Condensed Novels: New Burlesques* (London: Chatto and Windus, 1902).

Hope, Anthony, *The Prisoner of Zenda: Being the History of Three Months in the Life of an English Gentleman* (London: J. W. Arrowsmith, 1894).

Hope, *Sport Royal and Other Stories* (1893; New York: Henry Holt, 1895).

Hope, *Rupert of Hentzau* (Bristol: Arrowsmith, 1898).

Lehár, Franz, et al., *The Merry Widow, New Musical Play, Adapted from the German of Victor Léon and Leo Stein, Lyrics by Adrian Ross, Arranged for the Piano by H. M. Higgs, Vocal Score* (London: Chapell, 1907), 20–21.

McCutcheon, George Barr, *Graustark* (Chicago: Henry Stone, 1901).

McCutcheon, *Beverly of Graustark* (New York: Dodd, Mead, 1904).

McCutcheon, *Truxton King* (New York: Dodd, Mead, 1909).

McCutcheon, *Prince of Graustark* (New York: Dodd Mead, 1914).

McCutcheon, *East of the Setting Sun* (New York: Dodd, Mead, 1924).

McCutcheon, *The Inn of the Hawk and the Raven: A Tale of Old Graustark* (New York: Dodd, Mead, 1927).

Novello, Ivor, and Christopher Hassall, *Glamorous Night: A Romantic Play With Music by Ivor Novello, Lyrics by Christopher Hassall, Amateur Version Prepared by Sydney Box and Conrad C. Carter, Under the Supervision of the Author* (London: Samuel French, 1939).

Novello, *King's Rhapsody: A Musical Romance*, Devised, Written and Composed by Ivor Novello, Lyrics by Christopher Hassall (London: Samuel French, 1955).

Romberg, Sigmund, *Princess Flavia* (2 November 1925, Century Theatre).

Romberg, *The Student Prince* (2 December 1924, Jolson's 59th Street Theatre).

Rosalie (dir. W. S. Van Dyke), MGM, 1937.

Rose, Edward, 'The Prisoner of Zenda: A Romantic Play in a Prologue and Four Acts', unpublished typescript.

Stevenson, Robert Louis, *Prince Otto* (London: Chatto and Windus, 1885).

The Merry Widow (dir. Erich von Stroheim), MGM, 1925.

The Merry Widow, New Musical Play, Adapted from the German of Victor Léon and Leo Stein, Lyrics by Adrian Ross, Arranged for the Piano by H. M. Higgs, Vocal Score (London: Chapell, 1907).

The Mouse on the Moon (dir. Richard Lester), Walter Shenson Films, 1963.

The Mouse on the Moon (New York: William Morrow, 1962).

The Mouse that Roared (dir. Jack Arnold), Highroad, 1959.

The Princess Diaries (dir. Garry Marshall), BrownHouse, Walt Disney Pictures, 2001.

The Princess Diaries 2: Royal Engagement (dir. Garry Marshall), BrownHouse, Walt Disney Pictures, 2004.

The Prisoner of Zenda (dir. Edwin S. Porter), Famous Players, 1913.

The Prisoner of Zenda (dir. John Cromwell), Selznick International Pictures, 1937.

The Prisoner of Zenda (dir. Rex Ingram), Metro Pictures, 1922.

The Prisoner of Zenda (dir. Richard Quine), Universal Pictures, 1979.

The Prisoner of Zenda (dir. Richard Thorpe), MGM, 1952.

Where There's Life (dir. Sidney Lanfield), Paramount, 1947.

Wibberly, Leonard, The Mouse that Roared (New York: Little, Brown, 1955).

Yates, Dornford, *Fire Below* (1930; London: Ward, Lock, 1949).

SECONDARY SOURCES

Adamson, Joseph, and Jean Wilson, eds., *Northrop Frye, The Secular Scripture and Other Writings on Critical Theory*, vol. 18, 1976–1991 (Toronto: University of Toronto Press, 2005).

Alexander, George, *Parts I Have Played: Photographic and Descriptive Biography of Mr George Alexander* (London: Abbey Press, c.1910).

Allen, David Rayvern, *Sir Aubrey: A Biography of C. Aubrey Smith* (1982, Ewell, Surrey: J. W. Mckenzie, 2005).

Altick, Richard D., 'Nineteenth-Century English Bestsellers: A Third List', *Studies in Bibliography* 39 (1986).

Altman, Rick, *The American Film Musical* (Bloomington: Indiana University Press, 1987).

Arvidson, Linda, *When the Movies Were Young* (New York: E. P. Dutton, 1925).

Bachelard, Gaston, *The Poetics of Space* (1964; New York: Penguin, 2014).

Bakhtin, M. M., *The Dialogic Imagination: Four Essays*, trans. Caryl Emerson and Michael Holquist (Austin: University of Texas Press, 1981).

Barstow, Susan Torrey, '"Hedda Is All of Us': Late-Victorian Women at the Matinee', *Victorian Studies* 43.3 (Spring 2001): 387–412.

Barton, Ruth, *Rex Ingram: Visionary Director of the Silent Screen* (Lexington: University Press of Kentucky, 2014).

Bassett, Troy, 'At the Circulating Library: A Database of Victorian Fiction, 1837–1901' on Victorianresearch.org.

Bassett, Troy J., and Christina M. Walter, 'Booksellers and Bestsellers: British Book Sales as Documented by The Bookman, 1891–1906', Book History 4 (2001): 205–36.

Bergan, Ronald, 'Obituary: Ken Hughes: Director who Yearned for Serious Films but Won Fame with *Chitty Chitty Bang Bang*', *Guardian*, 1 May 2001.

Bloom, Clive, *Bestsellers: Popular Fiction Since 1900*, 2nd edition (Houndmills: Palgrave Macmillan, 2008).

Blum, William, *The CIA, a Forgotten History: U.S. Global Interventions Since World War 2* (London: Zed Books, 1986).

Bolitho, Hector, *Roumania Under King Carol* (London: Eyre and Spottiswoode, 1939).

Bordman, Gerald, *American Operetta: From H.M.S. Pinafore to Sweeney Todd* (New York: Oxford University Press, 1981).

Bowser, Eileen, *The Transformation of Cinema, 1907–1915*, History of the American Cinema, vol. 2 (New York: Charles Scribner, 1990).

Boyer, Paul, *By the Bomb's Early Light* (1985; Chapel Hill: University of North Carolina, 1994).

Brampton, Henry Hawkins, *Reminiscences of Sir Henry Hawkins, Lord Brampton* (London: Edward Arnold, 1904).

'British Book Sales as Documented by The Bookman, 1891-1906', Appendix 2, *Book History* 4 (2001).

Broad, William J., 'From the Start, the Space Race Was an Arms Race', *New York Times*, 25 September 2007.

Broad, 'Star Wars Traced to Eisenhower Era', *New York Times*, 28 October 1986.

Bruce Babington, Bruce, 'Herr Lubitsch Joins the Corps Saxonia: History, Gesture and Homosociality in *The Student Prince of Old Heidelberg*', in Phil Powrie, Ann Davies, and Bruce Babington, eds., *The Trouble with Men: Masculinities in European and Hollywood Cinema* (London: Wallflower Press, 2004), 122–33.

Bucur, Maria, 'King Carol II of Romania', in Bernd Fischer, ed., *Balkan Strongmen: Dictators and Authoritarian Rulers of Southeast Europe* (London: Hurst and Company, 2007), 87–117.

Buitenhuis, Peter, *The Great War of Words: British, American and Canadian Propaganda and Fiction, 1914–1933* (Vancouver: UBC Press, 1987).

Burnett, Frances Hodgson, *A Little Princess* (1905; New York: Charles Scribner, 1917).

Butsch, Richard, *The Making of American Audiences: From Stage to Television* (New York: Cambridge University Press, 2000).

Cabot, Meg, *The Princess Diaries* (New York: HarperTeen, 2000).

Cantu, Maya, *American Cinderellas on the Broadway Musical Stage: Imagining the Working Girl from 'Irene' to 'Gypsy'* (New York: Palgrave, 2015).

Carroll, David, *The Matinée Idols* (New York: Arbor House, 1972).

Cavendish, Richard, 'Death of Carol II of Romania', *History Today* 53.4, April 2003.

Cawelti, John G., *Adventure, Mystery, and Romance: Formula Stories as Art and Popular Culture* (Chicago: University of Chicago Press, 1976).

Chamberlain, Derek, *39 Steps to Stardom: The Life and Times of Madeleine Carroll* (Leicester: Matador, 2010).

Cohen, Samuel, *After the End of History: American Fiction in the 1990s* (Iowa City: University of Iowa Press, 2009).

Conroy, Sarah Booth, 'Star Memories', *Washington Post*, 12 May 1983.

Corbett, Sue, 'The Accidental Bestseller', *Publishers Weekly*, originally published on 24 November 2014, available on publishersweekly.com.

Craft, Christopher, 'Kiss Me With Those Red Lips: Gender and Inversion in Bram Stoker's *Dracula*', *Representations* 8 (Autumn, 1984): 107–33.

Cunningham, James P., '400 Do Coronation Job', *Motion Picture Herald*, 15 May 1937, 40.

Davies, Brenda, *John Cromwell* (London: BFI Publications, 1974).

DeGroot, Gerard J., *The Bomb: A Life* (Cambridge: Harvard University Press, 2005).

Denning, Michael, *Cover Stories: Narrative and Ideology in the British Spy Thriller* (London: Routledge and Kegan Paul, 1987).

Desmond, Shaw, *London Nights in the Gay Nineties* (New York: Robert M. McBride, 1928).

Donohue, Joseph, and Ruth Berggren, eds., *Oscar Wilde's The Importance of Being Earnest: A Reconstructive Critical Edition* (Gerrards Cross: Colin Smythe, 1995).

Douglas, Ann, 'Periodizing the American Century: Modernism, Postmodernism, and Postcolonialism in the Cold War Context', *Modernism/Modernity* 5.3 (September 1998): 71–98.

Dudley Edwards, Owen, *British Children's Fiction in the Second World War* (Edinburgh: Edinburgh University Press, 2007).

Duncan, Barry, *The St. James's Theatre: Its Strange and Complete History* (London: Barrie and Rockliff, 1964).

Dunlap, David W., '1950: "Atomic Bomb Is Not The Weapon"', *New York Times*, 10 August 2017.

Easterman, A. L., *King Carol, Hitler, and Lupescu* (London: Victor Gollancz, 1942).

Edel, Leon, ed., *Guy Domville: A Play in Three Acts* (Philadelphia: Lippincott, 1960).

Ellmann, Richard, *Oscar Wilde* (New York: Vintage, 1988).

Evangelista, Nick, *The Encyclopedia of the Sword* (Westport, CT: Greenwood, 1985).

Everett, William A., *Sigmund Romberg* (New Haven: Yale University Press, 2007).

Forman-Brunell, Miriam, and Rebecca C. Hains, eds., *Princess Cultures: Mediating Girls' Imaginations and Identities* (New York: Peter Lang, 2015).

Foucault, Michel, 'Of Other Spaces, Heterotopias', *Architecture, Mouvement, Continuité* 5 (1984): 46–9.

Ford, Elizabeth A., and Deborah C. Mitchell, *The Makeover in Movies: Before and After in Hollywood Films, 1941–2002* (Jefferson, NC: McFarland, 2004).

Freeman, Nicholas, *1895: Drama, Disaster and Disgrace in Late Victorian Britain* (Edinburgh: Edinburgh University Press, 2014).

Frohman, Daniel, *Memories of a Manager: Reminiscences of the Old Lyceum and Some Players of the Last Quarter Century* (New York: Doubleday, Page, 1911).

Furia, Philip, *Ira Gershwin: The Art of the Lyricist* (Oxford: Oxford University Press, 1996).

Gerstell, Richard, *How to Survive an Atomic Bomb* (New York: Bantam, 1950).

Gerstell, 'How You Can Survive an A-bomb Blast', *The Saturday Evening Post*, 7 January 1950, 23, 73–6.

Gerwarth, Robert, *The Vanquished: Why the First World War Failed to End, 1917–1923* (London: Allen Lane, 2016).

Gilloch, Graeme, 'The Word on the Street: Charles Baudelaire, Jacques Offenbach, and the Paris of their Time', in Christian Hermansen Cordua, ed., *Manifestoes and Transformations in the Early Modernist City* (Farnham: Ashgate, 2010), 59–76.

Glazener, Nancy, *Reading for Realism* (Durham, NC: Duke University Press, 1997).

Goldsworthy, Vesna, *Inventing Ruritania: The Imperialism of the Imagination* (1998; London: C. Hurst and Co., 2013).

Graff, Garrett M., *Raven Rock: The Story of the U.S. Government's Secret Plan to Save Itself—While the Rest of Us Die* (New York: Simon and Schuster, 2017).

Grieveson, Lee, and Peter Kraemer, 'Introduction: Feature Films and Cinema Programmes', in Grieveson and Kraemer, eds., *The Silent Cinema Reader* (London: Routledge, 2004), 187–95.

Gunning, Tom, 'The Cinema of Attraction: Early Film, Its Spectator and the Avant-Garde', *Wide Angle* 8.3 & 4 (Fall 1986): 63–70.

Guy, Stephen, 'Calling all Stars: Musical Films in a Musical Decade', in Jeffrey Richards, ed., *The Unknown Thirties: An Alternative History of the British Cinema* (London: I. B. Tauris, 1998), 99–120.

Hackett, Alice Payne, and James Henry Burke, *80 Years of Bestsellers, 1895–1975* (New York: R. R. Bowker, 1977).

Hagen, Joshua, 'The Most German of Towns: Creating an Ideal Nazi Community in Rothenburg ob der Tauber', *Annals of the Association of American Geographers* 94.1 (March 2004): 207–27 (213).

Hammond, Andrew, ed., *Global Cold War Literature: Western, Eastern and Postcolonial Perspectives* (New York: Routledge, 2011).

Harding, James, *Folies de Paris: The Rise and Fall of French Operetta* (London: Chapell/Elm Tree Books, 1979).

Harding, *Ivor Novello: A Biography* (1987; Cardiff: Welsh Academic Press, 1997).

Hart, James D., *The Popular Book: A History of America's Literary Taste* (Berkeley: University of California Press, 1950).

Haver, Ronald, *David O. Selznick's Hollywood* (Los Angeles: Bonanza Books, 1980).

Hebard, Andrew, 'Romantic Sovereignty: Popular Romances and the American Imperial State in the Philippines', *American Quarterly* 57.3 (September 2005): 805–30.

Holt, Henry, 'The Publishing Reminiscences of Mr Henry Holt', *The Publisher's Weekly*, 12 February 1910: 929–33.

Hope, Anthony, *Memories and Notes* (London, 1927).

Horak, Laura, *Girls Will Be Boys: Cross-Dressed Women, Lesbians, and American Cinema, 1908–1934* (New Brunswick: Rutgers University Press, 2016).

Hunner, Jon, *Inventing Los Alamos: The Growth of an Atomic Community* (Norman: University of Oklahoma Press, 2004).

Jaffe, Julian F., *Crusade against Radicalism: New York During the Red Scare, 1914–1924* (Port Washington, NY: Kennikat Press, 1972).

Jenkins, Simon, 'After Ivan Rogers, Britain Will Still Need Friends in Europe—and Diplomats', *Guardian*, 4 January 2017.

Jones, Henry Arthur, *The Triumph of the Philistines* (New York: Samuel French, 1899).

Kaplan, Amy, 'Romancing the Empire: The Embodiment of American Masculinity in the Popular Historical Novel of the 1890s', *American Literary History* 2.4 (Winter, 1990): 659–90.

Kaplan, Joel H., and Sheila Stowell, *Theatre and Fashion: Oscar Wilde to the Suffragettes* (Cambridge: Cambridge University Press, 1995).

Keil, Charlie, *Early American Cinema in Transition: Story, Style, and Filmmaking, 1907–1913* (Madison: University of Wisconsin Press, 2001).

Kestner, Joseph A., *Masculinities in British Adventure Fiction, 1880–1915* (Farnham: Ashgate, 2010).

Kilmer, Alfred Joyce, ed., *Literature in the Making, By Some of its Makers* (New York: Harper and Bros., 1917).

Knapp, Raymond, *The American Musical and the Performance of Personal Identity* (Princeton: Princeton University Press, 2009).

Knight, Grant Cohran, *The Strenuous Age in American Literature* (Chapel Hill: University of North Carolina Press, 1954).

Koszarski, Richard, *An Evening's Entertainment: The Age of the Silent Feature Picture, 1915–1928*, History of the American Cinema vol. 3 (New York: Charles Scribner, 1990).

Koszarski, *Von: The Life and Films of Erich von Stroheim* (1983; New York: Limelight, 2001).

Krasner, Orly Leah, 'Birth Pangs, Growing Pains, and Sibling Rivalry: Musical Theatre in New York, 1900–1920', in William A. Everett and Paul R. Laird, eds. *The Cambridge Companion to the Musical* (Cambridge: Cambridge University Press, 2002), 29–46.

Lambton, Antony, *Elizabeth and Alexandra* (New York: E. P. Dutton, 1985).

Langbauer, Laurie, 'Romance', in Stephen Arata, Madigan Haley, J. Paul Hunter, and Jennifer Wicke, eds., *A Companion to the English Novel* (Oxford: Wiley Blackwell, 2015), 103–16.

Lasch, Christopher, *The Culture of Narcissism: American Life in an Age of Diminishing Expectations* (New York: W. W. Norton, 1979).

Lazarus, A. L., and Victor H. Jones, *Beyond Graustark: George Barr McCutcheon, Playwright Discovered* (Port Washington, New York: Kennicat Press, 1981).

Leffler, Melvyn, and Odd Arne Westad, eds., *The Cambridge History of the Cold War*, 3 vols. (Cambridge: Cambridge University Press, 2010–12).

Leigh, Wendy, *True Grace: The Life and Times of an American Princess* (New York: Thomas Dunne Books, 2007).

MacColl, Gail, and Carol McD. Wallace, *To Marry an English Lord or, How Anglomania Really Got Started* (New York: Workman, 2009).

Mackerness, E. D., *A Social History of English Music* (London: Routledge and Kegan Paul, 1964).

Mallet, Sir Charles, *Anthony Hope and His Books, Being the Authorized Life of Sir Anthony Hope Hawkins* (London, 1935).

Mason, A. E. W., *Sir George Alexander and the St. James's Theatre* (London: Macmillan, 1935).

McCutcheon, John T., *Drawn from Memory: The Autobiography of John T. McCutcheon* (Indianapolis: Bobbs-Merrill, 1950).

McDaniel, Cadra Peterson, *American–Soviet Cultural Diplomacy: The Bolshoi Ballet's American Premiere* (Lanham, MD: Lexington Books, 2014).

McNulty, Thomas, *Errol Flynn: The Life and Career* (Jefferson, NC: McFarland, 2004).

Melman, Billy, *The Culture of History: English Uses of the Past 1800–1953* (Oxford: Oxford University Press, 2006).

Menke, Richard, 'The End of the Three-Volume Novel System, 27 June 1894', *BRANCH: Britain, Representation and Nineteenth-Century History*, edited by Dino Franco Felluga, an extension of Romanticism and Victorianism on the Net.

Migozzi, Jacques, Farid Boumédiène, 'Circulation transnationale des romans et séries de la culture populaire en Europe (1840–1930)', *Géographie poétique et cartographie littéraire*, PULIM, 2012.

Miller, John, *Peter Ustinov: The Gift of Laughter* (London: Orion, 2003).

Miller, Judith, 'Civil Defense Notions Change But the Skepticism Remains', *New York Times*, 4 April 1982.

Mirisch, Walter, *I Thought We Were Making Movies, Not History* (Madison: University of Wisconsin Press, 1988).

Miyao, Daisuke, *Sessue Hayakawa: Silent Cinema and Transnational Stardom* (Durham, NC: Duke University Press, 2007).

Moore, James Ross, 'Girl Crazy: Musicals and Reviews Between the Wars', in Clive Barker and Maggie B. Gale, eds., *British Theatre Between the Wars* (Cambridge: Cambridge University Press, 2000), 88–112.

Moran, Joe, 'Why Elizabeth II's 1953 Coronation is the Day that Changed Television', *Radio Times*, 2 June 2013.

Morley, Sheridan, *The Brits in Hollywood: Tales from the Hollywood Raj* (1983; London: Robson, 2006).

Morrow, Charles, 'It's Good to be the King: Hollywood's Mythical Monarchies, Troubled Republics, and Crazy Kingdoms', in Andrew Horton and Joanne E. Rapf, eds., *A Companion to Film Comedy* (Chichester: Wiley Blackwell, 2012), 251–72.

Mott, Frank, *Golden Multitudes* (New York: 1947).

Mundy, John, 'Britain', in *The International Film Musical*, edited by Corey K. Creekmur and Linda Y. Mokdad (Edinburgh: Edinburgh University Press, 2012), 1–28.

Mundy, *The British Musical Film* (Manchester: Manchester University Press, 2007).

Murray, Robert K., *Red Scare: A Study in National Hysteria, 1919–1920* (New York: McGraw Hill, 1955).

Musser, Charles, *Before the Nickelodeon: Edwin S. Porter and the Edison Manufacturing Company* (Berkeley: University of California Press, 1991).

Musser, *The Emergence of Cinema: The American Screen to 1907*, Volume 1 (Berkeley: University of California Press, 1990).

Nadel, Alan, 'Fiction and the Cold War', in John N. Duvall, ed., *The Cambridge Companion to American Fiction After 1945* (Cambridge: Cambridge University Press, 2012), 167–80.

Nairn, Tom, *The Enchanted Glass: Britain and its Monarchy*, New Edition (1989; London: Verso, 2011).

Napper, Lawrence, *British Cinema and Middlebrow Culture in the Interwar Years* (Exeter: University of Exeter Press, 2009).

'New McCutcheon Book', *New York Times*, 23 May 1908, 296.

Nicholls, Stewart, 'West End Royalty: Ivor Novello and English Operetta, 1917–1951', in Robert Gordon and Olaf Jubin, eds., *The Oxford Handbook of the British Musical* (Oxford: Oxford University Press, 2017), 199–223.

Niemeyer, Paul J., 'The Royal Red-Headed Variant: The Prisoner of Zenda and the 1893 Heredity Debates', *College Literature* 42.1 (Winter 2015): 112–38.

Niver, Kemp R., *Motion Pictures from the Library of Congress Paper Print Collection, 1894–1912* (Berkeley: University of California Press, 1967).

Noble, Peter, *Ivor Novello, Man of the Theatre* (1951; London: White Lion, 1975).

'Noel Coward and Ivor Who?', *The Economist*, 27 November 1993, 96.

Nordau, Max, *Degeneration* (1892; London: William Heinemann, 1895).

Novello, Ivor, and Christopher Hassall, *King's Rhapsody: A Musical Romance*, Devised, Written and Composed by Ivor Novello, Lyrics by Christopher Hassall (London: Samuel French, 1955).

O'Leary, Liam, *Rex Ingram: Master of the Silent Cinema* (1980; London: BFI, 1993).

Oakes, Guy, *The Imaginary War: Civil Defense and American Cold War Culture* (New York: Oxford University Press, 1995).

Parker, George, and Alex Barker, 'Intrigue and Betrayal Stalk UK's Corridors of Power', *The Financial Times*, 1 July 2016.

Parkinson, David, *The Rough Guide to Film Musicals* (London: Rough Guide, 2007).

Pearsall, Ronald, *Edwardian Popular Music* (Newton Abbot: David and Charles, 1974).

Piette, Adam, *The Literary Cold War: 1945 to Vietnam* (Edinburgh: Edinburgh University Press, 2009).

Pizzitola, Louis, *Hearst Over Hollywood: Power, Passion and Propaganda in the Movies* (New York: Columbia University Press, 2002).

Plunkett, Sir Horace, "Diary of Sir Horace Curzon Plunkett (1854–1932)" in the online collections of the National Library of Ireland.

Pollack, Howard, *George Gershwin: His Life and Work* (Berkeley: University of California Press, 2006).

Pope, W. Macqueen, *Ivor: Story of an Achievement* (London: W. H. Allen, 1951).

Pope, W. Macqueen, *St. James's, Theatre of Distinction* (London: W. H. Allen, 1958).

Prochaska, Frank, *The Eagle and the Crown: Americans and the British Monarchy* (New Haven, CT: Yale University Press, 2008).

Ramsaye, Terry, *A Million and One Nights: A History of the Motion Picture* (London: Frank Cass, 1964).

Reuven, Frank, 'The Great Coronation War', *American Heritage* 44.8 (1993). Online.

Richards, Jeffrey, *Swordsmen of the Screen: From Douglas Fairbanks to Michael York* (London: Routledge and Kegan Paul, 1977).

Richards, *The Age of the Dream Palace: Cinema and Society in Britain 1930–1939* (London: Routledge and Kegan Paul, 1984).

Roosevelt, Theodore, *The Strenuous Life* (New York: Review of Reviews, 1910).

Saunders, Frances Stonor, *Who Paid the Piper? The CIA and the Cultural Cold War* (London: Granta, 1999).

Schwaub, Thomas Hill, *American Fiction in the Cold War* (Madison: University of Wisconsin Press, 1991).

Schweitzer, Marlis, *When Broadway Was The Runway: Theatre, Fashion, and American Culture* (Philadelphia: University of Pennsylvania Press, 2009).

Shafer, Stephen C., *British Popular Films 1929–1939: The Cinema of Reassurance* (London: Routledge, 1997).

Shaw, George Bernard, *Dramatic Opinions and Essays*, volume 2 (New York: Brentano's, 1922).

Shuler, Sherianne, 'Raising (Razing?) Princess: Autoethnographic Reflections On Motherhood and The Princess Culture', *The Popular Culture Studies Journal*, 3.1 & 3.2 (2015): 458–86 (461).

Singleton, Brian, *Oscar Asche, Orientalism, and British Musical Comedy* (Westport, CT: Praeger, 2004).

Stewart, Susan, *On Longing: Narratives of the Miniature, the Gigantic, the Souvenir, the Collection* (Baltimore: Johns Hopkins University Press, 1984).

Stone, Oliver, and Peter Kuznick, *The Untold History of the United States* (New York: Gallery Books, 2012).

Symonds, Dominic, "The American Invasion", in Gordon and Jubin, *The Oxford Handbook of the British Musical*, 225–48 (239–42).

Taraborrelli, Randy J., *Once Upon a Time: Behind the Fairy Tale of Princess Grace and Prince Rainier* (New York: Grand Central Publishing, 2003).

Taves, Brian, *P. G. Wodehouse and Hollywood: Screenwriting, Satires and Adaptations* (Jefferson, NC: McFarland, 2006).

Thomson, David, *Showman: The Life of David O. Selznick* (London: André Deutch, 1993).

Tibbets, John C., *The American Theatrical Film: Stages in Development* (Toledo: Popular Press, 1985), 71–6.

Tomoff, Kiril, *Virtuosi Abroad: Soviet Music and Imperial Competition during the Early Cold War, 1945–1958* (Ithaca, NY: Cornell University Press, 2015).

Tooze, Adam, *The Deluge: The Great War and the Remaking of Global Order 1916–1931* (London: Allen Lane, 2014).

Traubner, Richard, *Operetta: A Theatrical History* (London: Victor Gollancz, 1984).

Treglown, Jeremy, *Roald Dahl: A Biography* (London: Faber and Faber, 1994).

Twenge, Jean M., and W. Keith Campbell, *The Narcissism Epidemic: Living in the Age of Entitlement* (New York: Free Press, 2009).

Ustinov, Peter, *Dear Me* (New York: Random House, 1977).

Walker, Alexander, *Peter Sellers* (London: Macmillan, 1982), 305.

Wallace, Raymond, 'Cardboard Kingdoms', *San José Studies* 13.2 (Spring 1987): 23–34.

Watin-Augouard, Jean, *Le dictionnaire des marques* (Paris: JV&DS-Sediac, 1997).

Watkins, Tony, 'Introduction', *The Prisoner of Zenda* (Oxford: Oxford World's Classics, 1994).

Weinberg, Herman G., *Stroheim: A Pictorial Record of His Nine Films* (New York: Dover, 1975).

West, James L. W., 'George Barr McCutcheon's Literary Ledger', *Yale University Library Gazette* 59.3–4 (April 1985): 155–61.

West, *American Authors and the Literary Marketplace Since 1900* (Philadelphia: University of Pennsylvania Press, 1988).

Westad, Odd Arne, *The Global Cold War: Third World Interventions and the Making of Our Times* (Cambridge, UK: Cambridge University Press, 2007).

Westad, *The Cold War and World History* (London: Allen Lane, 2017).

Wibberley, Anna, *Time and Chance* (New York: Simon and Schuster, 1973).

Wolf, Mark J. P., *Building Imaginary Worlds: The Theory and History of Subcreation* (New York: Routledge, 2012).

Wright, Adrian, *A Tanner's Worth of Tune: Rediscovering the Post-War British Musical* (Woodbridge, Suffolk: Boydell Press, 2010), 38.

Zukor, Adolph, *The Public Is Never Wrong* (New York: G. P. Putnam's, 1953).

NEWSPAPER AND OTHER REVIEWS

A. A. B., 'St James's Theatre: The Prisoner of Zenda Revived', *Daily Mail*, October 21, 1896.

Abel., 'The Student Prince', *Variety*, 10 December 1924.

'A Chat With Leonard Boyne', *The Era*, 7 July 1894.

Agate, James, 'The Prisoner of Zenda', *Tatler*, 24 November 1937, 332.

'American Film in London', *Weekly Variety*, 1 October 1915.

'Amusements', *The Record-Union* (Sacramento), 22 October 1896.

'Amusements', *The Sphere*, Saturday, 4 May 1901, 28.

'Anthony Hope's Debutante Daughter', *The Sketch*, 2 August 1922, 31.

'A-Raid Test Stills Boro: Imaginary "Bomb" Dropped Downtown', *Brooklyn Daily Eagle*, 14 June 1954.

Arnold, Gary, 'Hollywood Breaks Out Laughing', *Washington Post*, April 22, 1979.

'Author of "Mouse that Roared" Leonard Wibberley Dead at 68', *Daytona Beach Morning Journal*, 24 November 1983.

'Back to Graustark', *New York Times*, 1 October 1904, 661.

Barnwell Elliott, Sarah, 'Some Recent Fiction', part 2, *Sewanee Review* 3.1 (November 1894): 90–104.

'Bette Davis and Joan Crawford as Sisters', *Times*, 2 May 1963, 6.

'Beverly of Graustark', *Athenaeum*, No. 4044, 29 April 1905, 524.

'Beverly of Graustark', *Variety*, 21 April 1926, 34.

'Beverly of Graustark: Lovely Picture', *Athens Banner-Herald*, 18 June 1926, 3.

Blaisdell, George, 'Observed in the Audience", *Moving Picture World*, vol. 15 (Jan–March 1913), 871–2.

Blaisdell, 'At the Sign of the Flaming Arcs', *Moving Picture World*, vol. 15 (Jan–March 1913).

'Book Reviews: Truxton King', *Evening Star* (North Dakota), 25 September 1909, 5.

'Books in Demand', *New York Times*, 22 June 1901, 14.

Brown, Scott, 'The Princess Diaries 2: Royal Engagement', *Entertainment Weekly*, 20 August 2004.

Bushman, Francis X., 'From the Inside of the Studio', *Picture Play Weekly*, 10 April 1915, 1–4 (3).

'Carol's Crown', *Time*, 16 June 1930.

Caward, Neil G., 'Essanay's Graustark', *Motography* 13.19 (January–June 1915), 742.

'Chatter: Broadway', *Variety*, 22 October 1952, 62.

'Comments on the Films: Beverly of Graustark', *Moving Picture World*, 3 June 1916.

Conlogue, Ray, 'Ruritania Done For Good', *The Globe and Mail* (Canada), 28 May 1979.

'Courtesy of the Public Library', *New York Times*, 9 May 1937, 3.

Corry, John, 'Prisoner of Zenda is Presented on A&E', *New York Times*, 12 August 1986.

Crowther, Bosley, "Movie Review: The Mouse That Roared", *New York Times*, 27 October 1959.

Crowther, 'Screen: British Spoof of Space Race and Statecraft; "Mouse on the Moon" Opens at Cinema I; Tiny Duchy Is Victor Over Great Powers', *New York Times*, 18 June 1963.

'Daniel Frohman Gets Big Stars to Act for Movies', *New York Times*, 22 December 1912.

'Death of Sir George Alexander: A Quarter of a Century at the St James's', *Times*, 16 March 1918.

'Dramatic and Musical: Rudolf and Flavia Again', *New York Times*, 11 April 1899.

Eberhart, Wilfrid, 'Evaluating the Leisure Reading of High-School Pupils', *The School Review*, 47.4 (April 1939), 257–69.

Ebert, Roger, '*The Princess Diaries*', 3 August 2001, on rogerebert.com.

'Elspeth Grant on Films', the *Tatler,* 12 July 1961, 89.

'Emphatic Success of James K. Hackett in Rupert of Hentzau at the Hollis', *Boston Daily Advertiser,* 3 January 1899, 5.

Engleman, J. O., 'Outside Reading', *The English Journal* 6.1 (January 1917), 20–7.

'Extraordinary Special Feature: Palace Theatre', *Athens Banner-Herald,* 16 June 1926, 5.

'Extravagant Heroics of New Stage Duels', *San Francisco Call,* 2 February 1902.

Farjeon, Herbert, 'The London Stage: The White Camellia', *The Graphic,* 9 March 1929, 12.

'FBI Admits Spreading Lies about Jean Seberg', *Los Angeles Times,* 14 September 1979.

'Film First Night', *Times,* November 3, 1937, 17.

'Film Notes by Our Cinema Correspondent: Victory by Mistake', *Irish Times,* 5 October 1959.

'Film Reviews: *Glamorous Night*', *Variety,* 19 May 1937, 23.

Findon, B. W., 'The Naughty Princess: Opera Bouffe in Two Acts', *Play Pictorial* 37.225 (October 1920): 86–97.

Galbraith, 'Our American Letter', *The Bookman* 32.217, October 1909, 8.

'Geo. B. M'Cutcheon Dies at a Luncheon', *New York Times,* 24 October 1928, 1.

'Glamorous Night', *Play Pictorial* 66.398 (June 1935): 3–9.

Gliatto, Tom, 'The Princess Diaries 2: Royal Engagement', *People,* 23 August 2004.

Gordon, Devin, 'She's Getting the Royal Treatment', *Newsweek,* 8 May 2001.

'Grace Gatts Sues Ferris', *New York Times,* 1 December 1911.

'Graustark', *Athenaeum* review of the Grant Richards 6 shilling edition, 26 April 1902, 525.

'Graustark', *Spartanburg Herald-Journal,* 12 March 1910.

'Graustark', *Urbana Daily Courier,* 1 May 1903.

'Graustark', *Weekly Variety,* 23 May 1913.

'Graustark', *Weekly Variety,* 9 September 1925.

'Graustark at Harlem Opera House', *New York Times,* 21 January 1908.

'Graustark: Greatest of All Leading Romantic Plays Now On', *Athens Banner,* 13 October 1910, 3.

'Graustark Heralded as One of the World's Greatest Dramas', *Camas Prairie Chronicle,* 24 December 1915.

'Graustark-on-the-Mediterranean; Here are Some Scenes of the Improbable Land of Monaco', *New York Times,* 8 April 1956.

'Graustark: Revived in Sequel', *San Francisco Sunday Call,* 9 October 1904.

'Graustark to Play Return Date', *Bryan Times,* 10 November 1911.

'Hackett Revives His Biggest Hits', *San Francisco Call,* 14 August 1910.

'Hackett's Career Has Been Active', *San Francisco Call,* 10 July 1910.

Haldeman, Peter, 'The Princess Diaries 2', *Architectural Digest* 61.7 (July 2004): 152–5.

'Harlem', New York Clipper, January 25, 1908.

Harrison, Louis Reeves, 'Studio Saunterings: Stealing a March on the Famous Players Company', *Moving Picture World,* vol. 15, (January–March 1913), 26–8.

'Heidelberg to Music', *Sporting Times,* 6 February 1926, 7.

'His Majesty's Theatre', *Times*, 4 February 1936, 10.

'His Majesty's: The Student Prince', the *Stage*, 11 February 1926, 18

Hodge, Paul, 'Plans for City Evacuation in Case of Nuclear War Studied; Civil Defense Studies Plan for Evacuation of Washington Area', *Washington Post*, 20 January 1977.

'Hollywood Hatchet', *Time* 30.16, 18 October 1937, 30.

'Hollywood May Pick Up Wally–Windsor Yarn', *Boxoffice*, 15 May 1937, 43.

Jaafar, Ali, 'Princess Diaries 2: Royal Engagement', *Sight and Sound* 14.12 (December 2004): 59–60.

'John Gilbert Has Good Vehicle in George Barr McCutcheon Story', *Film Daily*, 4 February 1923, 15.

Kerr, Peter, 'Leonard Wibberley, 68, Dies; Wrote "Mouse that Roared"', *New York Times*, 25 November 1983.

'King's Rhapsody', *Yorkshire Post and Leeds Intelligencer*, 16 September 1949.

Knoblauch, W. V., 'Aus dem Englischen Buchhandel', *Börsenblatt für den Deutschen Buchhandel*, 6 April 1914 (Jg. 81) Nr. 79, S.497–9.

Koehler, Robert, 'The Princess Diaries', *Variety*, 27 July 2001.

Kroll, Justin, 'Princess Diaries 3 Is Not Currently in Development', *Variety*, 17 June 2015.

Kyriazis, Stefan, 'Princess Diaries 3 Confirmation: Julie Andrews and Anne Hathaway "Very Keen" to Start', *Daily Express*, 3 March 2017.

Lang, Andrew, 'Tendencies in Fiction', *North American Review* 161.465 (August 1895), 153–60.

Lang, 'Realism and Romance', *Contemporary Review* 52 (1887): 683–93.

Lawrence, Sidle, "Saccharine Drama: Whose the Blame", *Los Angeles Herald*, 31 May 1908.

Leydon, Joe, 'Review: "The Princess Diaries 2: Royal Engagement"', *Variety*, 11 August 2004.

'Literary Notes', *Freeman's Journal*, 3 May 1895.

'Literature and Art', *Sheffield Daily Telegraph*, 8 April 1903, 3.

'London Correspondence', *Freeman's Journal*, 26 October 1896.

'London Theatres: The Palace, King's Rhapsody', *The Stage*, 22 September 1949, 7.

'Lucky Girl', *Motion Picture Herald*, 2 July 1932.

'Managers Get The Results', *Motion Picture Herald*, November 22, 1952, 48.

Maslin, Janet, 'Screen: Sellers in New "Zenda": A Comic Version', *New York Times*, 25 May 1979.

'Matinée Idols, Past and Present', *Munsey's Magazine*, January 1904, 576–85.

'McGuire's MG *Rosalie* Readied for Cameras', *Variety*, 16 December 1936, 3.

Mills, Michael, 'A Mouse With Reason to Roar', *Irish Press*, 5 October 1959.

'Miss Evelyn Millard', *Times*, 14 March 1941.

Mitchell, Elvis, 'Film Review; Pygmalion for Another Fair Lady', *New York Times*, 3 August 2001.

Moses, Montrose, 'Geo. Barr McCutcheon: Believes in the Happy Endings not for its Commercial Value But Because of his Philosophy of Art', *New York Times*, 21 July 1912, 417.

'Mr George Alexander and His New Playhouse, Drama and Dog', *The Sketch*, 31 January 1900, 21.

'Mr George Alexander and the Police', *The Sketch*, 13 November 1895, 120.

'Music and Drama', *Milwaukee Journal*, 1 September 1896, 3.

'My Lips Betray', *New Movie Magazine*, February 1934, 101.

'My Lips Betray', *Screenland*, February 1934, 9.

Naylor, Hazel Simpson, 'As Others See You, or Gleanings from the Audience', *Motion Picture Magazine* (August 1915–January 1916), 132, 168.

'NBC, Selznick Plan Coronation Air Show', *Motion Picture Daily*, 24 April 1937, 4.

'New Books of the Month', *Bookman*, May 1902, 71

'New Publications: A Bright and Stirring Romance', *New York Times*, 27 May 1894.

'Newsreels Cover Coronation With Color, Television', *Motion Picture Herald*, 15 May 1937, 42.

'New Talmadge Vehicle', *Moving Picture World*, 22 November 1924, 345.

'Novels', *Saturday Review*, 13 January 1900.

'Novels and Stories', *Saturday Review*, May 26, 1894.

'Occasional Notes', *Pall Mall Gazette*, 6 February 1900, 2.

'Old Heidelberg', *The Era*, 23 March 1903.

'Old Heidelberg Again', *New York Times*, 13 October 1903.

'One Hundred Christmas Books: *Truxton King*', *New York Times*, 5 December 1909, 34.

'Original Performances of Plays at the Lyceum Theatre and The American', *The Sun* (New York), 5 September 1895.

Orme, Michael, 'The World of the Kinema', *Illustrated London News*, 13 November 1937, 858.

Pardy, George T., 'Beverly of Graustark', *Motion Picture News*, 8 May 1926, 2266.

'Photoplay Classics', *Motion Picture Magazine* (February–May 1916), 141–2, 181.

'Picturesque Ruritania: Production of the Prisoner of Zenda', *Pall Mall Gazette*, 7 January 1896.

'P.I.P. Playgoer', *Penny Illustrated Paper*, 7 March 1908.

'Playboy into Statesman', *Time*, 13 November 1939.

'Police', *Times*, 5 November 1895.

'Presenting Mr Pidgeon', *Picture-Play Magazine*, September 1926, 47.

'Present Road Shows', *Variety*, 27 March 1925.

'Prince of Graustark', *Weekly Variety*, 3 November 1916, 25.

'Prisoner of Zenda Again: Hackett's Revival of Hope's Play Warmly Applauded', *New York Times*, 22 September 1908.

'Public Amusements', *Lloyds Weekly Newspaper*, 12 January 1896.

'Punch and Judy at the Vaudeville', *Illustrated London News*, 30 October 1937, 772.

Rabinovitch, Dina, 'Author of the Month: Meg Cabot', *Guardian*, 27 October, 2004.

'Recent Publications', *New Haven Morning Herald*, 11 October 1894.

'Refugees Fill Torrance in Mock Atomic Attack', *Torrance Herald*, 17 June 1954.

'Reviews', *Times*, 6 February 1900.

'Romanoff and Juliet', *Variety*, 31 December 1960.

'Ruritanian Romance', *The Globe*, 16 March 1918.

'Ruritanians All', *The Stage Year Book* (1909), 26.

'Russian Ballet in Prince of Graustark—at Strand', *Athens Banner*, 22 April 1917, 7.

Schneider, P. E., 'Graustark Becomes A Boom Town', *New York Times*, 15 February 1959.

'See American Men Win Two Graustark Beauties', *Pittsburgh Press*, 26 May 1911.

Sennwald, Andre, 'The Merry Widow', *New York Times*, 12 October 1934.

'Sensational Magical Illusions', *The Strand*, January 1903, 63–66.

'Sir Anthony Hope Hawkins: The Creator of Ruritania', *Times*, 10 July 1933.

Sisk., 'Princess Flavia', *Variety*, 18 November 1925.

'Snub', *Daily Herald*, 17 July 1959, 2.

'Stage Scenery at Auction', *New York Times*, 27 July 1909.

Stevenson, Robert Louis, 'A Gossip on Romance', *Longman's Magazine* 1 (November 1882): 69–79 (73, 77).

'St James's Theatre', 25 November 1895.

'St. James's Theatre', *The Era*, 13 January 1900.

'Stroheim Plays Villain for Constance Talmadge', *Exhibitors Herald*, 8 August 1925, 39.

'Talmadge's Lot Move', *Weekly Variety*, 18 March 1925.

Tempest, Rone, 'Move Over, Charles and Di: The House of Windsor isn't the Only Royal Mess. Just look at the Grimaldis of Monaco', *Los Angeles Times*, 24 November 1992.

'Theatrical Gossip', *New York Times* 13 June 1901.

'Theatrical Gossip', *The Era*, 16 June 1894.

'Theatrical Gossip', *The Era*, 13 July 1895.

'The Balkan Princess', *Playgoer and Society Illustrated* 1.6 (June 1910), 99.

'The Charge Against Mr George Alexander', *Times*, 6 November 1895.

'The Drama in America', *The Era*, 21 September 1895.

'The Jean Seberg Affair Revisited', The Daily Mirror blog, *Los Angeles Times*, 22 March 2009.

'The King of Ruritania', *New York Times*, 5 September 1895.

'The London Theatres', *The Era*, 24 November 1867.

'The London Theatres', *The Scotsman*, 17 September 1949.

'The London Theatres: The St James', *The Era*, Saturday, 11 Jan 1896.

'The Matinee Girl', *Manchester Times*, 3 November 1899.

'*The Mouse That Saved the West*, by Leonard Wibberley', *Kirkus Reviews*, 22 April 1981.

'The New Pictures', *Time* 30.11, 13 September 1937, 36.

'The New Pictures', *Time* 60.18, 3 November 1952, 102.

'The Odeon's Gala Opening Performace: The Prisoner of Zenda', *The Sketch*, 10 November 1937, 252.

'The Prince of Graustark Filmed from Famous Novel', *Athens Daily Herald*, 25 April 1917, 7.

'The Prince of Pilsen Comes', *New York Times*, 18 March 1903.

'The Prisoner of Zenda', *Focus: A Film Review* 6.2 (February 1953): 36–7 (37).

'The Prisoner of Zenda', *Pall Mall Gazette*, 8 April 1895.

'The Prisoner of Zenda', *The Evening World*, 5 September 1895.

'The Prisoner of Zenda', *Times*, 3 November 1937, 12.

'The Prisoner of Zenda at the Palace Theatre', *The Sketch*, 14 February 1923, 318.

'The Prisoner of Zenda: New Film at Palace Theatre', *Times*, 30 January 1923, 8.

'The Prisoner of Zenda on the Film', *Times*, 10 March 1915.

'The Screen', *Brooklyn Daily Eagle*, 3 September 1937, 10.

'The Screen', *New York Times*, 1 August 1922.

'The Screen: The Merry Widow', *New York Times*, 27 August 1925.

'The Screen: The Prisoner of Zenda Opens at the Music Hall', *New York Times*, 3 September 1937.

'The Stage', *San Francisco Call*, 11 October 1896.

'The Student Prince', *The Era*, 10 February 1926, 8.

'The Sweet Yell of Success', *Daily Mirror*, 28 Nov 1968.

'The Theatres', *Times*, 16 February 1896.

'The Triumph of the Weak Brother', *Glasgow Herald*, 12 January 1895.

'The Uses and Abuses of Fictional Geography', *Academy*, 13 October 1906.

'The Week at the Theatres', *New York Times*, 16 April 1899.

Thirkell, Arthur, 'Not Two of the Best Sellers', *Daily Mirror*, 7 December 1979, 21.

'This is a Landmark Cinema', *Daily Herald*, 3 November 1937, 11.

'Three Films Have Premieres at Midtown Theatres—Hope at Paramount', *New York Times*, 25 December 1947.

Tilton, Jane, 'Beverly of Hollywood', *Motion Picture Magazine*, June 1926, 37.

'Tonight: At the Colonial, Graustark Beautifully Staged', *Athens Banner*, 15 October 1910, 1.

'Topics of the Drama', *New York Times*, 18 October 1903.

Trewin, J. C., 'The World of the Theatre: Off the Map', *Illustrated London News*, 8 October 1949, 552.

'Truxton King', *San Francisco Call*, 10 October 1909, 7.

'Truxton King: Class A', *Screen Opinions* 11.15 (March 1923), 232.

Weinberger, Aliza, 'Author Meg Cabot Returns to Genovia for More "Princess Diaries"', Mashable.com, 2 June 2015.

W. H., 'Notable Film: Success of the "Prisoner of Zenda"', *Pall Mall Gazette*, 30 January 1923, 4.

'When You Book a "Book Title" Picture, Remember the Bookseller in Your Town', *Exhibitors Herald*, 24 February 1923, 26.

Williams, Gilda, 'The Princess Diaries', *Sight and Sound* 12.2 (February 2002): 57–8.

Wilson, Jeff, 'A "Princess Diaries" Moment for Albert's Daughter', *Washington Post*, 5 June 2006.

Wloszczyna, Susan, 'Girls Will Royally Enjoy "The Princess Diaries"', *USA Today*, 2 August 2001.

York, Cal, 'Studio News and Gossip, East and West', *Photoplay*, 26 February 1926, 40.

'Zenda Licensed', *Weekly Variety*, 14 March 1913.

'"Zenda" Out In the Fifth', *Washington Post*, 25 May 1979.

Index

For the benefit of digital users, indexed terms that span two pages (e.g., 52–53) may, on occasion, appear on only one of those pages.